The Provisional City

The Provisional City

Los Angeles Stories of Architecture and Urbanism

Dana Cuff

The MIT Press

Cambridge, Massachusetts

London, England

This book was set in Sabon and Frutiger by Graphic Composition, Inc., Athens, Georgia, and was printed and bound in the United States of America.

Library of Congress Cataloging-in-Publication Data

Cuff, Dana, 1953–
    The provisional city : Los Angeles stories of architecture and urbanism / Dana Cuff.
        p. cm.
    Includes bibliographical references and index.
    ISBN 0-262-03276-7 (hc : alk. paper)
        1. Architecture, Domestic—California—Los Angeles. 2. Architecture, Modern—
20th century—California—Los Angeles. 3. City planning—California—Los Angeles—
History—20th century. 4. Public housing—California—Los Angeles—History—20th
century.   I. Title.
NA7238.L6 C84 2000
307.76'09794'9409044—dc21

                                                                        00-030379

to Amelia and Julian

Contents

Acknowledgments

I remember hearing my parents describe living in Los Angeles during the Second World War. My father worked in an oil refinery, and my older sister had just been born. They told of darkened streets, submarine attacks, Tin Can Beach, victory gardens, and block wardens. Somehow it all seemed dangerous and exotic at the same time, though highly remote. Perhaps that's how this study began. Maybe it started when I watched our citrus grove, which had been my grandfather's before us, plowed under to make way for tract housing. I was in the third grade, and I couldn't believe we were going to move south to plant another grove rather than stay to soak up what seemed like the start of a bonafide city. Why leave a place about to get sidewalks? Before long, we returned to our rural-community-turned-suburb, and I learned that the limits of roller-skating were tied not only to surface but to destination. And the project is at least partly due to my friend Lenwood Johnson, who introduced me the hard way to public housing and community activism. The work has many origins, but they are all based in an intermingling of intellectual contradictions, everyday life, and political biases that coalesce in the architecture of the city.

The ways cities change and the way land is manipulated in that process seem to me more significant to urban form than most urban observers admit. I wanted to catch something of the interchange between real estate as a cultural and economic practice and the designers and planners who work their optimism into episodic utopias. Big schemes began to seem brutally clear just by the scale they assumed, and thus scale seeped into all my thinking: from the size of the chapters that follow to the size of the projects they cover. The irony of our predicament was inescapable: the grander the plan, the more it seemed to undermine its own pretenses. This reflects my dual inclination toward cultural study as pure observation and uncompromised architectural propositions. Good design seems to require both but permit neither.

The moment when this book began can be pinpointed, however, to one day in 1996 when I went to the Los Angeles Public Library to look at photo archives of public housing. Getting there had been a typical LA experience—a twenty-minute trip extruded into an hour of unbearable traffic and impossible parking. When I arrived, Carolyn Cozo Cole haltingly informed me that she was unable to locate the requested files. To soothe me she dropped off a foot-tall stack of folders called "LA—Slums." There, as you will see in the pages beyond, was a startling Los Angeles that had existed alongside the victory gardens and blacked-out city, all gone by now. It became so much rubble beneath the public housing I was trying to track down. The struggle to make a home, with almost no means, was viscerally evident in these images. The places depicted were vulnerable and temporary in every aspect. It occurred to me that early low-rent housing advocates faced that same struggle, until they successfully commandeered federal funds to make what they believed would be permanent. Over subsequent decades, the public housing they built had deteriorated in turn to such an extent that land sharks were now swarming for the real estate. The appraisal photographs in the succeeding chapters reinforced these observations.

In my studies of contemporary urban debates between homeowners and developers, with designers skewered in the middle, I saw how people came to defend their small stakes with such vehemence. The faces in some of the appraisal photographs registered that same posture, as the origins of modern-day contentiousness took shape. Thus a story began to emerge about urban change and architecture's role therein, about homeplaces and their provisional status, and about the ways our conceptions of property filter into every spatial act.

Many individuals and institutions lent support to this project: the USC School of Planning, Adele Santos and my colleagues at the short-lived UCSD School of Architecture, and Sylvia Lavin and colleagues at my present home in UCLA's Department of Architecture and Urban Design. The staff there has been helpful beyond words. In 1992, Tridib Banerjee and I received a grant from the National Endowment for the Arts to write "Form in Contention," together with Ken Beck and Achva Stein. That is when the Playa Vista study began, though it seems it will never end.

Along the way, I have received inspiration and assistance from able students. Sylvia Darr, José Gámez, and Ken Gutierrez deserve special mention. Their help with the research and images was essential over the past four years. Wendy Bone provided powerful illustrations of the fundamental ideas of the book based on her own research; Sasha Ortenberg created the fine maps of the city; Tulay Atak and Therese Kelly conquered the bibliography; Duane Jackson drew early Playa Vista graphics; and Patricia Solis, Chuck Saltzman, Mark Fredrickson, and Karen Adhikari helped in the initial phases. The students in my "Provisional City" course at UCLA in the winter of 1999 gave me a needed intellectual boost with their creative energy for the subject.

It was my year as a Scholar at the Getty Research Institute that defined this work. There I was afforded not only the luxury of time, but the insight of others contemplating Los Angeles in its myriad forms Michael Roth, Roger Friedland, and Harold Zellman offered valued friendship and critique. The thoughtful weekly seminar and a number of its members were particularly helpful: Robert Davidoff, Brenda Bright, Phil Ethington, Bill Deverell, Susan Phillips, Becky Nicolaides, Mike Davis, David James, Robert Carringer, Doug Flammang, and Tom Hines. The staff at the Getty was exceptional, which contributed to our productive and provocative time there.

I am fortunate to have a circle of smart friends who have thought about the ideas in this book with me over the years. Don Parson was a generous and informed colleague. Michael Bell encouraged the property chapter through his own edited volume *Slow Space* (with Sze Tsung Leong). Michael Dear and Jennifer Wolch are key to any urban investigation. And I have benefited from conversations with Kevin Daly, Gerda Norvig, Frank Gruber, Janet Levin, Lisa Lowe, Chris Genik, Tom Buresh, Danelle Guthrie, Roger Sherman, Diane Favro, Sylvia Lavin, Richard Weinstein, Dagmar Richter, Beth Robertson, Sarah Jane Lind, Anne Fougeron, Russell Reiff, Michael Storper, Anastasia Loukaitou-Sideris, Greg Hise, Lars Lerup, Stephen Fox, Dolores Hayden, and Robert Gutman.

I could not have written the book without the generosity and assistance of community members across Los Angeles. These individuals knew the urban stories from the inside, and shared their experiences with me: Frank Wilkinson, Julie Inouye, Doug Gardner, Bill Goss, Jean Whinnery, Leota Smith-Flowers, Dorothy Sterling, Bill Hannon, Howard Drollinger, and Frances Camareno, among others. Their recollections brought the book's subject to life for me, and I have aspired to retain that vitality in the retelling. I have worked at a number of archives with fine collections and staff: I thank Carolyn Cole at the LA Public Library, Dace Taube at USC's Regional History Center, Mary Lou Crockett of the Westchester Historical Society, Loyola Marymount University's Southern California Collection, the Huntington Library, Berkeley's Bancroft Library, the National Still Picture Archive, and the Getty Research Institute. UCLA's Special Collections and the Air Photo Archives in the Department of Geography provided core documents. The Housing Authority of the City of Los Angeles, in particular George McQuade and Ugo Garcia, have shared resources that formed the foundations for the entire book. Evelyn De Wolfe Nadel, widow of photographer Leonard Nadel, has been especially gracious.

Finally, I can't imagine thanking my family—Dad, Penny, Pam, Bob, Tracy, Maria, Abby, and Annie—since what they give goes far beyond gratitude. In my own home, Kevin sharpens my architectural intellect, while Amelia and Julian make every day unpredictably fresh. I can't say what our children will recall about growing up in Los Angeles, but I'll remember that we lived a great, full life here together.

The Provisional City

No Little Plans

Extra-Large

It seems incredible that the
size of a building alone
embodies an ideological
program, independent of
the will of its architects
Rem Koolhaas

Make no little plans, they
have no magic to stir men's
blood. Make big plans, aim
high in hope and work,
remembering that a noble,
logical diagram once
recorded will never die.
Daniel Burnham

1 Cities across America are punctuated by large projects: housing developments, hospital complexes, public utilities, college campuses, office complexes, shopping malls. Some of these urban places have employed architecture's blood-stirring "magic" to create modern communities as well as to destroy them. Add nonarchitectural components like freeways and parks, and the city can be viewed as a dispersion of linked large projects that structure and dominate the fine-grained interstitial matter. The dominant places are sited upon others that have somehow lost their value in the city. And the new inhabitation comes into being convulsively, sometimes violently, leaving little trace of what it evicted. This book explores the conflation of three aspects of contemporary urbanism: scale, upheaval, and property. It does so in the context of Los Angeles, where the transformation of five distinct places illuminates a broader picture of the fugitive city.

As Koolhaas remarks and Burnham implies, the scale alone of a civic construction is deterministic. Large undertakings begin by piecing together a commensurably sizable field of operation—a site, from an assemblage of independently owned properties. Cobbling the site together is a long, arduous process, and the bigger the undertaking, the more effort required to move it toward realization. That effort is partly a matter of ideology, for there must be a motivational narrative to retell when energy flags over the years required to realize a big dream. At least to some extent, a utopia is conjured of a better city, and with it a better life. Architecture is an essential part of any big plan, for it must embody the aggressive optimism of those who initiate these fundamental alterations to the landscape. Burnham's professional faith, however, is overly optimistic: noble, logical diagrams—even very large ones—are readily erased.

In order to grasp the form of the contemporary city, and how it is significantly transformed, we can scrutinize the great schemes imposed there. Large-scale projects produce civic upheavals as they lurch into existence. Such convulsions demonstrate the inherent discontinuities of urban evolution, along with a fundamental provisionality characteristic of even those places that seem most stable. Particularly when homeplaces are at stake—either threatened with demolition or envisioned by new plans, or both—the assumption of permanence is shaken, to reveal the provisional city. In piecemeal fashion, each site's proposed utopia buries another part of the city, naive in its own vulnerability to the next generation's dreams.

The spatial location and limits of a big, urban scheme (that is, the site) are structured by the politics of real property. The evolving conventions of real estate and ownership create a dynamic playing field on which any project must prevail if it is to be built. Large projects bring added complications and opportunities insofar as they generally involve public funds and invoke public contention. As such, these undertakings must seek public concurrence in their visions of a better future, for which there can never be consensus. An expanding notion of ownership, the dominance of rights over duties, the arbitrary discontinuities of boundaries—such fundamentals of real property along with the practices of real estate reveal much about the shape of civic architecture.

This investigation of contemporary urban change focuses on large-scale constructions that erupt across the cityscape, as property relations shift to accommodate a debatable utopia. It posits the evolution of the modern city as a sequence of unrelated upheavals, in which big schemes overrun the territory they require, leaving no trace of the former land use. Each such architectural scheme denies the past as it manifests a temporary vision of a better future, for it too will experience the surges that it rode into existence, bringing about its own obliteration.

The fleeting city characterizes American urbanism and Los Angeles since the time of the New Deal and later World War II, when government and demographics conspired to effect radical change. In order to flesh out issues of scale, property, and provisionality, I have chosen to focus on residential settings because they evoke such compelling connections between architecture, space, and culture. Housing in Los Angeles embodies a series of contradictions that illuminate conditions of architecture and urban development: destruction is a fundamental part of construction; the physical building site is a social construct; the domain of privacy is made into a spectacle and politicized; the places we con-

The Flats/Aliso Village, 1941–1998.

2 Estrada Courts Public Housing, built 1942.

3 Parcel #48, Estrada Courts public housing; appraisal survey of existing buildings for eminent domain proceedings and eventual demolition.

sider stable are in fact fugitive; and today's solutions soon become the next problems to resolve.

The 1930s mark the beginning of the house as an affordable, mass-produced box, at first built well and quickly; then, later, just quickly. With the Great Society programs came a conception of a vast middle class that might be housed in a standardized, commodious manner. The box would be functional, as modernist ideology of the time promoted, and equipped with the conveniences afforded to domestic life. The role of architecture was to decorate the box without detracting from its affordability or functionality. With middle-class homeownership as the stated objective, federal and state governments restructured the building industry after the 1929 crash, from banking to construction to real estate development. That restructuring produced the seas of tract houses that comprise the suburbs. Ironically, the house became a standardized box at the same time as the population grew strikingly more diverse, through immigration, increasing numbers of women in the workforce, the undermining of racial segregation, and domestic migration.

Tales of urban upheaval are vaguely unsettling and simultaneously thrilling, as all disappearing acts tend to be. When the smoke clears, the former scene is gone and a new one has materialized. As big changes are wrought upon the city, a great deal is buried beneath the newly manifest urban future. When Burnham uttered his famous dictum, he had the whole of Chicago in mind. The same mixture of bravado, vision, rationality, and ruthlessness is needed to build large projects in any city. Rationality and ruthlessness are necessary because there is no big plan that can be accomplished without broad, sweeping approaches to a project, and without burying that place where the new project will rest. The new communities could be called utopias, since they purport a better life; but like the areas they interred, they are characteristically provisional in both physical and social terms.

Other studies of popular housing and modern city planning have generally ignored the politics and aesthetics of a place's metamorphosis, from one state, into a site, then to a superseding state. I selected the five LA cases because they represent a uniquely instructive range of temporary conditions and permanent implications within the architecture not only of Los Angeles, but of the modern city as it grew after the war into the postmodern conditions characterizing it today.[1] The projects investigated include early public housing, temporary veterans' housing, real estate subdivisions, and new town planning. They are all constructions of communities, ranging from 800 units for some 3,200 individuals at Aliso Village to Westchester's 13,000 homes for over 40,000 people. Each was framed from its conception as an event in the evolution of the city, in the evolution of community, as indeed they were, though not always in the ways their makers intended. This book stays close to these places, and to the people who shaped them, because they make solid that which melts into air but also because the charge of a vivid life in place is so compelling.

Domestic places of dramatic change have always held a certain attraction, a bittersweet quality. There are incredibly optimistic dreams involved, at best in my view by an avant-garde that will bring its creative force to bear upon the making of a new world, nothing less. But to accomplish big plans requires the kind of planning and foresight that must inherently make a cold, rational survey of the prospects. Calculating, measuring, averaging, the rational plan grazes over the vast, differentiated, and idiosyncratic circumstances alive on the ground, to make proposals that can be justified in their entirety, legitimated in positivist terms, and applied to a wide range of specific instances. This weird combination of faith and science, optimism and rationalism, is embedded within large-scale urban projects like those described in the coming pages.

4   The Los Angeles area as it appeared in the 1940s, highlighting the five case study sites: Aliso Village, Rodger Young Village, Elysian Park Heights, Westchester, and Playa Vista. Mapmaker: Alexander Ortenberg.

Scale and event, bigness and transformation, value and utopian thinking are topics that have occupied architects' and urbanists' attention in recent years. They are not new topics in the field, just newly viewed. Architect Rem Koolhaas in his well-known tome (1995) gives the brute classification of size to all building: like a T-shirt, architecture is S, M, L, or XL. Scale gives us a reading of the building, its ideological roots, as well as its impact on the city, on the public, on the architect. "Bigness destroys, but it is also a new beginning. It can reassemble what it breaks" (p. 511). What Koolhaas describes as bigness in a single building has parallels to bigness in urban plans comprised of many buildings. The stories in this text manifest destruction for the purpose of beginning anew; but they refute the claim that reassembly is possible. Not only is it rare for large-scale works to attempt to reconstruct what they have displaced, but it is inherently impossible. The destruction is severe and permanent; the optimism of new construction is its supposed utopian counterproposal.

Early XL

Soon after the 1929 stock market crash, an urban extra-large was formulated as a utopian counterproposal that would shape subsequent American housing policy. In 1931, President Hoover called a conference to deal with the worsening conditions of wage-earner housing in American cities (Gries and Ford, 1932). Of the four related committees, a certain modernist zeal permeated the one called "Large-Scale Operations," which proposed an alternative to the individually produced, single, detached dwelling. The Large-Scale Operations committee modeled an approach to popular housing on the practices of big business. Mass-produced, multifamily (and single-family) housing would supersede methods of small-scale homebuilding and would be appropriate to inner-city slums, intermediate areas of blighted districts, and the unbuilt outlying area. It would occupy large tracts of land which would undergo comprehensive planning, reaping economic benefits by efficiencies and by justifiable condemnations of land. I quote at some length from the committee's report, for it defines large-scale operations and lays out a rationale for bigness, the benefits of which were thought to be commensurately immense:

> 1. It is economical. The land is treated in large blocks, and is developed in one continuous operation to its final use for completed housing. . . .

> 2. It is modern. The community plan can be adapted specifically to the purposes it will serve, providing for gardens, a playground, and a recreational center, and in larger schemes, for shops, schools, and other community buildings.

5 Michigan Boulevard Garden Apartments, Chicago; an example of large-scale operations and segregation in the late 1920s. From Gries and Ford, *President's Conference on Home Building and Home Ownership,* 1932.

3. It is efficiently designed. Under large-scale operation methods, a group of one-family houses or a large block of apartments is designed as a single unit, thus utilizing to the maximum all space inside and outside the walls of the housing, and making possible beauty of design through the relation of the masses. . . . Small-scale operations are wasteful, because they must work within the frame of the single lot. . . .

4. It is a good investment. . . . By creating neighborhoods of a homogeneous character, it guards against the possibilities of deterioration through spotty or inadequate development and it preserves values for a longer time than does our present method.

5. It offers low rents. Loans on a greater percentage of value, with longer periods of amortization and a smaller interest rate are possible in large-scale operations. (Gries and Ford, 1932, pp. 70-71)

As early as 1931, large-scale land development was proposed as a key to the nation's housing problems. It is significant that the majority of architects at the President's conference—seven of the eleven in attendance—were members of the Large-Scale Operations group. The principal architect there was Henry Wright of New York, who was among Lewis Mumford and Catherine Bauer's crowd at the Regional Planning Association of America. The envisioned large modern housing was to be produced by private enterprise; the text gives as an example Sunnyside Gardens in Queens, planned by Henry Wright and Clarence Stein, and inhabited for eleven years by Mumford. Nearly twenty years later, Stein would come to Los Angeles and plan Baldwin Hills Village with Robert E. Alexander, refining some of the same ideas about large-scale developments (see Stern, 1981). Years later, it was Alexander and Richard Neutra who planned the modernist utopia at Chavez Ravine, which, instead of becoming a prototype, sparked public housing's demise.

The 1931 housing conference was propitious. It made explicit the ideology among planners and architects that would shape their later actions, and eventually also those of builders, from the Depression through urban renewal. In his foreword, the Secretary of the Interior, Ray Lyman Wilbur, issued a prescient warning to skeptics:

> To those who look upon government operations in the field of housing construction with abhorrence the challenge is definitely offered. . . . If business, financial, and industrial groups fail to take the task in hand and apply the large sums of capital required and the utmost of planning genius and engineering skill to the problem, it seems likely that American cities will be forced to turn to European methods of solution of this problem, through subsidization by State and municipal treasuries and probably through actual ownership and operation of housing projects by municipal authority. (Gries and Ford, 1932, p. xii)

This report was the precursor to federal policy that emerged in the Industrial Recovery Act, Public Works Administration, and the Housing Act of 1937.

When the subject is large urban zones rather than big buildings, the qualities Koolhaas describes need amendment. First, he states that the parts remain committed to the whole even while they have escaped control and confinement by virtue of the bigness of the design task. No architect or planner can control all the elements of big projects (Koolhaas, 1995, p. 500). But Koolhaas overlooks that a large project's relation to its surroundings are harsh and unrelenting, because it is focused on itself. Moreover, because large-scale operations require the recomposition of independent entities (the assembly of land, the coordination of jurisdictions, and so on), culture and politics become central players by necessity and definition. Second, where Koolhaas acknowledges the "honesty" or revelatory possibility of architecture—in general—before Bigness, the same might be said of specific urban neighborhoods displaced by a big move. When an area is composed of independent, small bits of land, the buildings, use, and ownership make a certain sense that can be discerned by a situated observer. When it is taken over, pieced together, and reworked, it no longer makes phenomenal sense. Instead, it destabilizes, disorients, and perplexes. Its authorship has unclear roots, except that something big was behind it. Surges of unseen federal dollars, back-room politics between mayors and baseball team owners, the crash of the stock market—these shape big plans beyond any local condition. Third, unlike Kool-haas's notion of Bigness as amoral, my work argues that large urban works are bimoral: they are inherently good and bad, simultaneously. They are, in fact, *anything but* "beyond" good or bad (Koolhaas, p. 502), and instead reverberate within good and bad, even if this is taken on purely aesthetic grounds.

To understand urban works implies knowledge of what formed their temporal, spatial, and political context. In practical terms, this means examining the architecture of bigness and the architecture of planned pieces, as they struggle to hang together. For large works to come into existence, the former inhabitants of the land in question are banished. The big plan takes priority over existing land uses and pursues this whole, envisioned utopia until it is realized, until it exists as a zone. It often fails at its first attempts at eviction, but the threat of seizure and subsequent forays generally prevail. Transformed by its own process, a large-scale operation leaves no traces of what was or what might have been. It takes Koolhaas's notions of dismantlement and disappearance to the next step, and, with the grave conceit of power, aims to supersede. A form of domestic colonialism, large-scale operations are initiated upon the weak or the outsider, with the intention of domination but also with material utopian objectives: a better city, decent housing, clean streets.

Koolhaas (p. 509) claims what is needed in architecture is "a theory of Bigness—what is the maximum architecture can do?" Along with that, we need a theory of large-scale operations—how much architecture can we or should we plan at one time to shape the city? In fact, large-scale operations focus upon that intermediate zone between cities and buildings that is both architecture and urbanism, and yet neither.

Large-scale operations were not the only strategy endorsed by the federal government, but they were the one with the greatest impact on the existing city. At the other end of the continuum, the National Housing Act, signed into law in October 1934, authorized property improvement loans ranging from $100 to $2,000 to private individuals (to be repaid monthly over a period not to exceed three years). While $2,000 would have built a new house from scratch in 1934 dollars, this piecemeal approach was not going to solve the larger problem of the slums.

The Event
Just after Koolhaas's manifesto on Bigness, he writes about the resolution of a personal quandary: "I realize that from now on, events will decide my dilemmas, instead of my dilemmas deciding the events" (p. 518). What does not en-

ter into Koolhaas's incisive theories of Bigness is that the city is driven in the same direction as he describes his own life: events shape the city by determining its dilemmas. In sociohistorical terms, the war and the Depression played roles of urban instigation in terms of policy, slum clearance, public housing, defense housing, and suburban expansion. The situationist view is particularly relevant when we step back from the building (which preoccupies Koolhaas) and focus on a collection of buildings, not on the architecture of the city as a whole but on those parts planned and carried out as a unit.

If scale is one dimension of an urban convulsion, event is another. Bernard Tschumi formulates the event as a way of stepping beyond program or function into "the movement of bodies, to activities, to aspirations; in short, to the properly social and political dimension of architecture" (Tschumi, 1994, p. 13). Large urban interventions are events in and of themselves, but they also make events out of their own creation. The large uses violent force to make room for itself, leaving a trail of demolition, displacement, and environmental havoc. The small, the weak, and the outsider are easy targets, the latent objective of the manifest utopian vision at a grand scale. The small can mobilize to stage attention-getting events, to unite with other entities into something larger, and generally to show strength where none is assumed. But the small always finds itself defending against the large, in a posture of resistance, which, in the long run, is exhausting and given to failure.

There are other types of event that are themselves nonmaterial but have rock-hard consequences. These include unseen events, like a funding authorization or policy shift from Washington, the transfer of property ownership, or new land use regulations. The creation of the Federal Housing Administration and its various loan programs greatly shaped the American residential landscape. Similarly, the 1931 conference had a committee on "Industrial Decentralization and Housing," which recommended suburbanization to cure the ills of "Blighted Areas and Slums" (the title of another group).[2] Together with the focus on large-scale operations, these reflected a national housing agenda built by the state inside cities atop demolished slums, and built by private enterprise at the urban periphery with indirect state subsidy.

As scale and event, or space and time, we can describe the political emergence of the physical city around us. Scale and event dominate the phenomena that preoccupy this book. The places reverberate between the S (or even XS) and the L, which moves in to eradicate it. When something big "takes place" in the city, a central issue is the metamorphosis of some collection of urban places into a site. This involves an idea of value when an existing use is considered of less value than a prospective one.[3] Such a determination is most complicated when existing homes will be demolished. In America, this was the legacy of the federal highway program, the urban redevelopment era, and slum clearance policy. In each, massive intervention removed people from their homes, fractured communities, shifted access, and reorganized topography, leaving little recognizable in its wake. Zones were formulated within the city by stringing together the real estate of many little pieces of property. These zones were then granted qualities of a unified place which came to dominate the identity of their constituent pieces. Rather arbitrary boundaries on a map can become definitive of a "place" that is viewed with more and more coherence, if the campaign to create a site is effective.

In Los Angeles, one of the first areas to become a site for federally supported housing was the Utah Street project, which roped together hundreds of properties deemed blighted. Conceived in the early thirties under the Public Works Administration's housing program, eventually it was constructed with 1937 public housing appropriations (see section III of this book). In Washington, D.C., the Southwest Urban Renewal Project Area comprised some 560 acres and took over a decade to piece together (see Garvin, 1996; Seligman, 1957). Nearly a square mile in territory, that area could have had different boundaries, and was certainly not internally homogeneous. But in order for unified redevelopment to occur it had to be viewed as a whole, independent of what existed all around its edges as well as of what it contained. In cities across America, the New Deal motivated the creation of "slum neighborhoods" out of unevenly substandard properties inhabited by poor people of color, primarily recent immigrants to the city. Large slums then became part of the redevelopment spectacle.

To build upon the ideas of scale and event, we must carefully examine the social and political context of particular architectural undertakings. Not only does such an examination enrich our understanding of architecture, but it also explains a part of urban architecture that has received little attention, that of jarring projects that are large and obliterating. Urban history has not paid such projects their due precisely because, by definition, they obliterate history. Alternatively, architectural criticism focuses on the new entity without delving into its connection to what was destroyed. There are some exceptions to this oversight. For instance, Haussmann's Parisian triumph of urban boulevards is understood also as an attempt to quell political unrest through the massive demolition of working-class housing (see Kostof, 1985). Dolores Hayden's *Power of Place* (1995) reveals and marks the buried spatial history of women and people of color. She provides theory and method for redressing those places that have been so readily obliterated.

We know the architecture of repression all too well, even though we may have learned little from it. The poor, immigrants, people of color, women suffer discrimination that has its spatial correlate in segregation and its physical manifestation in slums, ghettos, inner-city neighborhoods, marginal space, or whatever label is currently sanctioned. Architects and community builders in this plot are merely tools of repression. But with the end of the war and recovery from the Depression came a time, perhaps the last time, when the nation looked forward in modern terms: new technology could solve old problems, rational planning would restructure the city, every American could share the American Dream and own a home. Under this banner, a believing public granted architecture the right to be simultaneously utopian and destructive, with all the baggage that dual job must carry.

With the large urban projects in this study comes modernity, as both style and ideology. Large-scale operations and episodic utopias existed before, but the New Deal and postwar attempts to restructure the city were massive, and were fraught with consternation for architects and planners, politicians and citizens. Modern housing, as proponents called it (Bauer, 1934), was a profound ideal for the American city. Its original intent was to build complete communities in the city core, but not on top of slums. In fact, the liberal housing activists wanted to build on vacant land because it would be less costly, faster, and easier in terms of site design (Radford, 1996). Modern housing was to offer a clear and desirable alternative to speculative housing not just for low-income residents, but for the middle class as well. Instead of the cherished freestanding house that builders constructed on the urban fringe, housers proposed high-density, rationalist housing blocks based on the variety of European models constructed since World War I. This approach left open space for recreation and community amenities, but was less costly than detached dwellings due to various efficiencies, including the use of land. The emphasis on collectivity was meant to have beneficial social impacts on the modern residents. The housing would have International Style modernist aesthetics, at least as Bauer saw it, embody rational planning ideals, engage new technological developments in construction systems and materials, all inside the city and outside the speculative real estate market. But the real estate promoters were not ready to relinquish construction to the public sector, let alone construction on vacant land. As the case studies demonstrate, the public housing contingent was effectively barred from building in the urban periphery and from vacant land in the urban core. To continue their project, housing progressives had to embrace the paradoxical, conservative position advocating slum clearance.

The disruption modern housing caused was rationalized as a small price for such great civic betterment. Urban disruption is not uniquely modern; it must have begun before the first city was complete, though its methods and impacts have changed over time. The Romans' building of cities to lay claim to conquered territory, the governing of Spanish town planning in the New World by the Law of the Indies, the British colonists' construction of their version of Shanghai—these actions were relatives of the domestic or internal colonialism manifested by slum clearance and urban redevelopment agendas in American cities during this century (see McClintock, 1994; Murguía, 1975).

In focusing upon the modern American phase of this long history, I intend to lay the groundwork for understanding urban architecture as provisional, eruptive, episodic, and discontinuous. This postcolonial domestic usurpation of space, like its predecessors, had mixed results when it supplanted the occupants with imposed visions of a better life. It should not be assumed that some profit-grubbing developers were responsible for the most egregious civic works; the state and the progressives were leagues ahead when it came to disrupting communities. As one Florence Scala said about her experience of trying to save her neighborhood from University of Illinois expansion plans: "They can really destroy you, the nice people" (in Terkel, 1997, p. 229). Urban upheaval continues to trigger debate in public hearings and neighborhood meetings because residents place great significance on their homes and their material history, not to mention their land values. Particularly during the postwar period, what I call contentious development has been an important part of urban planning and design.

Scale and event are dimensions that properly belong within a time-space analysis. This excavation through sequential layers of the material culture of buildings and cities immediately invokes questions of time. Architecture carries presumptions of an inherent permanence. A building's materiality seems to transcend time; it is concrete—the material giving added meaning to the term. But this sense of architecture stems from histories of the monumental, while our daily lives are made of buildings much more fugitive. The buildings of the poor, particularly the homes they build themselves, are indeed almost fleeting. Still, the stories of built form are dominated by notions of duration such that timelessness is the aesthetic ideal if not the physical reality. The cities that contain these buildings, everyday and monumental, also have been conceived in terms of built continuity evolving in rather predictable ways. It is my contention that the flip side of continuity and permanence, namely convulsion and provisionality, characterizes many of the changes besetting the contemporary city.

In architecture, tangled conceptions of time intervene in works caught between the temporary conditions of their making, their intractable consequences, and, in some cases of particular interest, their effective transience. This material interplay of space and time is the domain of architecture and urban design. The paradoxes embodied in this interplay have been abundantly apparent in Los Angeles since World War II. The population surge, the equable climate for thin, quick building, the availability of empty lots in the center city, widespread racial segregation, and the powerful role of the private real estate industry, all created fertile ground for a fugitive architecture.

This study in LA explores what we've lost, how we lose it, and what comes to take its place in cities. It takes as its object large-scale residential additions to the city, examining how they come about and what they supplant. It is a study in the physical form of provisionality—a temporary permanence that captures the transformation of places within the city, and thus of the city itself. This provisionality is socially produced, governed by political and economic forces of change.

The Decline of Modernity

2   The crisis of the Great Depression made radical alternatives seem necessary and appropriate even in the most conservative circles. Nowhere was this as evident as in housing, when as many as a thousand foreclosures a day sometimes occurred (Abrams, 1946). Previously despised policies for noncommercial housing were uncontested, if not welcomed, by real estate interests (Radford, 1996). Through various efforts, particularly by Catherine Bauer and Mary Kingsbury Simkhovich (head of the National Public Housing Conference in the early thirties), Roosevelt's National Industrial Recovery Act (1933) was written to include housing. Although often ignored in historical studies of the Depression,[4] in retrospect the most progressive and radical part of the New Deal may have been the public-sector housing program in Title II's comprehensive program of public works. Rationality, efficiency, and planning—fundamental modernist principles—would be sought in International Style modern housing. American architects and planners had seen its successes in the European housing that began after World War I.

Ironically, the decline of modernity was accompanied by the last great wave of modern architecture. Sociologist Anthony Giddens (1990, p. 1) characterizes modernity as those "modes of social life or organization which emerged in Europe from about the seventeenth century onwards." Jean-François Lyotard (1985) represents the condition of modernity as having a dominant ethos that tries to ground epistemology while upholding faith in humanly engineered

6   Architects meeting to learn about new work from the Los Angeles Housing Authority, 1950. (Richard Neutra is visible in the last row, far right.) Photographer: Leonard Nadel.

progress. The subsequent revolts against modernism, by contrast, are character-ized by a shift away from these as well as from overarching narratives that rely on science to give coherent explanations of social life, and that imagine a know-able past and a predictable future. In terms of the physical city, the crises pre-cipitated by economic depression and war fueled the last battle of modernism, both in architecture and rational planning.

The belief in universal models of rational planning and the architectural modernism of function-based form was abundantly apparent in public housing in the thirties and forties. Historian Gail Radford (1996) argues that the early Public Works Administration housing program, which built a total of 58 devel-opments across the nation, offered the strongest challenge ever to market-based housing in America, and perhaps even its finest urban housing. I believe the pub-lic housing that followed (through the 1937 Housing Act), contrary to Radford's position, was in many instances superior to the PWA models. The best of that second wave of public housing is tied, paradoxically, to the eventual triumph of market-based housing. In any case, nearly all the early state-subsidized housing was modern. In no other building type was modernism in all its senses more ap-parent. Modeled after European social housing, particularly in its planning, American public housing embodied ideals of social reform, sanitation, commu-nity, family life, and healthy living. It was to address problems of delinquency, poverty, health epidemics like tuberculosis, and crime. Public housing was un-dertaken by some of the best architects in the country, anxious for public work to end the professional doldrums of the Depression years.

The purpose of the early public housing was threefold: to provide con-struction-related jobs, to eliminate slums, and to provide basic shelter to citizens who needed help getting back on their feet. All were to be accomplished as economically as possible. The notion of economy played well with the goals of modern architecture; while not always inexpensive, it manifested an aesthetic of simplicity and order. The typical building block at this time, whether in Los Angeles, New Orleans, or Denver, was a two-story structure optimizing access to light and air, organized around traffic-free green spaces (see U.S., Federal Public Housing Authority, 1946). The units themselves were efficient and small; the overall site plan showed greater variety from development to development than in later periods, and creative solutions were often achieved.

The decline of modernism, as style and ideology, was embodied by the downfall of public housing and the success of real estate entrepreneurs. As the war retreated into memory, single, coherent approaches to civic betterment were replaced by multifarious opportunity and a more fractured, individualistic approach to housing. The public sector retreated from its highly visible role as builder and owner, to the subsidy of housing via arcane means that actually subsidized lending institutions and the real estate industry (Abrams, 1946). Those groups, in turn, served the middle class rather than the poor who had benefited from direct subsidies to housing. Public housing itself incorporated qualities based on size alone that would lead it to be viewed as a social problem rather than as a model. Big and modern went together; both came under criticism eventually, but the first to be attacked was the modern, not only as an aesthetic but, in the case of public housing, as an ideology that viewed rational planning as a cure for urban ills like slums.

Emergenc(it)y

3   Emergencies spark behavior unique to their circumstances, actions that would not be tolerated otherwise. The Depression, the Second World War, and the perpetual housing crisis from the thirties through the fifties each demanded catastrophic response. In a lucid essay titled "Redevelopment: A Misfit in the Fifties," housing advocate Catherine Bauer argued that the greatest progress in public policy, and housing policy in particular, had always been shaped out of crisis. Whether we like it or not,

> a crisis that affects the conditions of living and social-economic organization is likely to do two things that have great potential significance for those who are concerned with improving the civic environment. It forces change, whether for better or worse, and often requires unprecedented action. And it may dramatize certain basic, long-standing problems in a way that clarifies them in the public mind and gives them here-and-now urgency. (Bauer, 1953, p. 11)

In retrospect, she saw that housing practices of the forties embraced ideas mismatched to the emergency at hand. Slum clearance programs emanated from the thirties, when there were high vacancy rates in slums nationwide paired with lower inner-city land prices. During and after the war, domestic migration and segregation, along with the urban spatial economics of cities, produced wide-

7   The Marina family in their tent home, 1948. Photographer: Otto Rothschild.

spread overcrowding in inner-city neighborhoods and increased land values. Progressive planners and housers failed to grasp the implications of this shift, and rooted their housing policy in an outdated understanding of conditions.

The contemporary city has its own development strategies to deal with catastrophe, as the city has had in other periods in history. Paris after the Revolution, Chicago after the fire, Delhi after British colonization, Mexico City after the Mexican Revolution: each urban transformation was temporally marked by an overwhelming event, sparked from crisis and characterized by the prevailing ideology and technology of urban building. With these examples sits Los Angeles after the Second World War, a case study of the postwar American city.

The America of the Depression and the New Deal faced a series of emergencies related specifically to housing. These structured the events, which in turn organized the way community building would transpire. One of the most significant crises concerned the slums. Probably since the turn of the century, when Jacob Riis's poignant photos revealed tenement life to New Yorkers and the rest of the nation, middle-class Americans were not only shocked by slum conditions but repulsed and afraid. From the thirties onward, slum clearance moved out of

8   One of the few multistory tenements in Los Angeles, with City Hall in the background. Photographer: Leonard Nadel.

the municipal arena to become a national objective. Racial prejudice was linked to slums, because of the predominance of people of color living there (or conversely, since slums were defined as areas where people of color lived). As Seligman pointed out in 1957, "The so-called hillbillies [from the Ozarks] . . . are about the only sizable group of white, Protestant, old-line Americans who are now living in city slums" (p. 147). The majority of ill-housed people were low-wage migrants and ethnic immigrants, blacks, American Indians, Puerto Ricans on the East Coast, and Mexicans and Asians on the West. A disregard for economic, political, and cultural factors led to the belief that slums were the inevitable products of their occupants:

> The migrants drawn to slums tend to be semi-literate, low-income, of rural origin and members of racial minorities. . . . The trouble with [white hillbillies] as with rural Negroes, Puerto Ricans, and Mexicans who invade Chicago, is that they simply don't know how to live in cities. Their standards of sanitation are wretchedly low; they are largely ignorant of the routines involved in building maintenance; their ignorance and poverty (and

the racial hostility they encounter) lead them to overcrowd any quarters they find. In brief, they create slums wherever they go (Seligman, 1957, p. 147).

A racist moral superiority dominated conservative thinking and, in a somewhat milder form, progressive thinking as well. The slums, poverty's urban setting, were to be cleansed from cities across the country. In Houston's oldest black neighborhood, the 4th Ward or Freedman's Town, public housing and freeways wiped away thousands of small homes, businesses, and churches (Cuff, 1985). In New York, when thirteen blocks around Lincoln Square were demolished, 6,000 black and Puerto Rican families were dislocated to make way for new housing and the performing arts center (Seligman, 1958). In Detroit, 3,500 Polish residents of Poletown on 465 acres were uprooted, their homes razed to make way for a General Motors plant (Schultz, 1992). The power of eminent domain featured in each of these cases. Every city had its deteriorated housing, located on sites adjacent to the downtown near early industrial locations. With the demographic shifts sparked by the Depression, the wartime defense industry, and the postwar economy, low-wage workers of color coming to the city crossed paths with the white middle class fleeing to the suburbs. Blighted properties became lucrative for slumlords willing to break land or buildings into many small pieces, each assigned its own rent. If the public sector was to address the emergency of expanding slums, it would have to acquire the property and redevelop it. But how could "fair market value" for such property be established if it were not to be based on the exploitative acts of its owners?

After early arguments against slum clearance by the likes of Mumford (1934) and Bauer (1934), it was not again until the early sixties that housers or planners went public with their reservations about slum clearance, most notably in two books: Herbert Gans's *Urban Villagers*, about Boston's West End (1962), and Jane Jacobs's *Death and Life of the American City* (1961). It was finally admitted by planners, sociologists, and housers, at least, that slum clearance was not only racially discriminatory but ineffective both in removing blight and in creating more vital cities. At the same time, rehabilitation, conservation, and historic preservation rose in political significance, to lend merit to smaller-scale solutions for poor and deteriorated neighborhoods. Prior to the sixties, whole-cloth demolition and the broad use of condemnation left no trace of civic history in many places. In Philadelphia, Society Hill's Dock Street Market was torn down and a new, modern market created on the outskirts of town (Garvin, 1996). Seattle's Pike Place Market nearly met the same fate, saved by the community's heroic efforts to stave off demolition (Langdon and Shibley, 1990).

In the housing emergency initiated by the Depression, broad popular support for federal policy was based upon personal experience. Housing starts in 1933 were 10 percent of what they had been in 1925, and half of all mortgages were in default (Radford, 1996). When Roosevelt took office that same year, he developed a plan that reflected the widespread loss of faith in the private real estate market. The Public Works Administration's housing programs, flawed as they were, and later public housing legislation were responses to that emergency. When America entered the war in 1941, the new emergency of national defense took precedence over that of the slums, and in fact exacerbated it in order to maintain an adequate supply of labor at defense production plants. National housing subsidies were aimed toward this same goal. At no time in American history either before or since has the federal government been so effective in the production of housing. After the war ended in 1945, several housing-related emergencies rose into public view: a shortage of veteran's housing, continuing blight in the cities, and a shortage of entry-level housing for the middle-class wage earner. Each one of these was the impetus for one of the LA cases narrated below, and it is the last that came to dominate succeeding decades.

Emergency is fundamentally a collective state of mind in response to trying conditions. An emergency is declared, and thus it exists. They have a material base but they are political and ideological in nature, and thus they are also fleeting.

Los Angeles in the American Scene

4 This inquiry into provisional urbanism looks at sites where homeplaces have been erased and constructed, beginning at the time of World War II when so much of the contemporary American residential landscape was built. The city of Los Angeles is an ideal case to examine, for it shows an exaggerated form of the transience extant yet less visible in other cities. From the West, the East was construed as a distinct collection of urban characteristics: besides its severe climate, the East had tenements, high densities, and an associated general overcrowding with all the commensurate health problems.[5] Los Angeles, by contrast, was a new city expanding rapidly. Optimistic visions of the future were untethered from entrenched problems, since the past was not perceived as having left an indelible mark. The propaganda of boosterism portrayed a land of sunshine for tourists who, if they were smart, would stay and become property owners (Klein, 1997). The real estate subdivision activity that would dominate suburban growth after World War II in places like Levittown had already been honed to perfection in Los Angeles. While the more established eastern cities like New York and Boston seemed tied to the places from which their Anglo-Protestant residents had immigrated, Los Angeles was more in keeping with "modern" cities that would erupt after World War II.

Los Angeles, particularly its postwar history, has been understudied until recently.[6] LA is a place we should know more about, since it is paradigmatic in some regards, exaggerated in others, and in some ways unique among American cities. There are many aspects of Los Angeles and the particular places I describe that are exemplary. The early days of public housing and urban renewal here are recalled by recognizable projects in nearly every city in the United States. Indeed, photographs of public housing from the 1940s are eerily without regional context. These developments were planned as islands at one point in architectural history, so that developments in Atlanta, Houston, or Seattle could just as easily have been placed in Los Angeles, and vice versa. The sites selected for public housing also varied little across the United States. Sites were located where slums had been, emanating from near the central business district and following flatlands, either along a river or along railways (see fig. 9). The federal program devised national policies and guidelines that were inflected only minimally by the local housing authorities, design community, or physical conditions. Likewise, similar opposition to public housing was expressed nationwide; Los Angeles was notable in experiencing the largest of all local struggles over the program (Freedman, 1959, p. 225).

There were other national trends as well. The war was an instrumental force in the national zeitgeist (indeed, I might argue that this was the last time the term would apply to America), as was the Depression, the housing crisis, and the belief in high technology's ability to remake housing production. These broad currents surged through Los Angeles as they did through other cities. Lastly, the political economy of real property in America was an important factor in the urban transformations of interest here, and Los Angeles shares in that political economy.

In the early part of the period studied here, perhaps the most obvious limiting factors affecting housing construction nationwide were the extensive shortages of materials and the various regulatory controls applied to construction during and following the war. In January of 1944, for example, materials prices were at a record peak, with supply still short of war-related need. It was predicted for that year that there would be a shortage of one billion board-feet of lumber, no aluminum at all for building construction, and a limit of 50,000 new bathtubs (*Architectural Forum*, January 1944). These shortages, coupled with a shortage of available construction labor, caused housing production to sink as slum populations rose. Los Angeles was caught in this bind, along with the rest of America's cities. These conditions worsened the deterioration of the little affordable housing available, and increased the unfilled demand for new housing of all types. Low-income neighborhoods, particularly those accessible to families of color, were invariably subjected to the greatest pressures. Yet, in a kind of national delusion, politicians, real estate interests, and even housers talked about slums as if they were internally self-generating and could be removed. Like a tumor, the slum would spread if not excised. The popular view

9   Federally subsidized housing in Los Angeles, 1937–1955. Mapmaker: Alexander Ortenberg.

Key:

Public housing, 1937 Act:
A   Rose Hill Courts, 100 units
B   William Mead Homes, 449 units
C   Aliso Village, 802 units
D   Pico Gardens, 260 units
E   Ramona Gardens, 610 units
F   Pueblo Del Rio, 400 units
G   Estrada Courts, 214 units
H   Avalon Gardens, 164 units
J   Hacienda Village, 184 units
K   Rancho San Pedro, 285 units

World War II and veterans housing:
1   Belvedere Park, 74 units / veterans
2   Rodger Young Village, 1500 units / veterans
3   Pacific Park Annex, 24 trailers
4   Pacific Park, 300 trailers
5   Corregidor Park, 110 PSUs
6   Corregidor Park Annex 1, 44 PSUs
7   Corregidor Park Annex 2, 44 PSUs
8   Corregidor Park Annex 3, 120 PSUs
9   Estrada Courts Annex 1, 100 PSUs
10   Estrada Courts Annex 2, 60 PSUs
11   Bonnie Beach Park, 339 units / veterans
12   Pueblo Del Rio Annex
13   Palm Lanes Homes, 300 units / veterans
14   Will Rogers Park, 168 units / veterans
15   Jordan Downs, 320 units
16   Imperial Courts, 100 units
17   Imperial Courts Annex 1, 40 PSUs
18   Imperial Courts Annex 2, 60 PSUs
19   Imperial Courts Annex 3, 22 PSUs
20   Alondra Park, 144 units / veterans
21   Lumina Park, 75 trailers
22   Lumina Park Annex, 30 trailers
23   Bataan Park, 240 PSUs
24   Normont Terrace, 460 units
25   Dana Strand Annex, 260 PSUs
26   Dana Strand Village, 384 units
27   Wilmington Hall, 1900 beds
28   Wilmington Hall Annex, 1000 beds
29   Western Terrace, 1000 units
30   Banning Homes, 2000 units
31   Channel Heights, 600 units
32   Portsmouth Homes, 128 TDUs

Public housing, 1949:
I   San Fernando Garden, 448 units
II   Elysian Park Heights, not built
III   Rose Hill Extension, not built
IV   Aliso Village Apartments, 336 units
V   Estrada Courts Extension, 200 units
VI   Mar Vista Gardens, 601 units
VII   Pueblo Del Rio Extension, 270 units
VIII   Jordan Downs, 700 units
IX   Hacienda Village Extension, not built
X   Nickerson Gardens, 1110 units
XI   Imperial Courts, 498 units
XII   Rancho San Pedro Extension, 194 units

Airplane factories:
1   Vega
2   Lockheed
3   Douglas
4   Hughes
5   North American Aviation
6   Douglas–El Segundo
7   Northrop

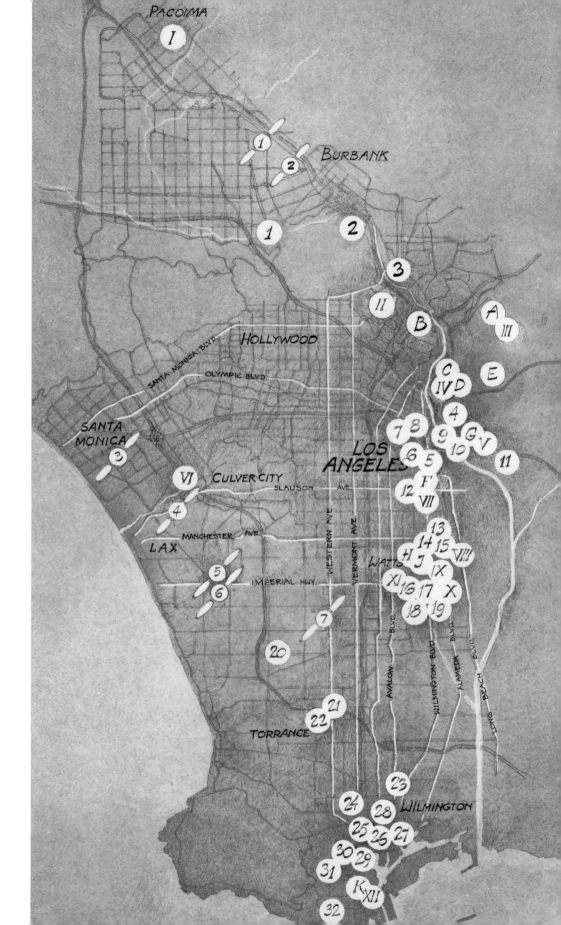

10   Kaiser Homes under construction, 1947.

was based on material culture: one shack's deterioration inspired its neighbor to a similar end, and so on in domino fashion.

In addition to the national scene, special local conditions were at play. California, and Los Angeles in particular, experienced dramatic population growth and resultant housing shortages in three distinct waves during the period of this study. First, the Depression pushed millions of people west during the thirties; then in the forties, millions of industrial workers followed, pulled to the West by jobs in the defense industries (Marchand, 1986). The war effort's effects on Los Angeles's economy were particularly beneficial, with its concentration of large aircraft production facilities and its important harbor, especially given the new priority on the Pacific theater after the bombing of Pearl Harbor. The third population boom came at the war's end, when many veterans moved to LA to raise their families.

Los Angeles was slower than most areas to recover from the Depression, with three of the region's predominant industries—petroleum, citrus, and film—remaining depressed after other sectors of the national economy began to experience some growth (Neff and Weifenbach, 1949). This may have made government props to the construction industry all the more important in the LA market.

Roosevelt's New Deal pumped money into social programs, economic restructuring, and public works programs, at its height about $8 billion a year. This number is dwarfed by the government's spending during the war, which reached $100 billion. In both forms, a disproportionate share of federal funds came to the Far West. Employment increased dramatically, and the gross national product more than doubled between 1940 and 1945 (Marchand, 1986). This was primarily due to government spending: in 1937, just 16 percent of the GNP was based on government expenditure; by 1944, this had reached 49 percent (Neff and Weifenbach, 1949).

Los Angeles's demographics shifted between 1940 and 1950 along with those of other cities in the West, but in a more exaggerated fashion. The population of Los Angeles grew by almost 56 percent, with the number of dwellings in the city increasing dramatically. Marchand estimates that housing construction outpaced demolition by a ratio of 18 to 1. By 1959, 38 percent of the buildings in Los Angeles had been built since 1940; 90 percent of the older buildings still remained, but they represented only 62 percent of all the buildings (Marchand, 1986, p. 114). It is significant that the geography of demolition and construction was unevenly distributed. Most demolition took place downtown, even though older buildings were dispersed in a crescent from Hollywood, through downtown, south to Watts (Nelson and Clark, 1976). In the urban areas of Los Angeles, about 2,000 dwelling units were destroyed each year. By contrast, new construction was undertaken primarily around outlying population centers like Santa Monica and Hollywood, particularly at their peripheries (Marchand, 1986, p. 113). Thus, a disproportionate number of older housing units was demolished in the center city without substantial rebuilding.

Real estate in Los Angeles held a peculiar status which, when coupled with tremendous in-migration, created a unique housing market. The city and California had been leaders in the real estate industry since the turn of the century. Tourism was key to an aggressive realty program of property subdivision and civic expansion. Vast territories of the city and its unincorporated regions had subdivision maps on file, far beyond what would be developed before war broke out. During the war, the West Coast, Arizona, and Nevada were the fastest growing regions of the United States in terms of population, and the construction industry could not begin to keep pace (*Architectural Forum,* April 1944). Overcrowding, temporary housing, and substandard housing were commonplace, and this situation was further exacerbated at war's end. As a port of dispatch for the Pacific theater, LA was etched in the memories of thousands of servicemen who fulfilled vows to return after their tour of duty.

Natural qualities of the region also have played a role in defining Los Angeles. Earthquakes, fires, and mudslides have lent a peculiar provisional quality to the buildings here (see Davis, 1998). The mild climate permitted the most minimal shelter, whether constructed by inexperienced builders with a modicum of materials or by adept modernists like Neutra, Schindler, and Ain. Barriers between inside and outside were deemphasized. In the early part of the century, concerned citizens discovered that this created a housing problem unique among established American cities. At first, newly arrived Angelenos paid ground rent to erect tents and "maverick shacks" of "scrap sheet iron, old bagging, and sections of dry goods boxes" (Los Angeles, Housing Commission, *Report 1906–1908,* p. 7). Later, when this practice was discouraged by city ordinance, self-built shacks hid behind only slightly more substantial bungalows. The further back from the street, the more insubstantial the dwellings became. This pattern was common in the poorer areas of the city, and provided livable if not comfortable accommodations to people of very low income.

The overall geography of the city has permitted great horizontal expansion, which, coupled with the dominance of the automobile and the demise of public transportation, has led to very low population densities compared to most large cities. This is especially relevant in a consideration of low-end housing. When housing experts argued the infeasibility of rehabilitating the slums, their reservations were based on New York–style tenements. Take, for example, the comments of the leader of the National Committee on Housing, Mrs. Samuel I. Rosenman, on rehabilitation: "While it often provides gadgets it sel-

11   Parcel #116, property appraisal for Aliso Village showing house at the back of a lot.

dom provides essential space, light and air" (Rosenman, 1944, p. 46). These were not the relevant inadequacies of Los Angeles slums, which had densities closer to single-family neighborhoods than to urban high-rise areas. Instead, the mild climate had permitted the construction of extremely insubstantial dwellings, without adequate infrastructure like plumbing and site drainage, with densities low enough to resemble rural poverty.

Thus Los Angeles shared certain conditions with cities nationwide in the first half of the 20th century, tweaked by LA's unique identity. When I selected the cases to study for this book, I initially used just one criterion: I looked for sites that were transformed by big plans which had housing as a major component. As it turned out, the places shared more than scale and use. They had a provisional quality, a sense of temporary permanence. They left no traces of what was buried beneath. Most assembled previously independent pieces of the city into sizable sites. They were intended to become neighborhoods of homes; indeed, each entailed a rather novel approach to housing. They embodied an episodic utopia, a momentary vision of a better life.[7] There were political ideals behind them. They sparked public debate. They hinged on a sense of emergency. They developed in a self-referential manner, internally whole with little relation to the surrounding context. This set of descriptors defines a class of architectural actions, that of large-scale operations and urban upheaval. The next few chapters take this description apart and examine its components.

Convulsive Urbanism, or Lurch City

5   The primary phenomenal characteristic of convulsive urban acts concerns their disruptiveness. The transformation which I call an upheaval or convulsion takes one land use, eradicates it, and replaces it with some vision of a better life; it removes numbers of people from their homes to build new housing; undeveloped land is built out. Tied to the degree of disruption is the matter of scale, since the larger the new project, the more it buries and the more comprehensive its utopian aspirations.

     The convulsive city lurches forward in time and material development as sites within the city are assembled and developed. Bits of its past are buried as if by volcanic eruption, in contrast to creating an "environment across time," as the historian Vincent Scully romantically suggests (1969). The present exploration of architecture and urbanism emphasizes the disruptive over the continuous, the spontaneous over the planned, short-term instability over long-term stability, the circumstantial over the referential. The places investigated give back to the student of architecture and urbanism a way of interpreting particular development activities. Eruptive building in cities dominates our phenomenal observations, while the historian's long view digests such episodes with narrations of constancy and progress. I will make the case for postwar urban change as multiple convulsions, weakly linked in the Los Angeles context by ideology, regulation, and infrastructure. The convulsion occurs to a part of the ur-

12   Houston, 1955. Freeway construction divided Freedman's Town, the oldest and poorest black neighborhood in the city, leaving the portion above the highway vulnerable to downtown development. The large public housing development just below the freeway interchange, Allen Parkway Village, had wiped out many blocks of the neighborhood two decades earlier. Photographer: Harper-Leiper Studios.

ban body which then becomes a discrete zone, operating with greater independence from its surroundings.

   If urban history tends toward steady evolution, economic history and particularly historical materialism are riddled with discontinuity (see Giddens, 1990). But as Giddens points out, even theories about discontinuity in Marxist thought have as a backdrop an overall direction for human history. The same might be said for urban historians, among whom discontinuity and convulsiveness are not exactly newsworthy. Instead, I here take the perspective Giddens describes as "accepting that history cannot be seen as a unity, or as reflecting certain unifying principles of organization and transformation. But it does not imply that all is chaos or that an infinite number of purely idiosyncratic 'histories' can be written" (pp. 5–6). Giddens identifies three features that distinguish the discontinuities of modern social institutions from traditional social orders: pace of change, scope of change, and the nature of modern institutions. These same three features appear in urban convulsions: radical changes are quickly effected, large sites are transformed, and new kinds of community are proposed.

Giddens describes modernity in the social order, whereas convulsive urbanism entails practices that may emanate from that social order but that have material consequences. Modernity in the physical, urban context is distinguishable also in terms of the relationship to the preexisting context, and in the complex agents of change. As the LA stories demonstrate, modern housing set itself apart as an island within its surroundings, to its own detriment in the end. The firm belief in rational planning was a purely "modern" ideology in Giddens's sense of the term. That modern idea met an increasingly postmodern world in which, for example, fragmented politics replaced centralized planning, fostering the independent, convulsive transformation of pieces of the city. Giddens describes the double-edged nature of modernity: opportunities for progress are countered by risks and dangers. Similarly, in urban housing, utopian possibility

13   Houston, 1980. The portion of Freedman's Town that was severed by the freeway has been redeveloped to become parking lots and a convention center. This photo clearly shows Allen Parkway Village's proximity to downtown, making the large site a target for a later wave of redevelopment. Photographer: Harper-Leiper Studios.

14   Houston, 1998. Heavy equipment demolishing most of Allen Parkway Village public housing to make way for a mixed-income residential development. Photographer: Dana Cuff.

is balanced by, indeed often overwhelmed by, racial discrimination, real estate speculation, and local urban politics.

Urban development hinges on the political economy of real property. While some overall logic of development might be discernible (e.g., highest and best use, racial segregation, slum clearance, etc.), it cannot adequately explain the selection of any particular property as a site. Time lapse, aerial photography would capture a John Cage-like performance in which individual properties undergo sporadic metamorphosis across the city. Most of these transformations remain isolated in the midst of the original surroundings, upon which they have little impact. This is inherent to their internally organized design, in spite of stated intentions to the contrary.

Several parallel themes emerge from an examination of cases of convulsive urbanism. First, the city is viewed in terms of discontinuities of a significant magnitude: its instabilities, the relative independence associated with individual pieces of property, and the episodes of development. Second, an underlying premise is that architecture and urbanism are social productions, embodying the political economy. Within this, public works and private development interact in relatively contentious ways. Third, since architecture posits what ought to exist and is inherently utopian, it should be recognized that architecture also makes claims about what is not worth saving. Part of an alternative urban history consists in interpreting the lost physical environment beneath each new architectural undertaking.

In this work, I reverse the emphasis of the broader space-time discourse in which theory is only beginning to grasp the import of space. Taking its perspective from the spatial disciplines of architecture and urbanism, this research considers place as the grounding for an expansion and revision of temporality and its aesthetic implications.[8]

This is an excavation into material culture deposited in a continuously sporadic manner, and as such it is a decidedly postmodern look at cities.[9] Though I am speaking of postmodern theory, not stylistics, there has been a startling shift in large urban interventions, from the wartime modernist utopias to the present New Urbanists' premodern design formulations. This contrast becomes salient in my final section with the most recent development case.

15 Architects' rendering of Aliso Village as a modernist utopia.

16 Architects' rendering of Playa Vista as a postmodernist vision.

A Steady Instability

6 When the history of urban form has been recounted, one of several models of transformation has usually been invoked: organic growth, cosmic order, geographic determinism, and mechanical systems are the most common. While each model has its particular features, all have two characteristics in common. First, they emphasize the long-term stability of the city and the resultant continuities. Short-term perturbations are recorded, but their meaning is gathered from the long view. Moreover, these theories implicitly posit evolutionary progress. They are very fundamentally modern in that sense. Second, models of the urban process consider the city as a "whole," not necessarily homogeneous but a set of inter-related parts. In his classic *History of Urban Form,* Morris contends there are just two types of urban growth: organic and planned. "This natural unplanned evolution of a town, usually from village origins, is termed 'organic growth' and it represents by far the broadest of two directly opposed continuing streams of activity whereby mankind, throughout history, has created and expanded his urban settlements" (Morris, 1979, p. 8). Organic growth was thought to be continuous, serial, and systematic, unlike current thinking about nature as discontinuous and riddled with essential mutations and unpredictable events. Morris describes the opposing process as "the planned, predetermined approach," of which few examples exist; but those American cities with planned beginnings exhibit "the least desirable characteristics of *laissez-faire* growth" (p. 288). Although Spiro Kostof, in his seminal work *The City Shaped* (1991), rejects the view of the city as a finite, static form, he too adopts a holistic analysis. He asserts that "a city . . . is never complete, never at rest" (p. 13). "We are recorders of a physicality, then, akin to that of a flowing river or a changing sky" (p. 14). Like the river or sky, the city is presumed to be a dynamic but unified field. Vincent Scully, in *American Architecture and Urbanism* (1969), states that "the architect should be regarded as a kind of physical historian, because he constructs relationships across time: civilization in fact. And since civilization is based largely upon the capacity of human beings to remember, the architect builds visible history" (p. 257).

What if we focus not on the urban narratives that fulfill the historians' professional bias of constructing an orderly, continuous past, but instead on the city's discontinuities? This view accepts the city as a mosaic of pieces that behave in relatively independent ways, and emphasizes the short-term perturbations as meaningful in their own right. The search for coherence has guided historians' interpretations, as well as planning policy. But a critique of modern urbanism can offer a different take on urban development—as something more akin to Brownian movement. Instead of reading Levittown with Scully (1969, pp. 161–165), as the offspring of Radburn, Ebenezer Howard, and Broadacre City, we could view it as a 4,700-acre intrusion into the potato fields of a rural community that had never before seen the like, with a nearly autonomous infrastructure of streets and a repetitive architectural visage that peppered flat modern lines with economically efficient symbols of home. This might be the start of a more phenomenological perspective, of the Levittown perceived by its neighbors as it was being constructed, describing urban process and urban form as social production.

Fernand Braudel is often cited as the historian who best understood and integrated place into his analysis. In the preface to his definitive work on the Mediterranean, he states that there are just three types of historical time: geographical time, the almost changeless history of people in relation to their surroundings; social time, the history of society's "gentle rhythms" that flow at "a thousand different paces, swift or slow," but with only rare breaks; and individual time, the history of events and individuals that create "a surface disturbance, the waves stirred up by the powerful movement of tides" (Braudel, 1972–1973, 1:12). In each of the three formulations, the underlying structure of continuity and natural placidity is evident, though Braudel leaves room for superficial unevenness. But it is an extreme version of unevenness, a violent upheaval in geographic, social, and individual times, that concerns me. I argue that these convulsions result from the political economy of property, urban policy and its federal appropriations, and contemporary design ideology. The convulsions have at their roots geography, social institutions, and individual people and events. Setting out from Morris and Braudel, I might formulate this as a fourth time, called urban time.

The historians' poetic metaphors of gentle rhythms and changing rivers are contradicted by the city's sporadic eruptions and spatial convulsions, due primarily to the particulate and relatively arbitrary world of property and the real estate market in which it circulates. Convulsions follow two contradictory logics, neither of which bear much relation to the larger urban pattern. First, a spatial and temporal *local* logic prevails, as when a subdivider sells sequential tracts of adjacent lands. Second, a spatially dislocated policy intrudes upon a particular place, restructuring its development potential, as·when the federal government appropriates funds for housing near defense industries. Planning serves to mediate between the local and the dislocated forces, but it is relatively weak. Such conditions spark the kind of urban convulsion that I believe characterizes the typical growth and change within a city. Not only are those transformations episodic, that is, fragmented in time, but they are also spatially discrete.

Preventing urban development from being totally unpredictable are the various contexts within which any particular project takes place. One context of particular interest is the physical architectural one. All but the oldest American cities leapt directly from a low-density, agrarian form to technologically driven, high-density development, so that preexisting conditions have not determined the emergent shape of American cities.[10] Still, the restraints are multiple: urban infrastructure such as streets, utilities, access; the specific geography of a site, its cardinal orientation, topography, climate; institutional guidance of planning, regulation, and finance, such as zoning, codes, specific plans, lending policy; and the real estate context, such as proximate land use and land values. While these may sound absolute, in practice they have been both dynamic and flexible.[11] This model of a pliable urban context is especially appropriate in American cities that experienced growth booms during this century, when real estate speculation came to dominate urban processes.[12] With use value liberated from exchange value, a new political economy of land was possible, and with it, new urban morphologies. The city is a construct of ownership (Kostof, 1991) which is largely private and independent. The piecemeal, powerful structure of real property sustains a fragmented urban process that is reinforced by the focus of current urban politics on specific sites, issues, and constituencies. The American emphasis on property rights, coupled with the perceived failure of planning, particularly in Los Angeles, produces ironies of urban politics and urban form: preservation groups battle for environmental or architectural causes, without much regard for large-scale planning issues; neighborhood organizations try to prevent a particular development in their vicinity but are not concerned that it is pushed into someone else's domain; activist organizations work to shape a proposed project to generate less local traffic but ignore regional transportation planning.

The Nature of Housing

7   I have taken housing as the starting point for several reasons. First, in the architecture of the American city, housing has played a singularly important role, particularly since the end of World War II. The so-called fabric of the city is made up of its residential neighborhoods. While our neighborhoods may seem like the urban zone most deserving of stability, they are, in fact, a part of the city that is highly vulnerable to large-scale change. Federal supports, as a commercial developer reminded me, always go to housing. State funding for new housing construction, whether direct or indirect, can have massive and most destructive impacts upon the existing city. In addition, federal housing programs at their foundation inherently embrace a set of sociopolitical goals. Their utopian underpinnings help to construct a social history of the city, but from afar. The spatial dislocation of what is fundamentally federal spatial policy is especially obvious in a place like LA, a long way from both Washington and New York, the cities that defined American housing concerns.

When suburbanization exploded in the 1940s, it restructured urban space, nowhere more evidently than in Los Angeles. This process of private residential development blended with programs of federal subsidies for housing. On one hand, public housing entailed the inner-city construction of very affordable apartment buildings, generally quite large in scale (between 200 and 1,000 units), paired with the demolition of slum housing. On the other hand, federal supports via the Federal Housing Administration created a massive market for small speculative houses. Not long after the war, the public housing program itself was virtually destroyed, with national battles waged in cities across America primarily by the private real estate industry. This book examines the constant interplay between publicly funded housing, demolition, and private residential development.

A second reason to focus on housing is because residential architecture has long dominated architectural discourse and is particularly significant in the evolution of modern design. A review of architectural magazines confirms this observation. In Los Angeles, for example, John Entenza's *Arts and Architecture* was filled with single-family dwellings until the onset of war in the early 1940s. For the next few years, the magazine began running stories about federally subsidized, multifamily housing in each issue. The best architects in California worked on federal housing here during its first decade. Although the magazine generally treated war housing as technical solutions to construction and schedule problems, its architects designed the housing in a sleek modernism that had few other venues (except perhaps schoolhouse and later office building design). That aesthetic, I will argue, distinguished public housing from privately developed mass housing, and came to symbolize its socialist base.[13] After the war, Entenza initiated the well-known Case Study House program to lay out modern goals for the detached dwelling. In practice, however, traditional imagery persisted in popular housing while modernist public housing projects were derided metaphorically as factories, rabbit warrens, prisons. The producers of popular housing were, however, far more sophisticated than Entenza's crew believed—

17   After the war, street after street of market-rate tract housing was built like this one in Azusa, California.

18   Joe Cannon sleeps through the days as he waits in an FHA line for new homes, 1945.

more so perhaps than the Case Study architects themselves. While the latter imagined themselves leading the way with new models of residential construction, large-scale builders had already studied (and employed or rejected) new developments in technology (see section VI of this book).

Housing warrants attention in an urban political history for a third reason: the house in the neighborhood is where the individual meets the public. In the residential domain, citizens construct their relation to the space of the city. Moreover, individuals seeking continuity in life gather a sense of well-being from the stability of the neighborhood. Thus, transformations or urban convulsions that impact the neighborhood spark highly contentious debates. In an examination of urban discontinuity, housing reveals an extreme case of social impact, public debate, and individual implications.

The house is a locus for those values by which people define themselves and structure their very lives: race, ethnicity, family, gender, health, morality. It becomes obvious to the student of housing that during the first half of this century residential choice and mobility, so highly valued, did not apply to the poor or to people of color, who would move "if restrictions and race feeling were not placed upon every new tract of land where lots are sold."[14] The legacy of prejudicial "race feeling" is abundantly apparent in housing demolition, regulation, and construction. Through housing, we can see the determining spatial role that racial discrimination played in American urbanism.

Additionally, housing drives the spatial practices of urban growth, as one commercial developer observed.[15] Among land uses, new residential or industrial development can spark growth and determine the subsequent location of commercial and institutional activities. When housing is wiped out or constructed en masse, it carries with it the businesses that depend upon its occupants.

The final reason to focus this work on domestic places stems from the previous ones: housing was the primary battleground of postwar urban politics in Los Angeles. A critical shortage of housing confronted returning veterans, just as the private real estate industry gained strength to structure government intervention to its own ends. The war effort's emphatic success in industrial, technological production created an unfulfilled faith that the same technology, coupled with a sound urban plan, could be channeled to eradicate the housing problem.[16] The vast acreage of outlying land subdivided and built out after the war left no doubt about the automobile's reign, if any had doubted after LA's electric car transit system was euphemistically retired. All these factors reinforce the story of postwar residential development as the consummate LA story.

What Ought Not Survive

8   The question of what should be built goes hand in hand with that of what ought not survive. Just as citrus groves were felled to make way for model suburban homes, so too districts of slums were razed to make way for the better life of refrigerators, copper plumbing, and 1.5 persons per room. Having gathered steam in New York, Boston, and Philadelphia, the federal low-rent housing programs (initiated first under the PWA, then in the late thirties under the Wagner Act) implicitly took dense collections of tenement buildings as the national epidemic (see for example, McDonnell, 1957). For the most part, Los Angeles's slums were neither physically dense nor consistently substandard. Still, entire districts were deemed not worth saving, and large solutions, "planned communities," were conjured by teams of architects to rehouse those who would be displaced. Under the Wagner Act, for every low-rent unit to be built, a unit of slum housing had to be demolished, if not on the exact site of the new housing then through "equivalent elimination" in some other part of the city.

The design theorist and methodologist Horst Rittel defined design as future plans that are "deontic" propositions: every design is a statement about transforming what is into what ought to be (Rittel and Webber, 1973). Rittel's "what is" recognizes the significance of the preexisting conditions of a design project, but architectural research has focused entirely on what is designed, ignoring what already existed. I would put the case even more strongly: in every instance of design, something is destroyed as another thing is constructed. Ex-

19   The first bite is taken out of Normont Terrace public housing, demolished in the 1990s to clear a site for mixed-income residential development. Photographer: Chuck Saltzman.

panding Rittel's deontic maxim: every design takes a position on what need no longer exist. In the most trivial case, the open space a building will occupy is usurped; more profound are the cases I will describe here in which one world of inhabitation is buried under another. No one has made this case more strongly than the environmental preservation movement.

If we are to read the urban and architectural landscape, and from it gather a sense of the culture, society, and individuals that produced it, then what of the lost city? Those places demolished to make way for the next inhabitation can tell us much about urban values and urban politics. This side of an urban narrative is by definition missing from view as we construct our interpretations. The Los Angeles cases begin, therefore, with the rationale for selecting the particular site to be convulsively transformed.

The LA Stories

9   I have tracked five stories of large-scale transformation in Los Angeles, beginning in the late 1930s and culminating in a contemporary, ongoing project. Although these cases are spatially independent, there are also a number of intriguing connections which I will point out. The first cases to be discussed are Aliso Village and Rodger Young Village, both conceived in an emergency and both challenging the traditional physical form of home. The second pair includes Westchester and Chavez Ravine. At these places, the battle between public and private housing forces was waged. Lastly, Playa Vista represents a recent manifestation of urban convulsions, of lengthy entitlements, environmental activism, and contentious civic participation in the planning process.

    Although ground was not broken until 1941, the site for the Aliso Village public housing project had been singled out some thirty years earlier. When Congress passed the Wagner Act in 1937, one of the first five projects of Los Angeles's public housing program was located at the northern portion of the Utah Street site later known as Aliso Village.[17] It promised to make rubble of what was variously called Russian Town, The Flats, or Boyle Heights Flats, widely considered the worst slum in Los Angeles.[18] Surrounding the Utah Street Elementary School was a multiethnic community primarily of Russian and Mexican descent, living in small houses near places of industrial work along the Los Angeles River and rail yards. The highway departments of the city and state played their part by restructuring circulation in the area via the Aliso bridge, the Ra-

20 Commissioners from the Housing Authority of the City of Los Angeles watch the start of construction at Aliso Village.

mona Parkway, and the Santa Ana Highway, with all agencies working together "to replace one of the worst obsolescent areas in the city at its figurative front door."[19] One individual who played an instrumental role in LA's public housing campaign was the dedicated young Frank Wilkinson. Operating under the parallel objectives of integration and better housing, Wilkinson would tour thousands through the slums to demonstrate the urgent need for public housing. In The Flats, some 417 dwellings were appraised, purchased, and demolished, their residents scattered until such time as the new, modern public housing development would be complete. Although 386 of these structures, or a full 92 percent, were classified as substandard, recently discovered photographs of each of the buildings indicate otherwise.

Had any of the former residents planned on moving into Aliso Village, they would have been disappointed. With the onset of World War II, war workers received housing priority and fully occupied the 802 units when they opened at the end of 1942. Designed by a team of architects including Lloyd Wright, Aliso Village still stands to manifest a then-utopian vision of modernist, large-scale planning, housing blocks with untrafficked green space, nursery and elementary schools, and all the latest conveniences. In 1998, Aliso Village was a typical public housing apparition: its thoughtful internal site planning seemed to set it outside the normal processes of urban transformation, except for severe decay. That year, a "demolition fiesta" was held at the adjoining public housing, Pico-Aliso, to celebrate the area's next convulsion: national and local housing agencies had decided to knock down the fifty-year-old modernist experiment to build a seemingly suburban neighborhood. It was thus demolished and buried under the same progressive ideals that it had been born under fifty years before. Though Aliso Village was labeled "permanent housing" by the housing authority that built it, in 1998 the president of its resident council joined federal and local administrators in hoping that a large part of Aliso Village would go the way of the public housing next door. That outcome is inevitable.

Los Angeles was port of dispatch and reentry for some 7 million men and women in the armed forces during the war. When the war ended, almost a third of the out-of-state veterans intended to settle here after the war, having caught just a glimpse of southern California's attractions.[20] One of the worst housing crises the area had ever witnessed began when thousands upon thousands of veterans returned to compete for housing with the "army behind the army" that had taken up residence in LA as defense workers. Federally subsidized housing considered temporary was retained to ease this housing shortage, and attempts were made to build new temporary veterans' housing. The largest such development in the Los Angeles basin was Rodger Young Village, a site filled with 750 Quonset huts each housing two families, a commercial center, a community center, churches, and an elementary school. It was located in the floodplain where the Los Angeles River took a sharp turn at the northeast corner of Griffith Park, its flat site converted from an airfield, with its hangars adapted to new uses. Since it was officially part of Griffith Park, the city could lend the site for housing, circumventing land costs and problems of acquisition. Built in 1946 over just 90 days, Rodger Young stayed in service through the Korean War and in spite of itself became home to thousands of families. Finally in 1954, after several post-

21　Quonset huts at Rodger Young Village get wired in 1946. Photographer: Louis Clyde Stoumen.

ponements of its scheduled demise, and over the protests of its remaining residents-veterans, primarily families of color discriminated against in the private housing market, the Quonset huts were dismantled and removed. The site was then transformed into what might be called no-place infrastructure: parking lots for the current Los Angeles Zoo and Autry Museum, and a freeway interchange. Virtually no trace of this temporary village remains.

While Rodger Young was serving its purpose, the housing authority gained federal funds to build 10,000 new units of much-needed permanent public housing throughout the city. At that time, in the late forties, market analyses indicated a need for 100,000 new units of housing a year for the next five years in order to satisfy demand. The site for the largest of these proposed public housing developments was Chavez Ravine, just north of downtown and adjacent to Elysian Park. The hilly 254 acres was agricultural grazing land and a brickworks, but there was also a substantial ethnic Mexican community of nearly a thousand homes, the Palo Verde Elementary School, and a variety of buildings affiliated with the Catholic Church. Like Rodger Young's vocal residents, Chavez Ravine neighbors fought demolition of their community. Undaunted, architects Richard Neutra and Robert Alexander, at the bidding of the

22 Architects Neutra and Alexander imagined replacing the unpaved streets of Chavez Ravine with garden apartments and towers in a park. This photo was taken on Effie Street in 1950. Photographer: Leonard Nadel.

Housing Authority of the City of Los Angeles and Mayor Fletcher Bowron, developed Elysian Park Heights, a modernist utopian vision of 3,300 units in both low-rise and high-rise buildings. This site, perhaps as much as any other in the United States, focused the controversy about social housing: eventually, not only the specific project proposed for Chavez Ravine was defeated but, it could be argued, public housing programs far beyond Los Angeles. Architecturally, it represented the finest example of modern housing that the U.S. public housing program would produce. In a highly contentious, well-publicized battle, public housing in LA virtually ended in the California state legislative hearings on un-American activities, with key members of the housing authority baited as communists and the mayor later voted out of office.[21]

Fritz Burns, a private developer in Los Angeles, was instrumental in the battle against public housing in general and Elysian Park Heights in particular. An effective organizer of the real estate lobby, Burns participated on many fronts at both the local and national level to defeat what he portrayed as federal, socialist intrusion into private enterprise. He began his career in Los Angeles in the twenties, when he represented the real estate company of Dickinson and Gillespie, setting sales records for lots across the basin. Burns was at his finest subdividing and marketing land overlooking the Pacific Ocean at Palisades del Rey. His interest in that particular area was evident again in the forties, when he subdivided agricultural land near LA's young airport, this time building the houses as well. By 1950, the city of Westchester comprised nearly 11,000 houses, thanks in part to the Marlow-Burns development company and Kaiser Community Homes, of which Burns was president. Burns's efforts, in the defeat of public housing, in the crafting of a more unified real estate lobby, and in the large-scale homebuilding industry, illuminate some of the principal forces of eruptive transformation in the private housing market in the postwar city. Burns himself represents the leadership of the national real estate industry as it came of age in modern America: its political role in local issues of land use and the building industry, its evolution as a nationally organized institution and lobbying bloc, its contribution to the dramatic transformation of the Los Angeles landscape after World War II.

Westchester's housing represents the middle-class model of the American dream (see Hayden, 1984), and its story helps portray why we came by so much of it. Westchester's planning took suburban privacy to a new level, with blocks of houses turning their backs on arterial streets that gave as few points of access into the blocks as possible. Stylistically bereft of architectural pretensions,

23   A Marlow-Burns house in Westchester, 1946. Photographer: "Dick" Whittington.

24   The land ripe for development at Playa Vista is visible here, surrounded by sprawling Los Angeles.

the houses were distinguished from one another primarily by the presence of thin, suggestive trim in Colonial, Cape Cod, or Western flavors. Instead, these houses were innovative in terms of their production and financing, turned out complete with blinds and lawn sprinklers for a lower monthly payment than the going apartment rent. They appealed to a broad range of potential owners of varying incomes and occupations, though racial restrictions excluded all but white families.

From the 1970s, the residents of Westchester were primary opponents to an extra-large-scale undertaking in their vicinity: Playa Vista. Billed as the largest development undertaking within a contemporary American city, Playa Vista is a 1024-acre mixed-use development, shaped in part by contentious public debate. This final Los Angeles story brings the construct of urban eruptions into the present context, notably to the highly politicized, participatory processes by which the contemporary city is shaped. It also demonstrates the evolution of utopian architectural imagery, from the European modernism of public housing to the nostalgia of neotraditionalism evident in the Playa Vista sketches.

It is significant that Playa Vista closes this study, with its messy combination of public and private interests that so characterizes today's urban residential projects. After some fifty years of postwar growth, the death of public housing, the private urbanizing of the country without any of the early advocates' ruralizing of the city (Los Angeles, Housing Commission, *Report 1906–1908*), there has evolved a new form of development. It is governed by some of the same forces as were visible at Chavez Ravine and Rodger Young Village, because a contentious and local activism responds to the convulsions in its vicinity. The geography of planning, then, is as convulsive as the developments that spark it. In concert with the architecture of a sporadic urbanism, itself politically charged, this constructs a new way of looking at city form.

Siting Land: The Politics of Property

Introduction to the Politics of Property

10 Maps make visible how the land, out of which a city grows, is invisibly subdivided, regulated, and owned. We see manifestations of that invisible property in the physical improvements: where individual buildings terminate reflects property boundaries; differences among buildings reflect something about their owners and the regulations by which they abide. But it is not possible to read accurately all the conditions of property from the surface structure. Within any city, land undergoes continual evolution through social and political processes, first when it becomes property, second when it becomes a site. As I will describe, land is converted to property when ownership comes into play; property is transformed into a site when some development is intended. There is probably no more famous case of this process than the one fictionalized by the movie *Chinatown*. *Los Angeles Times* owner Harry Chandler bought almost 50,000 acres of dry land in the San Fernando Valley between 1903 and 1909, and then, through elaborate political machinations, brought tax-funded water to it, rail lines, and city annexation. Land that cost him under $3 million, once wet, subdivided, and suburbanized, became worth nearly $120 million. For large-scale projects, the creation of a site is a real-life drama with significant repercussions.

In urban land economics, property has traditionally been modeled as a continuous phenomenon. For example, a land value gradient predicts decreasing property values as a linear function of distance from a highly desirable geographic point; the further one proceeds away from downtown, the less costly the

25   Hand-drawn boundaries circumscribe neighborhood and agricultural property to create the proposed site for Elysian Park Heights.

land. When such models didn't fit the facts, more complex topographical models could depress inner-city property and simultaneously heighten values for a ring of near-town commercial land uses. Most models of urban economics are based on continuities, in part because of the very nature of modeling. But a critical, cultural analysis of property suggests a more episodic and spatially uneven view of urban land development. A certain invisible illogic seems to reign over cities, which swamps any desire for predictable development behavior.

When a large-scale transformation of some part of the city occurs, it intrinsically involves the politics of property and land development. There are three steps necessary to ready such an area for development. The first is both conceptual and practical: property must be redefined as a site. That is, an existing land use is deemed disposable in light of a potential use, and loose boundaries are situated around the area intended for metamorphosis. Sites can comprise many independently held pieces of property which, when lumped together, form the tentative location for some urban plan. In the projects studied here, the sites vary from densely inhabited areas defined as slums to advantageously located open space and agricultural land. Slums, at least since the thirties, were inherently considered sites. Once an area was labeled a slum, it meant

26   Aliso Village, 1941–1998. This sequence of photos, all shot from the same position, illustrates the radical transformation involved in large-scale

urban development.

that plans for its general alteration not only could but should be created. Slums, as political constructs, embodied their own demise.

Second, the parcels within the site's boundaries must be assembled and readied for development. In large-scale urban undertakings, this process often provokes the use of eminent domain, whereby the forced sale of private property is justified by a planned use with public benefit, such as a park, freeway, or airport. As I will later analyze, the nature of eminent domain is of utmost relevance to understanding real property in the United States. Eminent domain is the extreme case on a continuum of urban land dynamics, specifically of the dynamics by which private property is transformed by public intervention.

Third, whatever presently occupies the land must be removed to make way for what private developers and urban economists call the highest and best use, or what public agencies represent as the common good. Thus visionary plans rest on incendiary tactics. Of particular interest here are cases where housing was demolished so that more housing could be built. In a process that became widespread with the Depression, areas of cities across the country were considered obsolete and their demolition necessary so that new seeds of a great metropolis could flower there. But this was by no means a natural process; rather, it was a highly political one.

A site is roughly sketched, the property is assembled, and existing uses are razed: only when these three steps have been accomplished can a large housing project begin. Land development and the structure of property relations are thus fundamental to understanding significant urban change. At each step of a public land development, the question of the commons arises: In what ways does the project contribute to some greater public good? A public agenda is explicit when the state undertakes urban change, as in the case of subsidized housing construction. But it is implicit in large-scale private development as well, most of which depends upon some form of public support. In America, the individual owner-occupied dwelling has historically received various state subsidies because of its supposed democratic benefits.

Whenever the pursuit of public good infringes, as it must, upon private interests, the potential for contentious disputes arises. Since large undertakings are likely to come armed with some form of public assistance, they trigger a debate over public and private interests. Counterintuitively, these large projects make the city a more provisional place, since they not only wipe out sizable territory in order to be constructed, but they are also themselves subject to later, large-scale transformation. Once land has been assembled into large pieces of property, it remains attractive when the next big plan needs a site. Thus, large urban transformations are rooted in issues of property, serve as breeding grounds for contentious debate, and become catalysts of fugitive urbanism.

27   Housing activist Frank Wilkinson addresses CIO members touring the slums, in the political battle to win support for slum clearance and new public housing construction. February 1952. Photographer: Leonard Nadel.

To grasp the convulsive growth of cities and the fugitive quality that large-scale undertakings lend to them requires a fuller understanding of land development. That means examining the ways people have thought about and behaved in relation to real property in American history. This legacy blurs the distinction between private and public rights in land, and explains why I will, in subsequent chapters, situate private real estate development in Westchester alongside public housing projects like Elysian Park Heights. Indeed, a brief historical survey suggests that the state was the original land speculator in America.

Perhaps a city's evolution would more closely resemble the natural processes urban design historians like to invoke, were it not for property. Urban property (that is, land in the city to which people lay claim) comes with rather arbitrary yet fixed spatial qualities paradoxically linked to a constantly evolving set of sociopolitical relations. Central to this story about provisionality in the city after World War II are the ways in which private individuals and groups construct their property rights, along with ways the state invokes its property rights. The sociopolitical evolution of property has strongly influenced the course of urban development. In the Depression era, New Deal ideas about real property gave great power to the state to remake the city. After the war, increased prosperity fueled private real estate interests in their bid to regain dominance, particularly in regard to urban housing. Commercial builders undertook ever larger residential projects with various public supports (most coming from the Federal Housing Administration), including land assembly, extended credit, and loan guarantees.

Two camps have played key roles in large-scale urban change in the modern residential environment: the state (most often, the federal government) as a public-sector developer, and private-sector developers, who are generally corporate developers or community builders, according to planning historian Marc Weiss (1987). Between corporate and community developers, boundaries are indistinct when it comes to homebuilding, but the battle lines are clear when it comes to urban policy. Although the present public-sector subsidy of housing is small and indirect (via various financial supports systems), New Deal policies sparked by the Great Depression substantially interjected the state as a significant player in real estate. The Second World War heightened government involvement in construction through defense priorities on housing and industrial location, construction materials, and rent controls. Throughout the past century, contentious debate over housing has provoked both the state and the real estate industry to generate propaganda steeped in myths of the American dream and inalienable rights.

Contention over Drastic Change

11   When areas of the city previously considered stable are razed, particularly homes, the upset is visceral; contentious debate over urban property will almost certainly ensue. But this is more common today than it was fifty years ago, as evident in the lack of organized resistance to Aliso Village from displaced residents of The Flats.[1]

We should distinguish at the outset between what I am calling urban contention or debate and Not-In-My-Back-Yard-ism. The latter is associated primarily with middle-class white suburbanites who resist any change to their communities, particularly changes that trigger demographic shifts or traffic-related problems. One might frame NIMBYism as simply a destructive force in urban planning and design, for by definition it aims to thwart action, asserting rights without commensurate duties of a constructive nature. Most urban debates take place over a long time period, however, and early no-growth, no-change stances may establish starting points for later negotiation. In contentious developments, unlike no-growth debates, eventually some change is recognized as desirable or inevitable.

In their efforts to shape the pending development, parties attempt to establish their property rights as well as the property-related obligations of others. Urban development is one of the only arenas where notions of duty are coupled with notions of rights in the formulation of a conception of justice. In a country dominated by "rights talk" to the exclusion of the correspondent re-

28 Life on this street would be drastically altered when K's Café became parcel #76 in the property appraisal that led to eminent domain proceedings and demolition for Estrada Courts public housing.

sponsibility (Glendon, 1993), urban negotiations warrant scrutiny beyond their already important role in shaping contemporary development. In fact, I contend that through such negotiations a cultural conception of environmental justice evolves.

As will become evident, the Los Angeles stories chart the increasingly deafening voice of citizen participation (particularly owner-occupant participation) in the transformation of the city. Indeed, planners and architects complain that participation has gone so far as to make forward progress interminably slow, when not impossible. Participation ranges from quiet backroom negotiations to vociferous, even violent battles. From the repressed disgruntlement of The Flats residents in the thirties, to Mayor Bowron's front-page fisticuffs with an opponent in the fifties, to the present noisy hearings about Playa Vista, a range of property debates are captured. The cases bear witness to an expanding notion of ownership. In recent contentious developments, the tireless citizen participation results, at least in part, from a generally broad sense of ownership and with it an expanded set of property rights. Between the thirties and the fifties, a political pressure wielded by residents emerged to shape urban development debates and form the basis for the broad powers of citizen groups today.

Underlying any discussion of property is the presupposition of scarcity, which also underlies urban contentions, as we shall see. Hilberseimer (1955) attributes the entire spread of civilization to scarcity of arable property, and argues that its expansion was inherently hostile: "Fertile land was probably not abundant, and the secrets of soil fertilization and conservation were undiscovered. . . . Young members of the settlement were crowded out to find new land to cultivate. They could possess the living space they required only through conquest. The people they conquered had to follow the same course. . . . Displaced populations were forced, themselves, to be on the move" (p. 18). While contemporary theories of urban growth and colonialism differ, this 1955 reading captures the idealized model operative in the postwar period. A scarcity of real property, inherent in settlements with growing populations, meant conquest and displacement. When the modern city grew or sought to rejuvenate itself, those same forces applied, with the same violence.

A basic American belief in the connection between work and property, embodied in the Protestant work ethic and articulated by philosopher John Locke in the seventeenth century, grants a person a claim over the land where he or she labors. This Lockean notion of property, coupled with a historical understanding of land in postcolonial America, upholds the primacy of residents' rights over their neighborhood and renders suspect development by external agents,

29   The Small Property Owners' League in 1954 invoked the Constitution and a general fear of Communism to keep state intervention out of their neighborhoods.

30 Following the 1949 Housing Act, the second wave of public housing sparked ongoing public debate, as at this Los Angeles Planning Commission hearing on the large (and eventually unbuilt) housing project at Rose Hills. Monsignor Thomas O'Dwyer is at the microphone. May 1951. Photographer: Leonard Nadel.

whether private developers or governmental agencies. It places the rights of tenants under those of title-bearers; and it places any government action in real estate on very fragile ground. In the American mind, where we mow, we expect authority.

Any contentious development documented in local newspapers will concretely exemplify these issues. When Los Angeles's Small Property Owners' League picketed against public housing and over 400 supporters protested at public hearings in June of 1951, their practices prefigured the more sophisticated but virtually identical acts of urban development debate forty years later at Playa Vista. The loud opposition that disrupted public housing in LA was also voiced in Pittsburgh, Seattle, and Chicago, among many cities (see Freedman, 1959, pp. 283–284). Though opposition at 1951 public hearings was directed toward government agencies, by 1992 citizen advocacy groups were protesting the actions of private developers.

The privatization of the public realm that scholars observe in physical spaces like shopping malls and corporate plazas is extended by this analysis (see for example Loukaitou-Sideris and Banerjee, 1998). The privatization of urban space has proceeded hand in hand with the shift in advocacy over those same spaces, away from public policy and toward special-interest citizen groups.[2] While the latter have tended to promote local concerns, they can be more representative than private developers operating without direct citizen input. And within public-sector development, as will be apparent in the LA cases, local concerns have been largely ignored in favor of some larger public good. In both public and private large-scale development, urban debate reveals a general lack of concern for the local good. Just how a local good should be merged with a broader public good is the substratum of most urban contention.

Although I argue that urban debates have taken their present form largely over the past fifty years, their origins go back as far as the city itself. Citizens had channels for public input about the shape of public works projects in ancient Greece. At the end of the nineteenth century, the Eiffel Tower proposal stirred Parisian debate. Indeed, close research into most large-scale urban undertakings would reveal some citizen reaction. What distinguishes the contemporary circumstance is the formalized channels for citizen input, such as public hearings, design review boards, and open planning commission meetings, the expanded basis for claiming rights in property, as well as the ultimate authority those claims carry.

Ideologies of Land and Property in America

12 The drastic urban developments covered in this book lay out issues of property in the city: public versus private, transformation versus stability, use value versus exchange value (see Logan and Molotch, 1987). In the case of real urban property, a tenuous balancing act between the public interest and the private landholder organizes all other dimensions of property. At no time in recent American history was this debate more focused than during the New Deal, and particularly at its demise. It was Roosevelt's plan to establish the great society through social programs serving that third of the nation that was ill clothed, ill fed, and, most important to this work, ill housed. And as the 1937 Housing Act hoped to demonstrate, a housing program provided jobs for workers so that they might be better fed and better clothed. While the federal housing agency retained vast authority, the 1937 Act conferred great powers upon the city and its agents working to improve poor housing conditions. Urban blight, and the slums it supposedly bred, were ready targets; eminent domain was revived with reinvigorated purpose.

The balance to which I refer is constantly restruck between private rights in land and public responsibilities (Bryant, 1972), although the latter are far more ambiguous than the former. The dynamic between the two is overtly apparent in development debates, in which both developers and community organizations claim their land rights, while simultaneously communities, government agencies, interest groups, planners, and politicians monitor public

31 Homeowners' resistance to eminent domain was rarely effective. Photographer: Otto Rothschild.

responsibilities. In a sense, most of these parties are manipulating property that by legal and popular opinion they do not own. While planners and politicians may have some jurisdiction over property, an expanding crowd of others acts upon their perceived right to control property to which they have no title.[3]

After life and liberty, "the third absolute right . . . is that of property" (Blackstone, 1765, Book I).[4] Property rights, so fundamental to the American system of law and thought, have developed to affect the very nature of the city. A steady stream of changes in the popular conception of real property rights (versus personal property) has influenced the evolution of property developments like eminent domain, slum clearance, emergency housing, or urban renewal. An exploration of property rights history and theory provides an intellectual context for large-scale urban convulsions.

The frontier, its history, and the theory of property rights reveal many factors that contribute to the dynamic between private rights, and public responsibilities in land.[5] In America, an aggressive legacy of taking and laying claim to land underlies contemporary development disputes. It also prefigures the violence of extra-large environmental undertakings, as they upset the existing social ecology and physical context.

The ideal of private property in postcolonial America has been one of complete freedom for the owner, as if, once across the property boundaries, the "law of the land" was one's own. No one was to tell an owner what to do on his or her land—a condition toward which every tenant farmer, immigrant, and later apartment renter aspired. Historically, this ideal of autonomy was never fully achieved, for communities, counties, and states always exerted some pressure on individual landowners. Generally, individual property rights have been struck down when some public good was assigned priority.[6]

Determining what constitutes a public good is a highly politicized process. Parties to a contentious project lobby with the explicit objective of transforming public opinion about what might serve its interests. Constructs of the public good are highly situational and are continuously being redefined. The changing use of eminent domain, for example, demonstrates the political malleability of public interest. During an economic downturn, powers of eminent domain have been granted to factories that will bring local jobs (e.g., Schultz, 1992), an authority not typically granted to private enterprise. As prosperity looms, eminent domain may be used to build baseball stadiums, downtown financial centers, and highways.

Because of the primacy of property rights in American social history, eminent domain could only be employed when public sentiment would permit it. Against it, notions of the pioneer spirit still figure in the contemporary landowner's mind. The ingenuity, temerity, and willingness to take risks typically assigned to pioneers are characteristics that might well be ascribed to present-day developers, but also to the most involved community activists. The land the pioneers settled was not free and open for the taking but was instead wrested by violence from Native Americans. The history of land during America's westward expansion implicates several complicating components of present-day contentions: a recognition that claim to land might involve usurpation, conquest, and displacement; a disregard for land as community property; the association of land with individual freedom; a Lockean ideal that ascribes natural ownership to those who mix their labor with the land; a disregard for geographically specific resources; and a general contempt for government restrictions on land. The latter retreats in economic downturns, when public opinion in general and the members of the building industry in specific admit a federal role in urban development.

A Wilderness for Speculation

13 Land, and the home built upon it, have played strong mythic parts in the American narrative. Here the danger of applying quick history to analyze current events is counterweighed by the simple myths that have so clearly shaped American views of land and property. These myths constitute the foundation that would be shaken by large-scale urban development and eminent domain.

The present sociopolitical system of land in America has evolved since colonial times, when land was the principal base for the economy and, along with religion, for the social order. Land ownership, with its prospects of independence and wealth, was a primary motivation for immigration to the New World. As land was plentiful and people few, the system of land tenure and attitudes toward the land developed accordingly. Although the colonies established a range of land tenures, there was a trend, according to the historian Clawson (1964, p. 37), "toward giving the landowner greater rights to use his land as he saw fit, and toward reducing controls and restrictions over land use, whether the controls were from government or landlords. The idea of unrestricted land ownership, in sharp contrast to feudal land tenures, was widely held by the time of the Revolution."

The end of the Revolution witnessed extensive land speculation along with the agglomeration of new large landholdings where Native Americans, farming, and smallholdings once dominated. This fundamental shift from individuals with claims on the land they worked to a system driven by speculative finance sowed the seeds of controversy between resident laborers and all others with interest in the land. Those same settlers who had not given credence to the claims of various Indian tribes now faced the threat, albeit less lethal, of speculative interest upon their own property rights. Contention developed over whose rights to property were the greater: the owner, the laborer, the resident, the speculator, or the state.

The Revolutionary War left the government impoverished but with large blocks of land. These became the means to replenish treasuries, through speculative sales that were held without an evaluation of their long-term impacts. "America got rid of feudalism at the price of handing over an altogether excessive part of the national patrimony to land grabbers, land jobbers, and profiteers. It was not an auspicious beginning" (Bryant, 1972, pp. 69–70). The concept of land as public trust was challenged from the nation's earliest hour. Two contradictory forces imposed limitations on the government's ability to manage the land: first, the colonists' disdain for any government interference, and second, the federal disregard for public land. Together, as we shall see, the same forces made their mark upon postwar housing.

With tremendous holdings of undeveloped territory (such as the Louisiana Purchase), governmental agencies appear to have given little thought to maintaining these lands. Instead, they sold them for little or nothing in what has been called "the great giveaway" of land in nineteenth-century America. Notable was the Homestead Act of 1862, by which one and a half to two million people acquired land (Bryant, 1972; Smith, 1950). Though the guiding ideal was the family farm, the reckless disposition of land fulfilled this ideal only modestly. In addition, natural resources were squandered as geographically unique ecologies were ignored.[7] Whatever the Homestead Act's impact in populating the country (the U.S. population grew by 32 million during the same period when less than two million homesteaded land), it certainly encouraged speculation by entrepreneurs, often leaving the small farmer to resort to squatting without payment to anyone. Over the following century, the gap between use value and exchange value of property would grow more apparent, as the real estate industry assumed a dominant role in the American economy.

Accurate land surveys were necessary if large blocks were to be parceled and sold without dispute to increase the national treasury. The coordinated effort of townships and sections, resulting from the Land Ordinance of 1785, laid a rigid grid over most of the United States west of the Allegheny Mountains (see Reps, 1965). The grid had little to do with local geography, ecology, or demography; instead, it had everything to do with neat subdivision and subsequent speculation, that is, the conversion of land into property. According to the American planning historian John Reps,

The gridiron spread across the country as the natural tool of the land speculator. No other plan was so easy to survey, and no other system of planning yielded so many uniform lots, easy to describe in deeds or to sell from the auctioneer's block. Everywhere there was gold in the land if it could be bought, subdivided, and sold, even in the hills, if promoted by a skillful operator. (Reps, 1965, p. 302)

The grid, molded over the hills of San Francisco just as it was laid flat across the Great Plains, became the accepted American standard. Into this nonhierarchical spatial system, communities organized themselves as best they could, making intersections or a stretch of Main Street the focus of town, rather than central open spaces. In most towns, like the nation itself, all land remained in the marketplace, relegating public space to the spaces in between. This settlement pattern reproduced the dominance of individual, privatized property rights while subordinating the collective, social order. It established the precedent that governmental action upon property was permissible when it enabled private development.

Precedents for community sentiment, however, should not be ignored. Early colonial townships shared a collective sensibility expressed in the subdivision of land. Rather than assuming more typical, dispersed, rural patterns, these farming communities organized into villages around a common green where livestock was penned. After collectively erecting the meeting hall on the common, the settlers built their houses close by with fields stretching out behind (see Reps, 1965; Jackson, 1970). Communal ethics did not meld readily with those of the pioneer, whose tough figure overshadowed the life of townspeople. Instead, a charged duality was established between the idea of the frontiersman and that of the gentleman. The American cultural geographer J. B. Jackson adds that the village model disintegrated as lots on the common were filled and villagers began speculating, selling their remote farmlands and woodlots to more recent arrivals (Jackson, 1970, p. 19).

The legacies of speculation, autonomous and government-spurning pioneers, and private property over public land remain with us today. The state role in real estate speculation not only blurred distinctions between private development and public undertakings, but left a vacuum surrounding the public interest—a vacuum that citizen groups would come to fill. Whereas the Great Depression briefly lent New Deal welfare programs a broad mandate and public support, the return to prosperity after World War II witnessed shifts in public opinion that encouraged urban contentions over places like Chavez Ravine and Rodger Young Village in Los Angeles. The national lobbying success of real estate organizations, coupled with local opposition to the specific sites where federal projects were to be located, effectively defeated subsidized housing and later large federal urban projects. The three organizations most potent in their opposition to public housing were the National Association of Real Estate Boards, the National Association of American Builders, and the United States Savings and Loan League (Freedman, 1959, p. 75). Their efforts helped to construct both the developers' belief in their own autonomy and the enabling policies favoring them, which are now regularly challenged by communities.

This legacy and the historically privileged position of the private right to property are variously embodied in the single homeowner who fights against any change that threatens property values, and the builder who believes restrictions on development are un-American. Arrayed against them are the modern "townspeople"—the progressive housing advocates of the 1940s, and the present community activists who organize to achieve a higher quality of life in their neighborhoods. While contemporary progressives take stands in property debates that are inherently complex and conflicted, nowhere are the contradictions more apparent than in the slum clearance and housing projects of the 1940s.

The Roots of Property Rights

14 In current debates about property rights, the conservative position seeks to produce a free market situation for land with greater control for the individual landholder and reduced control by government.[8] This position has been pitted against the so-called environmentalist position, which seeks to limit individual free choice related to property in order to protect some greater good. In general, the conservative view favors local control over the more remote regulations of federal and state authorities. There is an explicit spatial disparity framed by local versus state control. Neighborhood activism has upset this simple dualism, as individual landholders collectively exert their property rights over those of other individuals to regulate land use development in the interest of some greater good. I hesitate to call this collective good a public good, since community organizations often serve highly local objectives. Even so, neighborhood activism inserts itself, in theory and practice, in between a collective good and individual rights. The final case study in this book, Playa Vista, is an excellent example of this new spatial politics, with its struggles over local and public interests.

When a part of the city is transformed by upheaval, all those affected implicitly reevaluate their assumptions about property. Each individual holds some personal and probably tacit theory of property rights and property-related duties (although the latter seem to apply primarily to others rather than ourselves). Until an adverse court ruling in 1934, when the government took land for public projects most people accepted federal authority. Nowadays, when a community organization blocks the demolition of the derelict neighborhood school by a private developer who wants to build condominiums, both sides can claim proprietary interests. The community feels a sense of ownership of this once-central, public institution (and its land); the developer purchased the property with the right to transform it within existing regulatory constraints. As developers have discovered, entitlements are no longer sufficient to initiate construction, and even such imperfect entitlements have become difficult to secure. Through the public hearing process, the community can obligate the developer to mitigate the loss of this neighborhood resource. Although, as Weiss (1987) observes, it was real estate interests that lobbied most effectively for public-sector planning (e.g., zoning), they unwittingly empowered the very communities that now oppose urban development.

Beginning with the New Deal, we can see a dramatic change in conceptions of property rights that parallels drastic upheavals in the city. The early public housing that cleared away homes was built without much protest from those displaced. By the time of the second housing act, in the late forties and early fifties, occupants and interest groups were speaking out at public hearings, picketing, and using the media to register their views. Real property rights as legal scholars, political theorists, and philosophers conceive them had undergone a political metamorphosis that fueled development disputes. In constant evolution, these debates implicate not only that most fundamental right to property, but our ideas of justice, labor, and reward. If that were not enough, the very nature of land and the meaning of ownership are contested in legal theory.

Ownership of private property has long been associated with work, which is a specific case of the fundamental connection between effort and reward. In the seventeenth century, John Locke articulated a basis for property rights in "natural law" (written with the very pragmatic goal of undermining claims on property by royal absolutism), by which individuals make something their property, including land, when their labor is mixed with it. In *The Second Treatise of Government*, Locke states:

> Though the Earth, and all inferior Creatures be common to all Men, yet every Man has a *Property* in his own *Person*. This no Body has any Right to but himself. The *Labour* of his Body, and the *Work* of his Hands, we may say, are properly his. Whatsoever then he removes out of the State that Nature hath provided, and left it in, he hath mixed his *Labour* with, and joyned to it something that is his own, and thereby makes it his *Property*. (Locke, 1960, pp. 305–306)

Thus, when farmers till the soil, their labor (which they naturally own) mixes with the land and thereby gives them claim to it. In fact, it is the rise of agriculture that necessitated fixed property in land (Ryan, 1987). However, Locke believed the "invention of money" had distorted the natural law of property. In terms of property, the distinction between natural law and the invention of money parallels the distinction between use value and exchange value (Logan and Molotch, 1987), and it is a distinction that rears its head in urban development debates.

Industrialization in the capitalist state entrenched an instrumental attitude about the relationship between work and property, such that work yields wages, and wages (not labor) provide a means to secure property. With regard to land, however, a commutative interpretation of ownership did not apply as readily to other kinds of property, first because of the nature of landed property,[9] and then from the history of ideas about land in America.

Unlike other forms of property, land is a palimpsest of the activities that take place upon it. Traces of neglect or care are visible during the continuous life of a particular land use, but with demolition the slate is wiped clean. The architecture or buildings are provisional, yet the property as space and relations remains intact. "The ownership of land, therefore, offers opportunities for self-expression and allegiance, not simply for marketing farm produce or the extraction of urban rents by the slum landlord," explains political theorist Alan Ryan (1987, p. 72). This may be the reason certain land-related rights are informally granted dependent upon tenure, or strength of connection to that land. For example, the right to multigenerational family land is held more sacred than that to land recently acquired, or to rental property. In the Depression, the severity of economic hardship was registered when the government auctioned farmlands that had been held by now-bankrupt families who had labored there for generations. Likewise, the Homestead Act, a direct descendant of Lockean natural law, gave title to those individuals who demonstrated through agricultural labor their worthiness to own and commitment to maintain the land in a productive state. In the context of early modern upheaval, those least able to make claims on land were recent immigrants who had not yet had time to mix their labor with the land, and in particular those living in urban slums where little land was available to labor upon and most residents were renters. These factors lent further support, as if more were needed, to the demolition of poor immigrant neighborhoods.

Today, developers and even city officials will suggest that local homeowners, more than renters, are the vociferous stakeholders in contentious developments. Indeed, land has been viewed as a central element of democracy, an accessible form of property to the hardworking, a principal component in the

32   Well-tended gardens and houses testify to the sense of ownership renters felt for their homes. This house is one of three on a single lot, about to be demolished for Aliso Village.

establishment of home and livelihood (Cohn, 1979). When the city mapped, and thus defined, its slums, a high proportion of renters were located within the boundaries. Former residents register their dismay in recollections about their well-tended gardens, plowed under in spite of the labor they expended there.

With regard to land, the private developer's position, along with that of the state-qua-developer, contradicts Lockean reasoning and popular belief. While developers mix their labor with the land, it is indirect in comparison with the homeowner's labor. Instead, the developer's labor is concentrated upon assembling the site, subdividing the land, gaining entitlements, putting together the financing, and managing the process. Those homeowners who mixed their labor with the material property, as most must do, will feel justified in exercising their rights while extracting the duties of others. This, coupled with the culturally ascribed sanctity of a stable home, makes the demolition of any residential area controversial. In the early cases described here, beginning with Aliso Village, there was no manifest controversy. Residents, mainly poor households of color, were visibly angry in the appraisal photos but had no political clout. Their potential allies, the housing activists, were unwilling to forsake their own dreams of modern housing. The federal slum clearance program was billed accordingly as the means to establish stable homes among the poor. It was when Gans (1962) and Jacobs (1961) pointed out the intricate social solidity of existing communities that demolition propaganda began to ring hollow, or when poor, ethnic communities ceased to be viewed as sites.

Reading on in Locke's second treatise on government, we find the kernels of another challenge to the developer's property rights. Explaining that labor transforms into property what was found in a natural state, Locke qualifies that right according to the supply of land: property may be established by labor "at least where there is enough, and as good left in common for others" (Locke, 1960, p. 306). Beyond issues of scarcity and quality, Locke states that apportionment of land is fair when measured by its direct usefulness to the laborer, this being distorted by the "Invention of Money" (p. 311), with which possessions were enlarged beyond the basic needs of the possessor. According to Locke's reasoning, prior to the agreement to value money and prior to scarcity, there could exist a societal understanding of property rights without need of laws. "Right and Conveniency went together; for as a Man had a Right to all he could imploy his Labour upon, so he had no temptation to labour for more than he could make use of. This left no room for Controversie about the Title, nor for Incroachment on the Right of others" (§51, p. 320). The legitimate use of land

33 Poor communities of color were seen primarily as numbers of slum units to be demolished by housing progressives like these men, sitting before images of public housing developments in 1945. Photographer: Hoster.

is described in terms of sufficiency: in the state of nature, we take only what we need from the environment, leaving as much and as good for others. Those whose use of land respects the sufficiency rule hold claims perceived as more valid than those whose use of land exceeds natural rights. And it was upon the claim of insufficiency that housing advocates argued the need to build affordable accommodation for slum dwellers.

In post-Depression Los Angeles as well as other American cities, these underlying principles of property shed light on the emergent urban form. In the thirties and forties, as private homebuilding grew from a small-scale family operation into a full-blown industry, there was scant awareness that any scarcity of land at the periphery existed. Instead, there was a scarcity of affordable homes. Builders saw their task as a public service: to provide homes, and the public lined up for the opportunity to buy them.[10] Close-in agricultural land was seen as the logical place to build new houses. To serve the public interest, the government established programs under the Federal Housing Administration (FHA) to insure mortgages and create long-term, low-interest loans, as well as the Federal National Mortgage Association (Fannie Mae) to assure a good supply of credit, all so that homeownership was more broadly possible.[11]

An interesting variation on this conception of ownership and property rights occurred in the Chavez Ravine case when an extended family, the Arechigas, protested the compensation they had been granted for their property by eminent domain proceedings. At first they gathered tremendous public support for their plight, but it was later discovered that they owned some eleven pieces of property around the city. Immediately, public support was withdrawn, including the trailer loaned to the family as temporary quarters after their house was demolished. In the highly racialized social climate of the 1950s, a poor Latino family trying to live out the American dream in the slums played into scenarios of cultural assimilation and dominance, but there was no outpouring of sympathy for a wealthy Latino family that *chose* to live in such conditions and, moreover, expected to make more money than the government offered for their home's destruction. With racial views came the view predicted by this analysis, that property rights are strongest and clearest on a principal place of residence (labor and the sufficiency rule basically grant the right to have a roof over one's head). Given that the Arechigas seemed to have many alternative roofs, public support withered.

Locke's rather romantic portrayal of property corresponds more closely than formal property law itself to a tacit popular theory of property rights. Contentions over upheavals arise when builders act in ways that distort the legitimate use of property. In Los Angeles, the postwar building boom eventually convinced citizens that land was becoming scarce, and that further changes would diminish rather than enhance the quality of their community. Under these conditions, it is impossible to satisfy Locke's sufficiency criterion of leaving as much and as good for others. Moreover, the developers' interest in the land extends beyond what is personally useful, which gives them less moral standing than others whose rights they may encroach upon. There are of course laws that entitle developers to act as they do; my point is that those laws contradict the public's tacit, Lockean theories of property.

Comparing the American system of rights to those of other countries, political legal theorist Mary Ann Glendon (1991) makes a number of astute observations about Locke and the ideal of property. In Locke's formulation, starting from the unusual formulation that each of us is our own *property,* the rights that then befall us are not balanced by any sense of responsibility toward others. In the so-called natural state, our obligation to others is only to leave them land enough and as good as ours so that they can claim it with their labor. It follows that the resident-owner, equated with the laborer, has primary property rights without burden of reciprocal duties. If any duties are identified, they are assigned to the nonlaboring owner/speculator, who in turn does not recognize those duties, nor those of anyone else, but only the rights assigned to ownership. By contrast, when the state stepped into the builder's role, as with public housing, certain obligations were acted upon. Those residents displaced by slum clearance were to have first priority to rent the new housing.[12] Housing advocates, in turn, believed they had a duty to invent model dwellings, and dwellers, that would supplant the slums—though these were projections of their own middle class prejudices.

Few private developers, even in their propaganda, acknowledge duties to the community. Instead, what they consider extractions are publicly identified as gifts. By such reasoning, restoring a wetland is not the developer's duty but a generous donation. Glendon observes that our limited language of duties, overshadowed by rights-rich discourse, restricts the evolution of a more balanced social and legal system.[13] Ultimately, even neighborhood activists and preservationists frame what are easily considered responsibilities in the language of rights: the public has a right to a restored wetland. This formulation is unfortunate, since it makes it easier for the developer to claim generosity rather than obligation. Glendon summarizes American political discourse as uniquely exhibiting "a tendency to formulate important issues in terms of rights; a bent for stating rights claims in a stark, simple and absolute fashion; an image of the rights bearer as radically free, self-determining, and self-sufficient; and the absence of well-developed responsibility talk" (p. 107).

The adjudication of conflicting rights, or rights and duties, is fundamentally a debate about what is just, which is characteristic of development disputes in general. This core of urban disputes helps explain why NIMBYism and community activism are such powerful forces. Justice itself and property rights evolve together, according to Hume in *A Treatise of Human Nature* (III, ii 2). Ryan elaborates, "Were men to be spontaneously altruistic, or goods not at all scarce, property rights would have no point; there would be no need for rules to assign priority to some claims over others, and no need for authority to deter one man from invading another's rights" (1987, p. 96). In this light, present-day development disputes are readily seen as struggles for justice or, better, struggles to define what is just.

If justice and property rights arise in tandem, then so too arises injustice. The birth of fixed ownership of land is often cited as the basis for class inequality and, according to Jean-Jacques Rousseau, the basis for a government that favors the landed rich over the poor (Rousseau, 1973). In the contemporary American circumstance, regulation favors the owner over the renter; among owners, larger or more valuable landholdings outweigh those of individual homeowners, forcing the latter to organize to be heard. Moreover, people of color in America have been consistently discriminated against in terms of property, its ownership, and lending practices. In a clear battle about environmental justice, tenants fought city authorities over a Houston public housing project threatened with redevelopment. Residents tried to force the local authority to expend allocated renovation funds, while the authority simultaneously requested federal permission to demolish the project and sell the land (see Cuff, 1985). This heated debate raged for over a decade while tenants tried to establish the merit of their claims, the duties of city agencies, and at base a just solution. The public housing residents suffered the inequities of class, landlessness, and racial discrimination at the hands of the land-rich housing authority, whose privileged claims were mollified only slightly by the federal government's own requirements to address injustice and give residents some voice in the discussions shaping the future of their community.

The Los Angeles cases and the federal slum clearance program make abundantly apparent the injustices born of property relations. Locke believed that governments were created solely to protect citizens' property rights. No wonder, then, that the use of eminent domain by the state has been so politically charged.

Characteristics of Property Rights

15 Rights related to property are not singular and clear-cut, leaving much room for individual and circumstantial interpretation. A few key terms of property rights theory, drawn from the work of legal theorist Jeremy Waldron (1988), may frame the debate in urban development undertakings. These are: a dynamic system of rights, multiple claims, common and collective property, scarcity, and conflicts between rights and duties.

Property rights, including those related to land, must be considered as a construction that evolves over time from society to society. Private property is an abstract concept made concrete via a particular constellation of relationships, some of which fall within the category of ownership. The system of property in land is relatively ambiguous because land is both material, entailing mineral resources or arable soil, and spatial, a quite abstract location in three-dimensional space (Noyes, 1936; Waldron, 1988). These distinctions are challenged by actions like the transfer of development rights.[14] With such occurrences, the system of property in land evolves. In fact, Waldron argues that property is best conceived as a system of rules governing property relations and not as incidents of private ownership. For example, a corporation is "owned" by a collection of shareholders, who, according to a set of rules, have a degree of access to and control of the corporation. Waldron goes on to say that in modern economic life, the individual's "wealth is constituted for the most part by his property relations" (p. 37), in contrast to the preindustrial equation of wealth and land. Prop-

A DECENT HOME
AN AMERICAN RIGHT

5th, 6th AND 7th CONSOLIDATED REPORT • HOUSING AUTHORITY OF THE CITY OF LOS ANGELES

34   The *right* to decent housing; cover of a Los Angeles Housing Authority report.

erty relations are governed by rules that establish which individuals are entitled to realize certain options at a particular point in time in relation to some object (Nozick, 1974).

Property relations extend to city councils, planners, architects, interest groups, and community members who do not privately "own" a particular site, but who control its future to some extent because of existing rules of property relations. The architect owns access to and control of the design; the neighborhood, via the public hearing process, has right of review; planners utilize regulatory jurisdiction to set restrictions for development proposals; and in two of the cases in the following chapters, the voters exercised veto power. The "ownership" of these parties is defined by sets of property relations, established by social contract, law, common practice, and contention. I believe contentions establish practices and imply property relations in advance of the law. Through sequences of local urban debates, communities, architects, governing bodies, and developers come to understand the limits of their authority over property, the extent of their obligations, and the lengths to which they must go in order to prevail. An informal series of precedents is established by contentions, which set expectations for subsequent contentions. Thus, contention is an effective mechanism for pushing property relations into new terrain, for establishing new conceptions of justice.

Contemporary property relations have been fundamentally transformed by the development of more accepted, more complex, and more numerous claims on property. Several parties with rights in the same resource place multiple claims on a property. For example, in real property, claims may be held by the titleholder, the renter, the lender, the county, a regional body such as a housing authority or coastal commission, a smaller region such as the community designated by a specific plan, and the adjacent neighbors. Moreover, the claims operate in multiple domains, such as planning and zoning or design review, each of which has it own compliance procedure. In urban developments, the chaos of competing claims acts as a perfect medium for contention, as individuals and groups try to establish their theory of rights. Neighborhood opposition to affordable housing, for example, will focus on environmental protection (Frieden, 1979), historic preservation, or federal regulation about distributive equity, while the primary issue is actually xenophobia or property values.

Waldron (1988) distinguishes among three systems of property rights: private, collective, and common. The predominance of any one system is a sociohistorical phenomenon. While a system of private property has always dominated postcolonial America, a notion of collective property was also prevalent in the early colonial period (as discussed above). Some of the present contentions over urban development are struggles to relegate private property relations to a lower status in order to deny uses that detract from the collective social interest. For example, preservationists battle against the destruction of historic property in the interest of present and future generations. Similarly, the maintenance of parklands or undeveloped wilderness qualifies as a system of common property, intended to benefit all members of society. Contemporary development contentions often pit the developer-owner's private property against the community's common property.[15]

Common and collective systems of property are increasingly important in the context of scarce resources, explaining the vehemence of development debates in big cities where land is scarce in relation to population density. Indeed, scarcity is a presupposition of all talk about property (Waldron, 1988), and in all contentious development. A development undertaking that results in the loss of some resource constitutes grounds for community opposition. The loss of agricultural land or "rural atmosphere" in urbanizing areas, the loss of convenient parking and traffic-free streets, or the decline of natural habitats can exacerbate conditions of scarcity. The resources perceived as scarce are likely to become the hottest topics of debate. But since scarcity is politically determined, debates about urban upheavals reflect something about power relations in the city. For example, one effective argument in opposition to LA's public housing in the early 1950s concerned its use of large, undeveloped tracts of inner-city land. Such property was scarce, and private builders argued that they, not the government, had primary claim to it.

With regard to property, the clusters of associated liberties, rights, and duties are, in fact, the basic stuff of ownership (Waldron, 1988) since they establish the social relations that define property. The poorly developed sense of obligation within American legal institutions lags behind a popular perception of the builder's duties. Community members and city councils, primarily on opportunistic grounds, enumerate elaborate duties for builders who seek to implement a project. Thus the most explicit changes in property relations pertain to duties. Under the guise of exactions, impact fees, design negotiations, and other forms of mitigation and compensation, public and private developers are required to fulfill certain obligations determined to balance the impacts and gains of their own property against those of the community. Others suggest that these newly devised exactions demonstrate the increasing "police power" utilized in relation to property (Paul, 1987). But exactions have also been gleaned from the state. In the forties, one paradoxical duty assigned the federal government was to demolish a unit of substandard housing for every new unit built. This duty, nominally to eliminate slums, effectively maintained for private builders the existing level of housing demand.

Typically, we think of ownership as a relationship between a person and a thing, but in legal terms the relationship is among persons (since only people, not things like land or houses, can have rights or obligations). The term "owner" does not imply much about ensuing rights and duties, without reference to more specific legal relations (as, say, differentiate between the one who holds a mortgage, a general partner, a managing partner, and a leasor). If property ownership is a set of relationships among people, then it is little surprise that relations of racial domination and subordination have persisted in urban upheavals.

In the debate over rights and obligations, liberties are given their boundaries. In the urban development context, increased state, federal, and local regulation have placed greater restrictions on the liberties of individual property owners, even to the extent of legitimized taking of property via eminent domain. Compliance procedures and community opposition exert great control over those liberties. Duties, extending to land within some perceived jurisdiction, as by individuals living near a project site, are negotiated simultaneously with rights, bonded in one gelatinous mix. In the Playa Vista case, for example, wetlands restoration and traffic mitigation were identified as essential duties the developers must fulfill in order to receive necessary approvals. The extent of the duty, however, has been the subject of much heated controversy. Since the duties of property owners (or anyone else, for that matter) are not spelled out in American law, the landowner's duties are increasingly negotiated with a diverse group of experts (like traffic engineers), elected officials, organizations representing some public good (e.g., preservationists), and individuals with an interest in the project (adjacent homeowners).

Kant distinguishes two types of moral duties that are expressed by imperatives (e.g., "He ought to do X"). The first, which he calls hypothetical imperatives, involve "rules of action only for those who share the objectives they are intended to promote" (Rosen, 1993, p. 52). For example, if a developer wants to build a shopping center, then traffic impacts ought to be mitigated. The duty to mitigate traffic pertains because of the development plans; there is no a priori obligation to mitigate traffic. The second type of duty, a moral imperative, is an unconditional, universally valid rule of action for all rational beings. For instance, one individual should respect the home of another. I believe that communities often see moral imperatives in development disputes where developers see hypothetical imperatives. Whether or not legal restrictions apply, a developer who blocks the light of an adjacent property or inserts an incompatible land use is often considered to have disobeyed a moral imperative. The architect is implicated simultaneously, since any design solution translates moral duties, or their absence, into built form.

Land Regulation and Eminent Domain

16 While Locke emphasized the connections between property and liberty, there were multiple forms of regulation on property in early America, indicating that property rights were by no means absolute (Schultz, 1992). As long as agriculture was the basis of postcolonial society, wealth was equated with land. With industrialization and a growing commercial base, wealth was equated with money (see Ryan, 1987), and in this system, land needed to be easily convertible to cash. This required land to be subdivided into comparable lots, as accomplished by the grid, but also that it be maintained in terms of use and potential in the future. It is not, therefore, surprising that zoning became the most common means of controlling development. While generally acknowledged to be a clumsy tool, zoning regulations often embody the primary goal of preserving property values rather than formulating a rational urban structure.[16] In fact, Weiss (1987) points out that real estate interests were among the most adamant proponents of reliable zoning and stable urban plans. Indeed, "in North America, most people entertain the delusion that land is simply a particular sort of commodity" (Bryant, 1972, p. 9). While it can be bought and sold, land is not the same as other forms of property in that it can be transformed, it can itself be productive, it can be a vehicle of expression, and it cannot be consumed or replaced. Nevertheless, most regulations exist to protect land as commodity rather than land as resource.

35   The south side of Utah Street; Aliso Village appraisal survey.

36   The end of Las Vegas Street; Aliso Village appraisal survey.

37   The north side of Utah Street; Aliso Village appraisal survey.

Land and the dwelling that sits upon it remain symbolically and actually attached to wealth (see for example Cohn, 1979). The size of landholdings has decreased dramatically since America's farming era: from a country of small farms grew a patchwork of suburban lots, preserving the physical pattern of a detached dwelling surrounded by its own land and a territorial display of the subordination of the public domain to private property.[17] To mediate between public needs and private rights in land, the framework for fair taking of property had to be invented. More than any other limit to the rights of private property, eminent domain challenges the absolutist notion of real property.

Eminent domain is the power of government to take private property for public use. Both Locke and Blackstone accepted forms of eminent domain, and it was widely used by the 1780s to acquire land for dams, roads, and schools (Schultz, 1992). In the United States, the Fifth Amendment to the Constitution and its takings clause, in particular, set the stage for eminent domain, and for the slum clearance legislation that would appear a century and a half later. The amendment reads:

> No person shall be subject, except in cases of impeachment, to more than one punishment or one trial for the same offense; nor shall be compelled to be a witness against himself; nor be deprived of life, liberty, or property without due process of law; nor be obliged to relinquish his property, where it may be necessary for public use, without a just compensation.

"Just compensation" was less commonplace than the taking of property, since this amendment applied only to the federal government and not to the states, where property was often taken without any payment at all. The notion of public purpose is fundamental to eminent domain. The courts, sanctioning rather broad interpretation, in principle suggest that the taking of property under eminent domain should serve a primary public benefit with minor and secondary benefits to the private sector.[18] The right of eminent domain was extended past the government to any private entity's actions that served a public purpose, from railroads to grain mills with dams that would flood adjacent land. States, in the nineteenth century, used eminent domain as a form of economic development (just as was done in 1950s-style redevelopment projects), limiting compensation so that underutilized property of the landed gentry could be redistributed to an emerging class.

Slum clearance, particularly after the Housing Act of 1949, might be described by critics as the opposite strategy: taking of property used by the poor and redistributing it to the wealthy. At the least, condemnation of slum lands reversed the framers' intent: instead of taking property for future public use, slum clearance represented the elimination of what most considered a public nuisance. Eminent domain for slum clearance generally employed both purposes; this process had been tested in England in 1851, where the Common Lodging House Act cleared slums for replacement housing (Garvin, 1996). In 1887, New York state passed the Small Parks Act to permit slum clearance for public playgrounds (Garvin, 1996). For whatever eventual use, the economic benefits of eminent domain were unarguable. "Reduction in the cost of acquisition greater than can be achieved through condemnation is, by definition, impossible" (Garvin, 1996, p. 164).

Eminent domain for housing construction by the federal government was effectively terminated by a case decided in 1934 by the Sixth Circuit Court of Appeals, involving a property owner in Louisville whose property was condemned for a PWA project (United States v. Certain Lands in the City of Louisville). The court agreed with the property owner that his property could not be taken to provide housing for another individual, as this did not constitute a "public use." Two subsequent cases concerning the federal government's power to condemn land for housing were also decided against the PWA (Freedman, 1959). But the courts ruled differently with regard to states' power. In 1935, New York courts held that slum clearance and low-cost housing were public uses that justified the use of eminent domain. The PWA shifted gears accordingly, and began emphasizing local authority with less overt federal control, eventually via the Housing Act of 1937 (Freedman, 1959). Between 1934 and 1937, the PWA program had begun fifty projects in thirty five cities, for a total of 21,600 dwelling units, all in one- or two-story walk-ups (Freedman, 1959; Garvin, 1996). The subsequent reliance on local authorities, which received direct federal grants, remained in place for the urban renewal program initiated by the Housing Act of 1949.

In 1943, the first three states passed legislation to permit the use of eminent domain to condemn property for *private* housing development (Missouri, Pennsylvania, and New York; Garvin, 1996). In Missouri, this meant that cities could turn over power of eminent domain to private developers that planned to clear slums and build housing. In California, a statewide housing initiative was proposed by housing advocacy groups in 1948 which, according to critics, constituted "the most serious attack on private property rights ever launched in California." Had Proposition 14 passed, it would have authorized the use of eminent domain for housing and redevelopment authorities, specifically by defining slum clearance (as well as the better housing that would replace the slums) as within the public interest.

Inadequate housing and blighted neighborhoods represent impaired human, economic and civic values which affect the welfare of all. To the extent that private endeavor is unable to provide healthy and decent environment, it is a matter of public interest and concern. Advancement of the moral, physical and economic health and welfare of the people is a proper and necessary function of their government. The undertaking of such measures as may be effective to further these ends through better housing is hereby declared a public purpose and the policy of this State. (from the Proposition 14 housing initiative, published in *Southwest Builder and Contractor*, 1948, p. 3)

An expansion of the powers of eminent domain in 1954 permitted condemnation of any property, whether or not it was substandard, if a state legislature had deemed a public purpose for the land. Remarkably, it was not until 1970 that the first federal legislation passed which slowed slum clearance, by increasing the level of compensation required to victims of dislocation (Garvin, 1996). Since the late 1960s, land use regulation at all levels—federal, state, and local— has expanded dramatically (Paul, 1987), defining the liberties, duties, and rights associated with urban development. Urban development debates have contributed to that expansion, capitalized on those regulations, and at the same

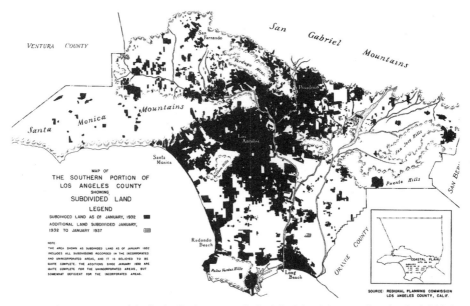

38   As early as 1932, most of the flat land in the Los Angeles basin had already been purchased and subdivided for future development. From United States Federal Housing Administration, *Housing Market Analysis, Los Angeles, California as of December 1, 1937,* vol. 1, pt. 2, p. 396.

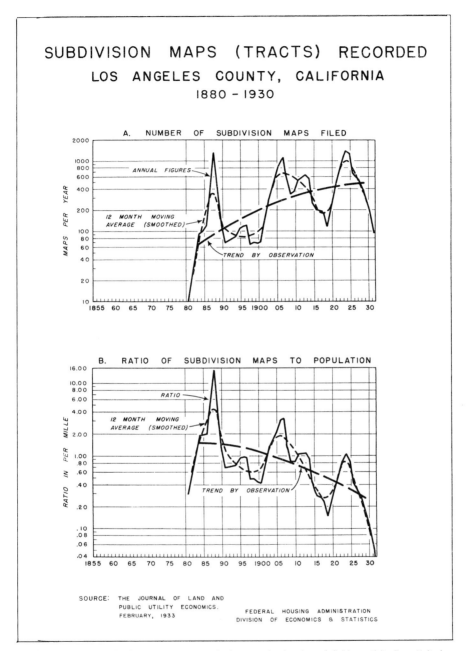

SUBDIVISION MAPS (TRACTS) RECORDED
LOS ANGELES COUNTY, CALIFORNIA
1880 - 1930

A. NUMBER OF SUBDIVISION MAPS FILED

ANNUAL FIGURES

12 MONTH MOVING
AVERAGE (SMOOTHED)

TREND BY OBSERVATION

B. RATIO OF SUBDIVISION MAPS TO POPULATION

RATIO

12 MONTH MOVING
AVERAGE (SMOOTHED)

TREND BY OBSERVATION

SOURCE: THE JOURNAL OF LAND AND
PUBLIC UTILITY ECONOMICS.
FEBRUARY, 1933

FEDERAL HOUSING ADMINISTRATION
DIVISION OF ECONOMICS & STATISTICS

39   Surges in real estate development are apparent in these graphs showing subdivision activity. From United States Federal Housing Administration, *Housing Market Analysis, Los Angeles, California as of December 1, 1937*, vol. 1, pt. 2, p. 399, chart 64.

time defined a separate territory of political pressure by which development can be influenced.

Eminent domain was but the extreme form of government intervention into private property; various forms of land regulation served more moderate ends. Even though urban policy at the federal level emanated from older, East Coast cities, it was Los Angeles that generated the first American citywide zoning regulations (1908), which, through several court decisions, established "the legal validity of regulating and separating land uses for the public purpose of sheltering and nurturing a home environment" (Weiss, 1992, p. 47). Zoning was one of the early ways to regulate private development publicly, particularly for the purpose of segregating residential areas of single-family homes from commercial and industrial uses. Weiss argues that New York's landmark Zoning Resolution of 1916 was actually anomalous in the context of the wave of zoning regulation that then swept the nation, for it was concerned less with residential land use than with height and bulk regulation in commercial and industrial sections of the dense downtown area. In low-density cities like Los Angeles, in midsized cities, and in the growing suburban regions, the primary concern in land use regulation was with the neighborhood.

In 1907, the first land use law was passed by the California state legislature, requiring land developers to file subdivision maps with the appropriate local government agency. This was in part to protect against "paper lots" (real estate swindles in which buyers purchased land that was unbuildable in some fundamental way, for example because there were no roads to it or it was on steep slopes). In 1929, the law was enhanced so that local governments could require developers to set aside land in their subdivisions for roads and other necessary infrastructure. In the thirties, the Map Act was further extended to allow cities to control the design and improvements of a subdivision (Fulton, 1991, pp. 106–107). Describing the way planning occurs in California cities, Fulton shows that, once land is subdivided, it is almost impossible to piece it back together (p. 248). Eminent domain is the primary mechanism by which older parts of the city can be reassembled so that a single owner, whether public or private, can redevelop the land. Eminent domain is basically the mechanism by which government can redistribute land ownership.

Finding Urban Slums

In other words, we have come to the conclusion speaking in medical terms, that there is a civic cancer which must be cut out by the surgeon's knife—and there is not any figure that describes a slum better. It is exactly like cancer in the human body. It can be cured by radium, if taken in time; but after it has gotten to a certain stage, it infects the body politic, and the only cure for it is to cut with the surgeon's knife. That is what we mean by a Slum Clearance Scheme.
Lawrence Veiller,
Housing Problems in America (1929), p. 75

17   The nation's public housing program was invented with an awareness of European solutions developed after World War I, all the more familiar in mass society once soldiers returned from overseas duty. Planners, architects, and housers like Mumford and Bauer had toured Europe to see the new housing (much of which was built on large empty parcels of war-cleared land), and they came back to tout the lessons from abroad. Los Angeles architects, including the best among them, were commissioned to build the city's first ten public housing projects: Paul R. Williams, Lloyd Wright, Richard Neutra, Welton Beckett, Eugene Weston, Reginald Johnson, Roland Coate, and Sumner Spaulding.[19] Many of these designers were proponents of European residential planning. Weston, for example, one of the architects at Aliso Village and Ramona Gardens (the first public housing development in LA), delivered a talk to the Southern California chapter of the American Institute of Architects, later published in *Southwest Builder and Contractor*, about European housing models, primarily from England and Holland. Weston thematized his observations in terms of the catchword of the day, community planning. The model of community planning was invented in England in 1851: low-rent housing built atop slums (Garvin, 1996). By this means urban property became a political tool to effect social ends as well as physical transformation.

In early twentieth-century America, there were few state or municipal programs to improve housing, let alone to construct new housing. Not until the

40   A child returns home through the debris of a Health Department slum "rehabilitation," or demolition, at Hunter Street in Los Angeles, 1952. Photographer: Leonard Nadel.

41   Early public housing was depicted as giving each family its own turf, preserving an illusion of homeownership. Photographer: Leonard Nadel.

42   Los Angles viewed as a scattering of possible new public housing sites. From left, Monsignor Thomas O'Dwyer, President of the Citizens' Housing Council, Housing Authority Director Howard Holtzendorff, and Deputy Mayor Caldwell, ca. 1949.

Great Depression did the housing problem strike middle-class awareness, as expanding slums became a national problem, a threat to American cities, rather than a local problem of locally manageable magnitude. There was both a quantitative extension of housing problems and a qualitative shift in the ways of thinking about them. The slums, most now believed, needed more than local regulation if they were to be stopped or cured, as New York housing advocate Veiller warned: slums always connoted a creeping malignancy.

Housing and health were directly linked in the first half of the twentieth century, a matter of special concern in southern California where a great number of migrants, rich and poor, came for their health. Tuberculosis was thought to spread via damp, poorly ventilated environments. Dust, like moisture, was believed to breed disease. Bubonic plague, of which the last U.S. epidemic broke out in LA in the twenties just north of The Flats,[20] was known to be connected to rats. And the health problems associated with substandard housing, like rats, were fearful because those problems could spread beyond the slums.

When citywide surveys were made of land suitable for public housing—that is, "slums"—evaluators looked at poverty, disease rates, overcrowding, juvenile delinquency, aging building stock, the adequacy of the plumbing, the proportion of renters, and racial concentrations. These descriptors, almost entirely demographic, of *residents* became the criteria for appraising *property*. This equation of social fact with physical consequence went unchallenged for at least a quarter of a century. In fact, the Home Owners Loan Corporation institutionalized what had been argued in the past: that socioeconomics influenced property values more than physical characteristics. Accepting the theory and research of University of Chicago professors Homer Hoyt in real estate and Robert Park in sociology, the HOLC systematized property appraisal based on ethnic and racial residential patterns, particularly in relation to African Americans (Jackson, 1985). One black family in a neighborhood was enough to warrant a "red grade," the highest investment risk category.

Slum clearance and subsidized housing "were undertaken primarily to create employment and stimulate the building industry rather than to wipe out the social evil of the slums" (Freedman, 1959, p. 22, quoting a New York City Housing Authority document). When the Wagner-Steagall Housing Bill finally passed both houses of Congress and was signed into law as the United States Housing Act of 1937, it was written as both a jobs program and a housing program. Its objective was "to promote the general welfare of the nation by employing its funds and credits ... to alleviate present and recurrent unemployment and to remedy the unsafe and unsanitary housing conditions and the acute shortage of decent, safe, and sanitary dwellings for families of low income." Thus its priorities were ordered: first jobs, then slum clearance, and last housing construction.[21] It was widely understood that the building trades experienced the greatest unemployment nationally of any occupational group in the 1930s, since more than a third of all those unemployed were connected to the construction industry (see Jackson, 1985).

The slums had been a national obsession since Jacob Riis's powerful photographs showed the horrors of New York slum life in the early 1900s. Attempts to improve slum conditions were replaced by slum clearance schemes, as invasive and extreme as Veiller's rhetoric suggests. It must have become evident that the urban experts had no better way of curing slums than doctors had for cancer. Hoover's 1931 conference had examined increasingly problematic "housing conditions of the wage-earning population of American cities," meaning not only blighted areas and slums but also middle-class neighborhoods (Gries and

43, 44   Block by block, surveys of physical and social conditions determined which areas were blighted and ready for clearing. Two of the case study sites are visible: Elysian Park Heights, south of the park between Boylston and Figueroa; and Aliso Village, north of First between the river and the extension of Boyle Avenue.

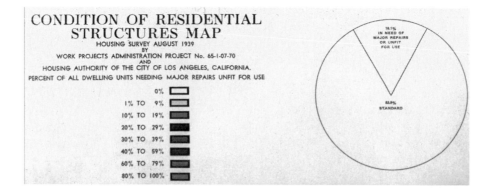

CONDITION OF RESIDENTIAL STRUCTURES MAP
HOUSING SURVEY AUGUST 1939
BY
WORK PROJECTS ADMINISTRATION PROJECT No. 65-1-07-70
AND
HOUSING AUTHORITY OF THE CITY OF LOS ANGELES, CALIFORNIA.
PERCENT OF ALL DWELLING UNITS NEEDING MAJOR REPAIRS UNFIT FOR USE

Ford, 1932, p. xi).[22] By 1933, a full half of all home mortgages were in default, threatening "the foundation of a sound economic and social system." In the thirties and especially the forties, housing activists appealed for improved conditions on general economic grounds: "Slums cost money. They are the most expensive form of housing known, and it is the community that pays for them. . . . However great the cost of wiping out slums, it is not so great as the cost of maintaining them" (Gries and Ford, 1932, p. xiv). Since they required the expenditure of public funds, slums were thus considered part of the public domain. The reports from the Hoover conference suggested "reconditioning" buildings as a part of "district replanning" with "modern housing"; where slum conditions were extreme, they saw building sites and recommended "complete demolition and large-scale operations" (pp. 3–4).

A national slum clearance program was soon set forth by the National Industrial Recovery Act of 1933 (Garvin, 1996), which authorized the Public Works Administration to build low-income housing to fulfill three objectives: to create jobs, to eliminate slums, and to provide decent, affordable housing. Because every public works program was limited to activity that did not compete with private enterprise, slum clearance was a necessary part of the policy equation. Eradicating blight was the public work that enabled an affordable housing construction program, which in turn could provide much-needed jobs. "The broad social objectives of slum clearance were, of course, subordinate to the main purpose: lubricating construction" (Abrams, 1946, p. 214).

A year later, the Real Property Inventory conducted by the Department of Commerce in 64 cities representing every state looked at over 2.5 million dwellings. Of those, they found that 15.4 percent needed major repairs, 17.1 percent had no indoor toilets, and 23.3 percent had no baths or showers.[23] These figures seem modest compared to the way substandard housing was presented over the coming years. Substandard housing was transformed into threatening

45 Frank Wilkinson leads society ladies through the slums to garner their political support for demolition and replacement by public housing.

slums by New Dealers and housing activists to gain support for low-rent housing as a public good, which would then enable the use of regulatory power and eminent domain.

While every city had its run-down neighborhoods, some of these had to be defined as slums in order to gain federal funds. Defining slums meant locating a confluence of characteristics: communities in which people of color, renters, and the poor coincided; land uses that interspersed residential with industrial buildings; housing that had poor plumbing, overcrowding, and a fair proportion of dilapidated structures. An area that could be described by such features was also generally associated with a high rate of juvenile delinquency, a high rate of communicable disease, and thus a disproportionately high demand on public services like police protection and medical care. These correlations were regularly pointed out and publicized in pro-housing propaganda to help convince a fearful, racially biased, and money-minded public that slum clearance and subsidized housing were in everyone's interest.

It is no surprise that from the outset, slum clearance was not just spatial cleansing but racial cleansing. This remained true through the urban renewal period, until the civil rights movement and later race riots erupted throughout cities across America. Policy toward slums can be viewed, in the continuum of imperialism, as "domestic colonization," whereby a dominant element within a nation treats some other, subordinate group as if it were a foreign colony. According to cultural theorist Edward Said, this requires an ideological formulation in which those people and areas to be colonized require and even "beseech" domination.[24] Slums were conceptualized epidemiologically: they were urban diseases, whose blight would spread outward from the point of infection. In the literature written for public consumption and in support of slum clearance programs, this threat was addressed to middle-class white citizens, because crime and disease could extend beyond the present slum boundaries into any neighborhood. Slum clearance was a racialized policy, and an anti-immigrant policy. Reversing the American dream of homeownership, slum clearance took the homes of poor, immigrant, and ethnically diverse people, consistent with their historical weak property rights.

In terms of property, it is interesting to note that a slum, like any other neighborhood, consists of multiple parcels. Thus, areas and boundaries had to be defined for a slum to become a site. To outsiders, these neighborhoods were plotted by their commonalities: people who looked alike or shared a language other than English, structures that appeared run-down or self-built, a district of mixed residential and industrial uses, and so on. This neighborhood-scale property, then, was assigned certain qualities and was seen as a whole rather than as individual pieces of property.

A moral code was often written into the definition of a slum, which further denigrated poor communities of color and recent immigrants that offended or seemed to threaten the Anglo community outside their boundaries. The seeming obsession with plumbing conflated health concerns and puritan ethics about bodily functions, sex, and cleanliness (see Douglas, 1966). In housing reports, mention is made of the deplorable condition of toilets shared by unrelated members of the opposite sex. The solution was for each house to have its own toilet inside the dwelling proper, and shared toilets, including those shared among dwellings on a single site occupied by members of the same family, became statistics in support of slum clearance.

Few buildings in the areas to be demolished were actually unsafe. Instead, the "physically substandard" category was generally assigned on the basis of insufficient plumbing. The possibility of retrofitting houses with adequate plumbing was rarely considered. Indeed, many houses in the Los Angeles neighborhoods targeted for demolition had new toilets, but these too were considered unacceptable by authorities. They were described in appraisal reports as toilets "on the front porch," where small bathroom enclosures had been located.

The additional category of overcrowding, or "occupancy substandard," points out just how socially defined blight was. Perhaps we could objectively de-

46 At the turn of the century, courtyard housing like Lopez Court, shown here, was considered to have the worst conditions. This photo was intended to illustrate the model toilets constructed at the back of the court. From *Report of the Housing Commission of the City of Los Angeles 1906–1908.*

fine a structurally unsafe building (whether it should be demolished or rehabilitated remains debatable). For overcrowding, a numerical criterion was established: more than 1.51 persons per room qualified a house as "occupancy substandard" and counted against the area. But even if you agreed that one and a half persons per room was too many, why was overcrowding a threat, and moreover, why did it require demolition of the structure? The problem was rarely put in terms of fire hazard, which might have been a likely rationalization. Instead, the implications of overcrowding stemmed from East Coast tenement life where children and adults had to bathe, dine, cook, and change clothes in very close proximity. Captions to photos of such conditions described the horrific closeness of ad hoc bathing facilities to likewise ad hoc cooking facilities. This has less to do with health or safety problems (boiling water from cooking pots splashing into the baby's bath) than with moral codes of privacy and decency. Like plumbing, overcrowding held nuances for morality and cultural coding. How was a citizenry to evolve, particularly from immigrant conditions, toward the ideals of the dominant white culture if general levels of an imposed "common" decency were not maintained? Overcrowding was generally decried by liberals and conservatives alike, who agreed that urban densities were a far cry from the standard set by the preferred suburban home (Jackson, 1985).

Poor neighborhoods were an undeniable part of American cities when slum clearance and housing construction were paired in legislation starting in 1933 and 1934 (with the National Industrial Recovery Act). But slums were defined more by social and economic than by physical or structural conditions, particularly in the low-density slums of cities across the nation, including Los Angeles, Houston, New Orleans, and Boston. Indeed, *slum* was a well-understood code word for "non-white," and it embodied the fear among whites that the center of the city was being taken over by Others. It is no wonder, then, that real estate interests moved quickly into the urban redevelopment arena of low-rent housing, seeing the progressives' program as a way to rid the city of a racial threat.

Robert Kohn, an architect who was appointed to head the Housing Division of the PWA in July of 1933 (Radford, 1996, p. 92), did not want his programs tied to slums. He had participated in the Regional Planning Association of America, with Clarence Stein, Charles Harris Whitaker, Henry Wright, Frederick L. Ackerman, Benton McKaye, Edith Elmer Wood, Stuart Chase, Catherine Bauer, and Lewis Mumford, all part of a progressive housing constituency. The group advocated garden city planning as the best means to make neighborhoods more humane, and as an alternative to uncontrolled, incremental urban growth. They saw the speculative homebuilder's profit motive and the dearth of modern industrial production in the construction industry as the main causes of deficiencies in affordable housing (Radford, 1996). They were more or less agreed that slum clearance was a mistake: it was more expensive than vacant land both to purchase and to clear, it complicated land assembly and acquisition (in many cases, it was difficult to locate owners and gain clear title; Radford, 1996), it triggered the unpopular use of eminent domain and the problematic

47   Children playing in the center of an inner-city block where many crudely constructed dwellings were located. Los Angeles, 1940.

issue of what constituted public use, and its preexisting street patterns restricted the planning of "modern community housing" (see Mayer, 1934; Wright, 1934; Mumford, 1934; Mayer, Wright, and Mumford, 1934). Slum clearance, from this perspective, was a second-level priority of urban revitalization, less important than the shortage of affordable housing. Its inequities were less relevant than its costs.

Kohn and his colleagues had only limited effect upon federal housing policy. The PWA was guided by the overbearing Interior secretary, Harold Ickes, who had great ambitions for its housing program but an inability to see his goals made into effective action.[25] As he moved the Housing Division into the direct production of low-rent housing in February 1934, he described slum clearance as one of the agency's central purposes. Slum clearance had wide middle-class appeal, and Ickes was a smart politician looking to gain support for his programs. From this earliest association of slum clearance and low-rent housing, progressives believed that "the government has temporarily given in completely to the demands of the financial and the realty interests and has no serious intention of lending money for any modern community housing whatever" (Mumford, 1934, quoted in Radford, 1996, p. 101). Slum clearance became such a popular part of subsidized housing that the progressives did not return to the problems of slum clearance until the whole of public housing was at stake in the 1950s.

No Public Works Administration housing was built in Los Angeles, even though three sites had been selected, including the Utah Street site, part of which eventually became Aliso Village public housing. Litigation shut down the Public Works Administration program after four years, during which time over 20,000 units in 58 separate developments had been constructed (Radford, 1996, p. 91). The PWA housing program laid the groundwork for subsequent public housing initiatives. Public housing, as defined in the Housing Act of 1937, was unambivalently tied to slum clearance. At no time was the ideal of a single-family detached dwelling displaced, but it was accepted that a submerged middle class needed transitional housing as they established the means to own their own homes. Public housing was thus accepted even though it offended the American dream in three significant ways: first, it took private land and converted it into publicly held land; second, public housing residents were renters rather than owners, and subsidized renters at that; and third, the housing itself was mass housing, with shared facilities and without the trappings of the single-family dwelling. Architects deepened this last cultural chasm by developing a stripped-down modern aesthetic that would dominate public housing imagery, and later symbolism.

Pairing the construction of affordable housing with slum clearance was not a uniquely American idea, but it gained peculiar strength in this country because of backing by the real estate industry and the savings and loan associations. These groups, nationally represented by the National Association of Home Builders, the National Association of Real Estate Boards, and the United States Savings and Loan League, were adamantly opposed to public housing because of their belief, both in heart and in wallet, that private enterprise could best provide homes for all Americans. Instead of the negative campaign against federal housing, these associations launched upbeat programs like ACTION (American Council to Improve Our Neighborhoods) to eradicate slums (Freedman, 1959). In effect, the slum clearance campaign was always a device by which private real estate interests could redirect federal support to create a greater market for homebuilders, away from the competitive provision of affordable homes. This extended to the industry's strong support of the Federal Housing Administration or FHA, which has been criticized as serving the interests of homebuilders rather than the public (Abrams, 1946; Freedman, 1959; Boyer, 1973). Indeed, the National Association of Home Builders' policies included supporting bigger and better FHA legislation (Freedman, 1959).

Policy and Property: The Federal Housing Administration

No agency of the United States government has had a more pervasive and powerful impact on the American people over the past half-century than the Federal Housing Administration.
Kenneth Jackson (1985, p. 203)

18 Created in 1934 primarily to alleviate massive unemployment in the building trades, the Federal Housing Administration was intended to stimulate construction by private enterprise without relying on government spending. It was secondarily expected to raise housing standards and stabilize mortgages. The FHA expanded the possibilities of homeownership to a greater proportion of Americans by insuring loans by private lenders and reducing their risk almost to nil. Based on prevailing bankers' standards for "economic soundness," FHA policies discriminated against poor and minority neighborhoods as bad credit risks while strongly promoting all-white, new suburban development (see Checkoway, 1986). For the preferred builder and buyer, the effective results of FHA policies were to lower the required down payment on home purchases, lower the monthly mortgage payment, and reduce foreclosures. In turn, this stimulated the housing market, which began its resurgence in 1937. In its first forty years (it is still in operation), the FHA helped 11 million Americans to purchase homes and 22 million to improve homes, and insured 18 million units in multifamily projects. During that same period, homeownership rose from 44 percent to 63 percent of all households (Jackson, 1985, p. 205). Just what this meant in the Los Angeles context will become clear when we look at Westchester, where the FHA regional representative, Fred Marlow, teamed with builder extraordinaire Fritz Burns and eventually with Henry J. Kaiser.

"ACCEPT THIS BRAND NEW HOME FOR YOUR VERY OWN!"

Enjoy the respect, happiness and security you and your family will find within it.

YOUR GOVERNMENT, with an unstinting hand, has cleared the way to provide you with life's most cherished possession... A BRAND NEW HOME OF YOUR OWN.

Uncle Sam, with kindly benevolence, stands ready and willing to enable you and your family to enjoy the great American Heritage, A BRAND NEW HOME OF YOUR OWN.

ARE YOU GOING TO TAKE IT?

Thousands upon thousands of American families through the new government F.H.A. are awakening to that bright new interest in life which home ownership alone can bring.

Surely you will not deny your family and yourself a proper share of the joy, contentment and independence which is within your grasp today!

F.H.A.

48   Uncle Sam's platter; emphasis on "own" and "new." Property of Dana Cuff.

The Federal Housing Administration put into policy and practice the basic American principles that it was better to own than to rent, that housing was better built by private enterprise than public endeavor, that life was better outside than inside the city, and that it was better to be white than anything else. The FHA was strongly biased toward all-white, single-land-use suburbs. Government agents had the specific responsibility of keeping people of color out of FHA-sponsored subdivisions (Hayden, 1984). It strictly privileged neighborhoods "occupied by the same social and racial classes" (see Underwriting Manual of the FHA, 1938, 1947; reported in Jackson, 1985, p. 208), and particularly discriminated against African Americans.[26] Even after the Supreme Court ruled against racially restrictive covenants in 1948, the FHA continued to work with builders who would not sell to blacks (Radford, 1996). If the American dream was not fully defined before the Second World War, the FHA made it crystal clear thereafter. At just the time when the majority of Americans were to become homeowners, federal policy institutionalized the ideal American family in the ideal American house in the ideal American neighborhood. That vision discriminated against the inner city, against people of color, against those of low income, against renters, against multifamily dwellings, and against mixed-use areas. If the neighborhoods called slums were not deteriorating on their own, they certainly were helped in that direction by the state.

Essentially, the FHA made it cheaper to own than to rent, if a household could indeed find a house or the lot and materials to build, if it had the required down payment, and if it were a white household choosing to reside in a segregated neighborhood.

Moreover, minimum standards for home construction set by the FHA formalized building standards nationwide. A conventional house was institutionalized with a few small bedrooms, traditional construction methods, and no flat roofs. Planning guidelines were also set which, if followed, assured a builder of low-interest loans and a buyer of low monthly payments. Physically, this meant common building setbacks, cul-de-sacs, and purely residential land use. Through its construction and planning directives, the FHA shaped the American residential environment physically. And it won the support of builders because it set up policies based on those already practiced by large developers, and in terms of incentives rather than regulations. The FHA's commitment to large-scale building practices sped the restructuring of the building trades from small to large scale operators (Weiss, 1987).

Conclusion

19 The mythical status of land in America is reinforced by the tremendous economic power wielded by real estate interests. This dynamic exists in exaggerated form in Los Angeles. California realtors led the nation in the 1920s in shaping urban planning policy and practice. Nowhere did real estate play a larger role in tourism and attracting home seekers than in the Land of Sunshine. In 1908, the Los Angeles City Council established the nation's first zoning law, the Residence District Ordinance, not coincidentally focused on maintaining an attractive housing environment. It protected three large residential areas from unwanted, conflicting industrial uses that ranged from carpet-beating establishments to fireworks factories (Weiss, 1987). If LA's ideal—a never-ending real estate boom—were indeed to be achieved, an unwavering push for tourism would have to be waged (see Klein, 1997), along with the establishment of assorted protections for the area's greatest draws: a pleasant climate and an attractive setting.

Deteriorating neighborhoods of poor immigrants could hardly help Los Angeles's image, particularly in those locations where visitors were likely to enter the city. These slums had no place in the City of Angels. Sadly, government housing policies were never as concerned with housing as might have been implied. Neither the dwellings to be razed, nor the modern communities to be built, nor the cities in which they all were located were of substantial interest to the state. They were instead means to other ends, such as jobs, or federal appropriations, or Americanization.

As it turned out, physical places were in fact more important to the citizenry than the state understood. Before long, the anger registered in appraisal photographs shot in The Flats would metamorphose into effective organized opposition. The best catalysts for the political transformation were extra-large urban developments. When the City of Los Angeles wanted to build ten thousand units of new, low-rent housing, where were the most feasible sites? Such a decision has many considerations, and a multitude of consequences for everything from timing to design. If some of the issues were physical, such as topography, a far greater number were cultural, political, social, and economic. By turning specific pieces of property, with all their associated rights, duties, and relations, into sites, the politics of urban form is born.

Provisional Places with Fugitive Plans: Aliso Village

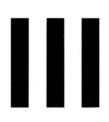

Introducing The Flats

If we were able to examine the part of Los Angeles called The Flats from the turn of the century until the present day, we would first observe small, piecemeal changes, overtaken in the 1930s by massive upheaval.[1] There, following the Depression, a plan for large-scale intervention succeeded and 800 units of public housing were built atop the rubble of private houses. Part of a wave of federally subsidized apartments, early public housing represented a nation's response to three crises: unemployment, slums, and a shortage of housing. These were big problems; they needed big solutions.

According to Koolhaas (1995), architectural "bigness" breaks apart architecture's traditional connections to program, composition, ethics, and context. Although he refers to extra-large projects of recent vintage, evidence for his argument is available from at least as early as the 1920s, when a shift in scale was formulated by modernists with radical plans for the new American city. That emergent extra-large embodied utopian goals as well as their existing urban antithesis, which would have to be destroyed. Prevailing ideas about property, the creation of a site, and its ultimately fragile nature were made visible as The Flats became Aliso Village. Here, in The Flats, we can see the provisional city. It is a story that could also describe events in Little Rock, Houston, Boston, Seattle, and most other American cities.

Modern housing, modern communities, modern town planning were more than rhetorical manifestos; they were ideologies that carried large physi-

49   Aliso Village public housing plan laid over the existing neighborhood of The Flats. Mapmaker: Sylvia Darr.

cal consequences. Small thinking was intellectually as well as practically diminutive. The promise of immense undertakings was epochal: they would be efficient, sanitary, mass-produced, rational, and economically sound. The positivist utopia would be clothed in modernist architecture, its clean elegance reflecting the era's values in bold, some would say brutal, form. The rational city could be scientifically planned via statistical surveys, careful measurement, detailed maps, and high-capacity infrastructure. Its grand physical scale reflected its megalomaniacal pretense. Where to put all this future city? This modern housing? The answer was only too obvious: atop that fine-grained city that not only embodied the past but portended a troubled future.

The principles of modern housing helped shaped the first federal housing programs. As Catherine Bauer documented in her 1934 book of the same name, "modern housing" was based on the "complete neighborhood" as the social unit. Such housing was planned, nonspeculative, and affordable, with basic community services and dwelling unit amenities.

50 Splash pools and the good life.

A modern housing development does not, therefore, constitute a mere mechanical extension of streets and agglomeration of individual, competitive dwellings. It has a beginning and an end, and some sort of visible, organic form. One part is related to another part, and each part serves a particular, predestined use. It can never deteriorate into a slum, or a "blighted area," or a case for expensive remedial city planning (Bauer, 1934, p. xv).

Bauer had observed this form of housing in Europe, whereas "very nearly none at all" could be found in the United States. Projects designed by fellow members of the Regional Planning Association of America, like Sunnyside Gardens and Radburn, were the exceptions.

While the radical possibilities of a well-planned, publicly supported housing sector were never realized in America, New Deal projects started to appear in the thirties. Big federal public housing developments were constructed, sometimes thousands of apartments at a time, rationalizing the sediment of poor, little houses under their foundations. The architecture of public housing was as clean, efficient, and rational as the domestic life it was to shape. Even though architectural design was hardly a priority, the projects were well planned, designed

51   Land use in The Flats prior to demolition (school not shown): *black,* factory; *dark gray,* commercial; *light gray,* church; *dotted,* apartment. Mapmaker: Sylvia Darr.

52   Mrs. Teckinoff returns, unsuspectingly, to her home next to the Chili King Cafe on North Utah Street.

along modernist tenets by a cadre of talented, underemployed architects. When these modern housing developments were built, they were at once visionary and modest. This reflected the belief that new community plans could heroically and deterministically lead common people to a better everyday life.

The new subsidized apartments obliterated the slums, yet they too would deteriorate drastically in the decades that followed, contrary to Bauer's predictions. Public housing built in the forties now sits on prime urban real estate, once again attracting the attention of redevelopers, both public and private. In such places, contradictions intertwine: abandonment and dreams, construction and demolition, utopia and distopia. These immense places are themselves provisional, and the upheaval that brought them into existence will also characterize their demise, as the next generation's utopia gains force.

To explore this slice of urban architectural history, I offer an analysis of one place and its upheavals. The area called The Flats is wedged between the Los Angeles River to the west and the bluffs to the east, upon which rest two neighborhoods: Brooklyn Heights and Boyle Heights. In this case study, several qualities characteristic of provisional modern cities can be observed. First, The Flats was radically transformed into Aliso Village, constituting an urban upheaval. Aliso Village is now vulnerable to the next metamorphic wave of development. Both transience and permanence are paradoxically evident here, where provisional urbanism prevails. Second, the specific site for demolition and rebuilding was a sociopolitical construction, rather than some natural or inevitable choice. While there were households there living under extremely distressed conditions, this was not the case throughout the neighborhood, nor were these conditions determined by the physical housing stock. Lastly, the destruction of The Flats

and the design and construction of Aliso Village represent an episodic utopia. The actions in this part of Los Angeles in the first half of this century show the uneasy marriage of large-scale, quantitative planning efforts with progressive-minded idealism. In retrospect, the visionary acts of our forebears have a dated patina, as will our own in generations hence.

The Fine-Grained City

21 Over the course of twenty-five years, between about 1910 and 1935, the downtown zone of poor, working neighborhoods was physically and conceptually reinvented as a "slum," transformed through a process triggered by "blight." The mechanisms needed to effect the metamorphosis included policies like a fortified eminent domain, institutions such as the Home Owners Loan Corporation,[2] and funding like that appropriated to the Public Works Administration. Segregation by race and land use fed these mechanisms, as when LA's Chinatown was literally buried in 1933 to make way for the new Union Station (Kronzek and Greenwood, 1996). By such means, existing neighborhoods could be converted to sites: tabula rasa for the architect's drawing board. Slums were important inventions to the cause of civic change.

Long before the Depression and America's engagement in the war, we can see the first signs of later housing events in The Flats. Overcrowding and the proliferation of house courts in that area sparked the city to establish its very first housing commission in 1906. "Ruralize the city; urbanize the country": this was the recommendation of the housing commission in its report of 1910. Little did the commissioners realize how dominant the second part of their charge would become in past–World War II Los Angeles. In 1910, however, the commissioners were worried about overcrowding in the central city, where a proliferation of tents and wooden shacks was attributed to the peculiar circumstances of LA.

53 Self-built housing clusters made of scrap materials by Mexican laborers were called "Cholo courts." From *Report of the Housing Commission of the City of Los Angeles 1906–1908.*

House courts, defined as three or more habitations on a lot with the unoccupied portion shared (Los Angeles, Housing Commission, *Report 1906–1908*), were a rational outcome of circumstances in Los Angeles at the turn of the century. The eastern banks of the never-navigable Los Angeles River were flanked by railroad tracks, small industrial enterprises, livestock-related businesses, and housing for low-wage workers and recent immigrants (Spalding, 1992). The generally low population density left plenty of open land near downtown and the railyards, that is, near jobs. Since most of the rest of the city was segregated, people of color lived primarily in concentrated communities along the river and the Alameda corridor (see fig. 9). The vacant land there became house sites for workers who paid about a day's wages for ground rent and the right to erect tents, shacks, and other thin, simple buildings, habitable because of the region's mild climate. After a year's study, the commission concluded that LA had a unique problem for which no parallel could be found in other cities. The crowding of "foreigners" into these small, poorly built houses in the center of the city was "deadly to health and morals."[3]

House courts were built in one of three ways: by an employer that provided worker housing (rail courts for railyard laborers is a prime example); by residents themselves who paid ground rent to a landlord; or by a property owner who rented out units. Two of the largest and worst house courts were the Aliso Street Court and the Utah Street Court.

54 The notorious Utah Street Court, with proper water hopper at the fore. From *Report of the Housing Commission of the City of Los Angeles 1906–1908.*

Utah Street court in the days of its most flourishing condition comprised a tract of land equal to one-third of a city square. On this ground were sixty-eight houses of various styles of architecture and material, depending on the choice and ingenuity of the builder. Between four and five hundred people, including children, lived in this area, and for their convenience and accommodation they were supplied with seven water faucets and eight toilets, which were used promiscuously by both sexes. We who live in the better parts of town can scarcely realize that human beings could exist under such horrible circumstances. (Los Angeles, Housing Commission, *Report 1906–1908*, pp. 7–8)

The house courts catalyzed the fears of the general public: they were breeding grounds for disease, sites of moral decay, places that might infect the civic body. In 1907, the city adopted its first housing ordinance. This law was not intended to rid the city of house courts, but to rehabilitate them with more substantial construction, more toilets, and better ventilation (Los Angeles, Housing Commission, *Report 1906–1908*).

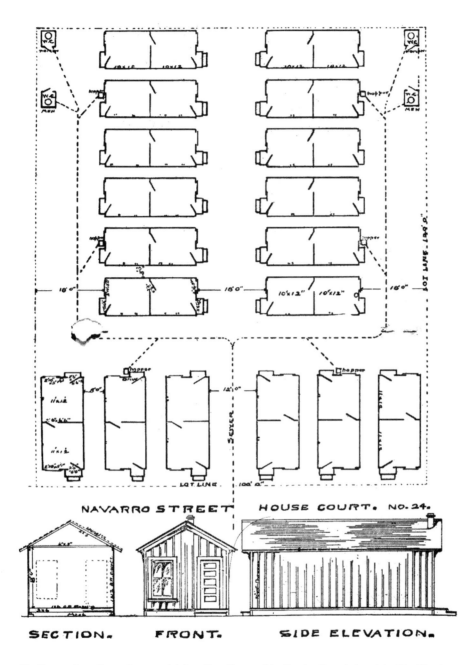

55　Navarro Street House Court, model plans. From *Report of the Housing Commission of the City of Los Angeles 1906–1908.*

56　Navarro Street House Court. From *Report of the Housing Commission of the City of Los Angeles 1906–1908.*

These early solutions proposed by the Housing Commission were small in scale. Floor plans were recommended for house court sites and units, with two-room houses sharing outdoor water hoppers and outdoor toilets. Ironically, those very recommendations condemned the area as blighted in the thirties. There were examples of modest improvements to extant house courts: drain basins so water runoff would not pond and create mosquito breeding grounds, or a reasonable number of bricked-in toilets. In one instance, when an area considered irreparable had to be demolished, the residents were reportedly relocated to land furnished by the city. The problems were surveyed and addressed by an inspector who was expected to educate house court dwellers in sanitation and moral decency. In 1909, a woman was hired because "the mother of a home must be educated along sanitary lines" and women living in house courts would "welcome into their homes and pour out their troubles to [an inspector] of their own sex" (*Report 1906–1908*, p. 23). She came with high-powered credentials from New York, the capital of American housing woes. She spoke several languages, and had a college degree in health. (All this helped justify awarding a relatively large salary to a woman.) Thus, the housing problem, as it was constructed at the beginning of the twentieth century, was both feminized and racialized. Solutions and political action, it should be noted, were coming from women at the time, but nearly all the prominent players in the housing scene, both women and men, were Anglos.

Before its first years of work were complete, the commission sought expanded power: they argued that the problem went beyond house courts to lodging houses and tenement houses (*Report 1906–1908*, p. 25). Of particular concern were diseases spawned in overcrowded rooms, including tuberculosis, cholera, typhus, and pneumonia. These were believed "to mount with exact ratio as the density of the population increased and the lack of sanitary conveniences increased" (Weston, 1936, p. 10). Rather than expand its jurisdiction, however, the city made the commission part of the Health Department. The perceived link between housing and health was so strong that bad housing and overcrowding were considered the cause of disease. Indeed, urban reform was dominated by physicians and philanthropists until the 1920s, when planners and architects began to make their mark (Radford, 1996). An underlying environmental determinism guided the thinking of middle-class reformers: improved housing was the key to a better life. Tuberculosis and an outbreak of plague in the twenties in Los Angeles commanded public attention. The city's explicit focus on housing resurfaced in institutional form a decade later, when federal housing appropriations became available.

57   Los Angeles's female housing inspector talks with slum residents. From *Report of the Housing Commission of the City of Los Angeles, June 30, 1909–June 30, 1910.*

For the present analysis, there are two significant implications from the early housing reports: small-scale improvements were considered viable; and The Flats had been singled out among other low-income areas as an area with housing problems. In some ways, the most telling aspect of this early phase is that, unlike subsequent programs, early efforts to improve housing conditions in The Flats did not comprise a massive, totalitarian scheme. The housing commission had neither the budget nor the authority for this, probably because the problem had not yet been defined as a catastrophic threat. The "emergency" did not become apparent until the Depression. No grand urban architecture was imagined, only slight improvements to benefit health and morality. Little by little, lot by lot, The Flats would be rebuilt, starting with the worst structures. There was, however, the constant underlying issue of race, and early documents record the commissioners' consistent stereotyping and discrimination.[4] Not only was The Flats a highly concentrated center of low-wage, immigrant workers, but with them came the concentration of troublesome house courts. Together, the population and the building stock helped outsiders draw a loose boundary around the area, which eventually would be transformed into a bona fide site. The city's intense focus on The Flats persisted for the next five decades.

The housing commission's garden city goal to ruralize the city with one hand while urbanizing the country with the other makes apparent that little was expected to remain static. Indeed, in the poorer, crowded parts of the central city, ruralizing meant demolition. Physically, it implied the reintroduction of green spaces into otherwise densely built neighborhoods. It also meant the imposition of social ideals by a dominant culture upon the personal, economic, and social lives of those taken to be Other. A glance at the photos from the housing commission's early reports reveals a Los Angeles now lost. Nothing from those images exists today: both deplorable housing and new construction were removed. Good and bad alike, the house courts that preoccupied these reformers were eventually eradicated by various forces, including their own fragility, regulation, the car, and finally public housing.

Turning Neighborhoods into Slums

We moved into the area in the thirties, and I went to grammar school at the Utah Street School. We moved there in the first place because most of the people my father knew from Zacatecas moved there, and from Durango, so they all knew each other. We all spoke Spanish, but there was a night school to learn English. We kids did the clean-up after dinner while our parents went to that school.

We lived in the middle of the block and the school was at the corner. We would run down five minutes before the bell would ring, so we wouldn't get dirty before class. My mother was pretty strict about those things.

I lived on Utah for about ten years; my youngest sister was born there in 1933. That was the year they had the big flood. Luckily, the homes were high up off the ground, or they would have been taken. We were scared. We heard policemen coming through the neighborhood—they woke us up—saying the river was overflowing and that families in lower homes had to get out. The water came right up to the floor boards; it flooded our streets. It was very scary, but I was 13, and we older kids thought the whole thing was fun. The Red Cross brought our food, and everybody was stuck there for a couple days. It ruined everyone's garden. Everyone there had gardens, and everyone tried to outdo each other. Before that the river was really nice. The neighborhood boys spent most of their time at the river. We had picnics there under the trees. The water was clean and pretty, except for at the Cudahy meat packing house—their water was really dirty. Then after the flood, they covered the river up.

Most days the women stayed home. The men came back around 6 by streetcar or they walked. My father worked for the Santa Fe railroad like a lot of the men. On payday, we'd go out to eat, maybe to a French restaurant on Alameda Street or to the Chinese place called The Far East on First. When we went downtown, we'd go as far as First, but I didn't like going past Second or Third because we weren't accepted there, for being Mexican. There was a lot of discrimination. I remember, because I was older than the other kids.

First Street had everything: a beauty shop, a bakery, grocery store, meat market. And there was a laundry, a milk factory, a chili factory, and a stable. And every day the rag man would come and buy rags and bottles from you. There was a Helms bakery truck. We had our own vegetable man, a Greek fellow. He had a beard that he never cut. He came every day and he wouldn't sell to everyone. If you weren't a good woman, say if you smoked, he wouldn't sell to you. For my sweet saint of a mother, he'd bring her things right into the kitchen. The streets were clean, because people swept the sidewalks. Then they'd even sweep the street itself. There were only about three cars in the whole neighborhood, so we could play in the streets. At 9 every night a whistle blew from somewhere down around Cudahy, and then we all had to go inside. But you could walk the streets at midnight and no one would bother you. I won't say there was no crime, but they didn't do anything compared to now. We never locked our doors.

Then when they started to do away with the homes where Aliso Village was coming, we moved a few blocks away to Gless Street. But in about 1950 or '51, they took those houses down too [for the Aliso Extension housing project]. All the homes there—everyone was going to stay. We always wondered why they chose our neighborhood to tear down. They just decided it had to be cleaned up, and that's it. To me, it was good, happy memories. It was sad when they tore it down. People didn't want to go.

My father wouldn't have wanted to move into the projects. I don't think there was one family who would have wanted to move in. Everyone left instead. I don't even know where they got all the people to live in them. There was nothing in between—no yards—they were just like apartments. People had chickens, rabbits, vegetables. Now where was all that supposed to go?

—Mrs. Frances Camareno[5]

58 Aliso Village public housing, looking northeast.

To build public housing in any city began with locating some slums to remove. In Los Angeles, The Flats was a prime target because of its location adjacent to downtown, at the eastern gateway to the city (*Housing Headlines*, 1940). While housing activists in the thirties or forties might generally have agreed that the worst housing in the city was located northeast and especially southeast of downtown, specific sites for slum clearance were politically determined. Correspondence from architect Lloyd Wright is revealing about site selection for what he hoped would be the first federally subsidized housing in LA. In a letter to an administrator at the Housing Division in Washington, DC, he writes:

> Have been working quietly in line with your suggestions and have consulted with many sincerely interested workers here. After the decision on land condemnation, went to work with others to dig up sites that could be obtained by option suitable to the low cost housing objective.
>
> As you know, we need a demonstrator to check the present and future creation of potential slums. . . . After the check of many sites, we selected a property on the east side of Los Angeles to submit to the Housing Commission. An excellent low cost Housing Site, located adjacent to Ninth and Marietta.
>
> I do not know whether the site is acceptable to the Government or whether we on this coast are going to be shelved for more pressing eastern

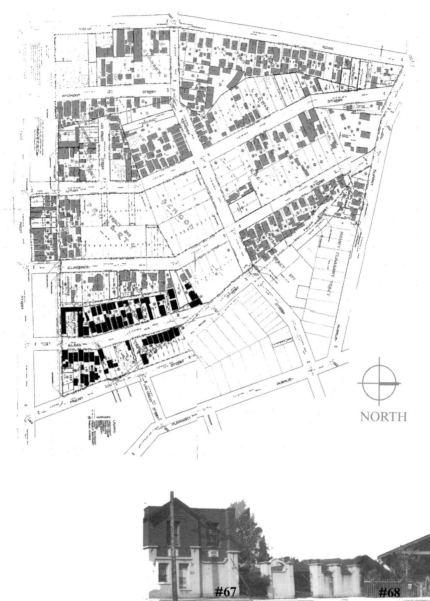

NORTH

#67
115–121 N. Gless
(Industrial bldg.)
$3200

#68
123 N. Gless
$1150

59   Appraisals of buildings on North Gless Street. Layout by Ken Gutierrez.

131 B N. Gless (Rear House)
Built 1915, 1922; 500 s.f.
"This is a very cheap maverick
Calif. type house."
Tenant: Jesus Palafos ($12/mo.)

133 N Gless St.
Built 1900; 850 s.f.
"This house is extremely poor and is
of very little value."
Tenant: Sofia Olasara ($15/mo.)
(other apt. vacant)

NORTH

131 N. Gless St.
Built 1898; 930 s.f.
" This is a very cheap, poor old building
in bad condition…almost shack-like."
Tenants: Alexander Erdugo ($15/mo.) &
Emma Ybarro ($15/mo.)

133 1/2 N. Gless St.
Built 1916; 620 s.f.
"This is a poor house in a little better
condition than the others on this lot."
Tenants: Carmen Mortago ($10/mo.) &
Hope Gonzales ($10/mo.)

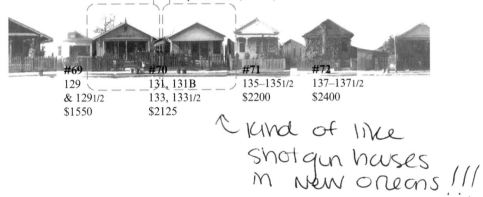

#69
129
& 129 1/2
$1550

#70
131, 131B
133, 133 1/2
$2125

#71
135–135 1/2
$2200

#72
137–137 1/2
$2400

↖ kind of like
shotgun houses
in new oreans !!!

projects. I hope not. To be abandoned to the tender mercies of the high pressure realtors—the Chandlers et al. would be bad news indeed.[6]

This letter and others in his files support the following conclusions I have drawn elsewhere: that site selection was relatively arbitrary, and then backed by subsequent surveys rather than originally determined in some scientific way; that condemnation and slum clearance policy "created" areas to demolish; that the West Coast was not a high priority for federally subsidized housing in part because East Coast cities were setting housing policy; and that advocates of subsidized, low-rent housing were operating in direct opposition to real estate interests.

The Flats, or Boyle Heights Flats, had long been occupied by a diverse population. There, Jews (probably including Mrs. Camareno's "Greek fellow"), Molokan Russians (a pacifist Christian sect of the Russian Orthodox Church), and Mexicans lived side by side and worshiped according to their traditions (Spalding, 1992). Early Americanization programs, some of which were housed at the Utah Street School, taught language in the evenings, but explicitly also sought to impose the values of second- and third-generation Anglo immigrants upon those of other ethnic origins. Irish, Russian, Armenian, Mexican, Asian, and Italian residents were subjected to this structured assimilation, but so were Mexican Americans and African Americans, despite their citizenship. The northern end of The Flats, where Aliso Village was built, was populated at the time of its demolition in 1941 primarily by poor people of Mexican and Russian descent (about 70 percent and 30 percent respectively).[7] It contained a mixture of land uses, including 417 dwelling units (not counting those removed by the freeway's construction) which were almost entirely single-family detached dwellings, several to a lot, and duplexes. On a typical residential site, the streetfront might be occupied by a small, well-crafted bungalow, behind which would be one or more auxiliary units, generally less well built, and in some cases very poorly constructed. There were a dozen small commercial enterprises (corner markets, beauty salons, cafes), several rather small industrial ventures (the largest being The Mission Winery and XLNT Spanish Food), and a few churches. At the heart of the neighborhood was the Utah Street School, a well-regarded, progressive institution that served the specific needs of its population more compassionately than most public schools at the time (see Young, 1932). It still stands. While much transformed, the school is the exception to the rule of complete erasure.

Appraising The Flats

23 In 1940, architect Lloyd Wright, son of the American master Frank Lloyd Wright, prepared for a meeting with LA's Housing Authority to review plans for Aliso Village: 800 units of housing funded by the Federal Housing Act of 1937. Some six years earlier he had lobbied successfully in Washington for a chance to build housing on the same site, but that project had fallen through with the collapse of the Public Works Administration's housing program. Somehow, the loose consortium calling itself the Utah Street Architects had hung together, and this time their modest plans for modern housing would finally be built.

At almost the same time, on October 24, 1940, Charles Shattuck's team drove into The Flats: a photographer, his assistant, a hand-held camera, a sheaf of paperwork, and a small chalkboard. Their project took a couple weeks, but it wasn't hard; they found just what they were looking for. The pair stopped at the corner of Mission and Kearny and started to work, one man behind the shutter and the other holding the chalkboard marked number 1. They knocked at Bruna Perez's door to ask her a series of impertinent questions: How much rent do you pay? Do you have a toilet, and can I see it? How about hot water? They repeated the inquisition at each of the three houses on the lot, filling out surveys while forming an impression: "The three houses are typical of the houses in the area which once were good but which suffer from hard use and neglect" (Los Angeles, Housing Authority, 1940). Their generous conclusions waned during the following weeks, particularly for Mexican homes; they wrote: "very cheap,

60   Las Vegas Street, north side.

61   Las Vegas Street, north side.

62   Las Vegas Street, south side.

63   Utah Street, north side.

poor, old building in bad condition," "hardly fit for human habitation," "shack-like," "makeshift bathroom," "building is a wreck."

The coincidence of ethnic prejudice and slum clearance was absolutely unified in the person of Charles Shattuck. Not only was he the appraiser for Aliso Village, President of the California Real Estate Association, and the president of the National Association of Real Estate Boards, but he was also an official of the Home Owners Loan Corporation, which redlined neighborhoods as bad investment risks if they had the "threat of infiltration of subversive races." That could mean one black family. Shattuck's overlapping roles indicate the extent to which racism was structurally and institutionally embedded.

The appraisal was completed by bits and blocks between October and December of 1940. The boundaries of the site had been sketched at least ten years earlier, when Utah Street was singled out for public housing projects along with two other sites in Los Angeles, none of which was built under Public Works Administration appropriations. By the end of the 1930s, all the pieces were in place for the demise of The Flats: funding, housing program, plans, public support, and perhaps more importantly, no public opposition. As the appraisal survey continued, the photographs indicate that the neighbors had got wind of what was happening. In one image, a shadow behind the screen door hints at someone reluctantly observing the brash intruders. In another, a few men gathered, glowering enough to make the chalkboard man sweat a little. A group of kids followed from house to house, until they were called back closer to home. Some women defiantly refused to let the appraisers in. They had to imagine the insides, but these places all seemed pretty much the same to them. And they knew it would all be torn down anyway. This appraisal had followed many other surveys, and they all led to the same conclusion: slum clearance. Still, the residents couldn't understand why. They kept up their yards, they went to work each day, their children went to the Utah Street School; what was so bad about that?

Emergency in The Flats

24
> The unemployment emergency yesterday, the post-war emergency today, the social emergency tomorrow—we may soon realize that emergency has become part of the very scheme of modern life and that we must plan for the emergencies as well as for the easeful interims. In fact, housing in the twentieth century has been one continuing emergency. (Abrams, 1946, p. 346)

Perhaps Mrs. Camareno was right and there wasn't enough wrong with The Flats. Nor was there strong conviction that a federal housing program was a good solution. Neither mattered, since a number of crises afforded the opportunity to make urban progress. Housing activist Catherine Bauer (1953) assessed the potential a catastrophe might hold for civic improvement, suggesting two significant effects: it can clarify long-standing problems, and it can force change. From 1929 right through the 1950s, catastrophes were readily available in American cities, beginning with the 1929 stock market collapse, the ensuing Depression, the war in Europe, and America's entry into the war. Crisis was identified first in economic terms (employment, banking, industrial production, real estate, commercial enterprise); then in military terms (defense production, the war effort, threats to security, and so on). On the home front, a national emergency took shape not in any of those domains, but in neighborhoods and over housing.

64   Overcrowding was a serious problem in the slums.

The Flats was a microcosm of a national urban crisis: the proliferation of slums. In California, this threat was answered by statewide legislation embodied in the California State Enabling Acts of 1938. These "emergency measures" permitted public bodies engaged in federally subsidized low-rent housing to "do any and all things necessary or convenient to aid and cooperate in the planning, undertaking, construction, or operation of housing projects," including the power to close roads, rezone, and make exemptions from building regulations (Los Angeles County, Housing Authority, 1944). This constituted a vast redevelopment authority armed with federal funds. State and local authorities took advantage of the right to demolish parts of the city via eminent domain. All this was framed as "in the public interest." The proliferation of the slums was a problem that could be addressed by demolition paired with construction of modern, affordable housing. The real estate lobby, which was quickly gaining momentum, made sure that government housing would not undermine the private market. Their insistence on "equivalent elimination," one unit destroyed for every unit built, soon became law. All these programs—assessing blighted neighborhoods, demolishing them, planning and building new communities—had the principal effect of creating jobs.

CAL 4.5-ALISO VILLAGE.
POINT #3 SEPT. 6. 1941

65   The Flats before demolition, 1941.

As early housing policy was shaping up, activists resisted pairing new construction with slum clearance. Not only was vacant land less expensive, but street patterns could be newly established and urban redevelopment could wait. But slum clearance was popular, and the Public Works Administration made it the agency's central purpose. (Radford, 1996, p. 101)

Out of political necessity, housing activists eventually advocated modern housing construction paired with slum clearance. They would remind us that housing and health conditions were horrific among the poorest residents of Los Angeles, particularly those of color. They not only decried poor housing but segregation and racism in all forms. In Los Angeles, activist members of the Citizens' Housing Council protested against the housing authority's policy of segregating its first housing projects. These individuals led many battles to improve housing conditions for Los Angeles's poor people of color, with complicated results: first, their overall programs and policies were adopted only partially and sporadically; and second, some of their plans had undesired consequences (see for example Abrams, 1946).

There was always a strong countermovement to the modern housing philosophy, which argued the benefits of single-family detached dwellings. Not only did the house on its own land denote a dedication to democracy, but apartments were downright un-American. Consider the monograph by Dr. S. James Herman of the Michigan Housing Association called "Why Do You Live in an Apartment? A Study of a Sinister Trend in American Life." He writes,

> It is generally conceded that apartment life has a deleterious or even destructive effect upon American ideals and institutions, the basis for which has been the traditional integrity of the American home. . . . It is a matter

66   The Flats after demolition, ca. 1943. Modern housing for this little boy's future. Photographer: Julius Shulman.

of common agreement that sound health, clean morals, and a love of honest endeavor are largely a part of home training, and that the most powerful influence in America's rise to greatness has been the integrity of the American home.[8]

New, detached, privately owned houses: this was the ideal prevalent as the housing crisis loomed during and after the war. Indeed, only these deserved to be called "home." It was this ideology that modern housing hoped to break, given the emergency conditions that shook American's ideals.

Creating Aliso Village

> I first heard of the proposed building of Aliso Village about eight years ago. I thought it was something that was so remote it would probably never materialize. I see now that I was mistaken. (McMahon, 1942; entry for March 25, 1942)

These are the first lines of a diary kept by K. McMahon, a teacher at the Utah Street School, as she and her pupils observed the surrounding upheaval from the windows of their classroom in the Utah Street School.[9] As early as 1934, but surely by 1938, it was public information that The Flats would be demolished for a new housing development (*Los Angeles Times,* 1938). Shattuck's documentary photographs (throughout this section) show The Flats just prior to demolition. While a large number of the houses appear to be in good shape, it is instructive to examine the worst property. The harshest appraisal was reserved for one of the few remaining house courts, at parcel number 41 on the corner of Kearny and Utah streets (see fig. 67). There, a collection of five lots was filled with residential buildings for 34 families and two commercial enterprises, described by the appraiser thus: "This land . . . is improved with 24 houses of the cheapest, poorest kind. All the buildings are in bad shape. These buildings are the poorest in the area, and the property is an eye sore from one end to the other. It is decidedly slum property" (Los Angeles, Housing Authority, 1940).

67 Several dwellings of parcel #41; the rear building has lumber yard signage, indicating that these structures were built as worker housing. Appraisal photograph.

Residential rents ranged from $6 to $15 a month (in 1940 dollars), with much higher commercial rents at almost $26 for the tortilla factory and $18 for the grocery store. Every unit was occupied by tenants with Latino surnames. The original buildings on this property were constructed for the primarily Russian lumberyard workers at the turn of the century. By 1940, all units had water, electricity, and heat, although only one had hot water and about four had toilets located outside the dwelling. The plumbing was described as "makeshift" probably because it was added in recent years. Appraisers sought inadequate plumbing because this immediately categorized the place as slum property, but even this site hardly seems to have warranted such a negative appraisal, particularly compared to some of the shoddy defense worker housing provided by the government just four years later. If slum clearance was widely supported in principle, distance masked the violence and disregard with which it overtook the older neighborhoods. In the Utah Street School teacher's journal, we catch a melancholy glimpse of demolition up close:

> The Haprov house is down. For many years it has been shaded and protected by a huge pepper tree on the top of Gless St. Hill. A neat little gray house, its starched white curtains visible from the road. Its starched white linens on the interior almost visible too. And the pepper tree familiar to us

all is lying with its roots in the air, its heavy branches far down the slope of the hill. At this moment a fast truck going past throws a cloud of dust over it. (McMahon, 1942; entry for June 4, 1942)

From a review of the building footprints, photographs, and parcel ownership patterns, it is obvious that this part of The Flats was braced for some kind of development. Over half the lots (55 percent) were aggregated into multi-lot parcels.[10] The land in the area was zoned for heavy or limited industrial use, and the appraiser gave disproportionately high value to large parcels with industrial masonry structures. The failed PWA project initiated in the early 1930s sparked the exaggerated decline of The Flats, creating more of the blight it was to remedy. Still, the photographs record several blocks along Las Vegas, Utah, Gless, and Clarence streets where neat houses were occupied by the owners, while their grown children lived in other buildings on the property. For example, in one block around Las Vegas and Utah, ten of the eighteen residential properties were owner-occupied. This is particularly striking since homeownership in 1940 was far less common than at present.

From a contemporary perspective, it is difficult to understand two factors that were accepted indicators of blight: mixed use and an older housing stock. Characteristic of The Flats is the mixture of commercial, industrial, and residential uses, undeniably negative from the appraisers' perspective. But sources other than the HOLC also saw mixed use as a neighborhood problem. For example, a pamphlet called "Homes for Workers" stated: "A corner gas station, a few stores, or excessive traffic contribute to the decline of a neighborhood" (UAW-CIO, 1943). In addition, negative associations clung to old buildings, positive associations to the new. The derogatory caption in figure 69 makes little sense unless we acknowledge that old connoted substandard in the same ill-founded way that a romantic nostalgia presently surrounds similar buildings.

There was a widespread faith in the new, in the promise of planning, in the modern, and, among housing advocates, in modernity (cf. Robbins and Tilton,

68   Composite street elevation of structures on parcel #41.

1941). Some fifty years later, in 1997, Frank Wilkinson examined the appraisal photographs. The former housing authority official and advocate of slum clearance in The Flats was surprised: "I don't remember these houses," he said, as he looked at slides of some of the trim bungalows that had stood on Gless Street. "We wouldn't have torn those down. They must have been moved." There is evidence that at least some houses were relocated,[11] but these better houses were neither defining nor perhaps even memorable. The old neighborhood could not stand up to the promise of modern mass housing. As Ms. McMahon wrote in her diary on May 21, 1942:

> There was a lessening in the heat wave to-day. It was pleasant to go into the cool dark aud and view another short film on Mass Homes of America. It proved that in large (mass) production the builder and home buyer both profited. Many features were made possible because the building was done on a large scale. The small power saws shown in the film were at that moment being using [sic] north of the new building across Kearny St. or rather what was once Kearny St.

It may have been sad to see the old homes destroyed, but the new "mass homes" justified the means.

In 1936, the Home Owners Loan Corporation assigned the red grade to (redlined) Boyle Heights, of which The Flats was a part. This prevented virtually all lending, and thus hastened overall deterioration. The HOLC, under Charles Shattuck, had this to say about Boyle Heights at the time (this predates, indeed enables, the Aliso Village appraisal report):

> This is a "melting pot" area and is literally honeycombed with diverse and subversive racial elements. It is seriously doubted whether there is a single block in the area which does not contain detrimental racial elements, and there are very few districts which are not hopelessly heterogeneous in type

70   Here, the bungalow has been remodeled into a builder's idea of the contemporary house. Note the enlarged photo of the original bungalow to the left of the front door, showing the before-and-after transformation to prospective buyers. *Western Building*, January 1954, p. 18.

of improvement and quality of maintenance. Schools, churches, trading centers, recreational areas and transportation are all conveniently available. Many of the thoroughfares are arterial in character and constitute traffic hazards. This area is wholly in the City of Los Angeles. It is hazardous residential territory and is accorded a general medial red grade, although in many parts slum conditions prevail. The Federal Government, in conjunction with the city government are undertaking a slum clearance project covering 41 acres in the extreme northeast part of the area.[12]

Hopelessly heterogeneous, melting pot, diversity, racial elements: this critical assessment justified the multiagency offensive that eventually cleared The Flats. The 54 acres north of First Street in the PWA project had by 1936 shrunk to 41 acres, later to become the 34.3 acres of Aliso Village. A new highway wiped out hundreds of additional houses in the area, consistent with the national use of highway construction for slum clearance purposes. The elevated thoroughfare gave the housing project its rigid northern and eastern boundaries, a supposed barrier from surrounding blight. It also led into downtown, with the new housing creating a worthy gateway. To the south, Pico Gardens housing development opened in 1942 with Aliso Village, to further seed the intended community transformation.

Aliso Village: Modern Housing, Modern Community

The utopian thinking of modern architects, their belief in the rationality of the site plan, the importance of function, access to light and air, ease of circulation, the separation of vehicular traffic from children's play, all became part of the American low-rent housing program. Housing advocates and architects traveled to Europe to see the high-rise social housing built after World War I, and came back to the States to help solve the American housing emergency in a similar way. Not until the early 1950s did these same individuals begin to criticize towers-in-the-park solutions for low-income family housing.[13]

In Los Angeles, by the end of 1942, ten new public housing developments had opened as a result of the 1937 Housing Act, all of which were low-rise garden schemes and nine of which were converted to give priority to low-wage war workers. Together, they contained almost 3,500 apartments. The largest concentration of these developments was just east of downtown, where four projects with 61 percent (2,121 units) of all the apartments were located: William Mead Homes, Ramona Gardens, Pico Gardens, and Aliso Village. The last two were built in The Flats and together housed 1,062 families, or nearly a third of all the subsidized units in LA. The largest of the ten public housing projects was Aliso Village (given the official designation Cal. 4-5), designed by a group of architects led by Ralph Flewelling and Lloyd Wright. The latter was an articulate believer in the redeeming powers of large-scale, mass housing:

There is no reason except the limitations imposed by unimaginative and improper economic control, to hinder the immediate and effective use to the fullest extent of the modern methods of quantity production, of standardization, of concentration without congestion, of perfection and interest of form and ideality, thru [sic] it, the discarding of unnecessary, ugly and confusing details, and the producing thereby of units far below present costs, furnishing a service far ahead of the work done by the clumsy, redundant forms, methods and details of the present building industry, not to mention the enhanced and immensely increased value of that romantic element that is so frantically sought for by human beings—that element that lifts them above lower animals, that keeps them from becoming mere machines, that in fact makes them masters of the machine, and their present opportunity, so that they may use it for their enjoyment and for the enjoyment of their children and their children's children.[14]

Ground was broken in February 1942 for Aliso Village, and its opening dedication ceremony was held in October of the same year. During those eight short months when Aliso Village was under construction, the radical transformation was vividly apparent from slums to rational modernism, or community modernism, as public housing scholar Don Parson calls it (Parson, forthcoming). The idiosyncratic bungalows in various states of repair metamorphosed into the largest public housing development in the city.

Aliso Village was a traffic plan and housing development in one, with federal and state funds constructing the Santa Ana Speedway (now Highway 101) to form the north and east boundary. By reordering the surface streets, Aliso Village eliminated The Flats' distorted city grid, replacing it with a careful circulation system that separated children from cars, moving all through traffic to the perimeter. On 34 acres of land, the repetitive courtyard buildings held 802 apartments in nearly identical structures, forming 22 courtyard blocks con-

72　Aliso Village fans out as construction nears completion, December 1942. Photographer: Luckhaus Studios.

structed simultaneously. The two- and three-story buildings were made of brick, concrete frame, and masonry. Units had access to the ground, to light and ventilation from two sides, and were equipped with all the modern conveniences. The buildings exhibited a functional aesthetic characteristic of residential modernism.

Lloyd Wright was no fan of international modernism. He wrote to his father about the seminal exhibition organized by the Museum of Modern Art in 1932 that it was "an excellent example of the worst of the 'Industrial Age'. Sadism cannot go much further. They can have their 'international Architecture', and I hope they are forced to live with it and in it" (quoted in Hines, 1998, p. 29). This is telling in relation to Aliso Village. The architectural aesthetic there was driven less by the International Style, and more by the need for economy of means. Likewise, Ralph Flewelling, who was trained at MIT, was "not strictly a modernist, but certainly modern" in his architecture, according to his long-time associate Jean Whinnery. Whinnery remembers that when the construction bids came back over budget, the housing authority suggested cutting costs by converting masonry structures to wood frame. Flewelling, in spite of the paucity of work at the time, threatened to quit if the three-story structures were switched to wood framing, since he firmly believed this would not be a durable solution.[15] The housing authority acquiesced. At every step of the project, the team of architects had to struggle with an inadequate budget.

73   Aliso Village site plan. Drawn by Sylvia Darr.

74   Architectural rendering of a ramada at Aliso Village.

The site plan was a better representation than the building form of Wright's idea of an American modernism. The large housing blocks were composed according to an internal logic of paths, streets, and open spaces, all of which were designed of a piece. Architecturally, Aliso Village was a good but not great example of what was possible under federal housing programs (in Los Angeles, the work of Neutra at Channel Heights is certainly more significant; see figs. 88, 156). But Aliso Village's architectural strength was greatest at those points where the building design asserted the order of the site. This occurred with the ramadas, or bridgeways at the base of each U-shaped housing block, which opened circulation and created visual interconnections between courts. The site plan was clearly the major achievement at Aliso Village, and was the primary concern of the architects.

> Out of the Architects' experience has come the conviction that the site plan is of prime importance, particularly where group housing is concerned. . . . Because of rigorous cost limitations inherent in low cost group housing, such architectural amenities as could be obtained would have to come largely from the inter-relationship of dwelling house units established by the site plan.[16]

In an early site concept, sets of four bar-shaped buildings slipped past one another to form a four-sided courtyard. Then, as the buildings were considered in more depth, the bars were strung together by habitable bridges. The bridges of rooms form both linkages and outdoor rooms in another early, schematic site plan, in which the building blocks themselves are pure bars tied together by the bridges.[17] Only later did these become more articulated three-sided courts with highly defined corner elements. Within the blocks were the service courts containing laundry lines and utility spaces. The separation of uses extended to residents and automobiles, such that only one thoroughfare curved through the development linking Kearny and Clarence streets, with traffic that was local and slow. Parallel to this street but internally oriented was a continuous, protected "paseo," a "wide, tree-lined lane for pedestrian and playground use," where wading and spray pools were located.[18]

Planning with regard to traffic circulation meant that the edges of the project were as well structured as the center. The southern boundary was the busy, commercial First Street. The administration building for all of LA's public housing was located here. The north and east boundaries were created by the junction of the Ramona and Santa Ana expressways crossing the Los Angeles River at the new Aliso Viaduct. All this work aimed to redefine the primary eastern portal to the downtown business district. A visitor virtually soared into Los Angeles unaware—above the river, the railyards, the public housing, and any remnants of the working-class neighborhoods below.

Building design for public housing, in short, was a matter of economy: the costs were to be low, the design simple, and the planning efficient. In a federal document intended to guide the design of low-rent public housing, the first page admonished that attention to minute detail saved much-needed money through the example of eliminating the usual baseboard from all closets.

> Disregard of the importance of such details, as well as in the major items, can readily result in excessive project cost. . . . But in no other field of architectural and engineering design are the qualities of simplicity and restraint more important; such austerity as this demands can be softened if the designer starts with a clear and sympathetic concept of the real nature of the problem and directs all of his resourcefulness in that direction. (Housing and Home Finance Agency, 1950, pp. 1–2)

It is not surprising, with so little vision and so much emphasis on cost, that talented architects focused attention on the site plan. In the stronger examples of public housing, the architecture of economy melded with a stripped-down modernist aesthetic to produce rather striking results, as in the case of Aliso Village.

Perhaps the most distinctive aspect of the site plan was the central location of the school, which organized the surrounding housing blocks. A nursery school was built adjacent to Utah Street Elementary, to serve the children and parents of Aliso Village. Given the emphasis on the future, it might seem contradictory to orient the new buildings in relation to the old. However, I believe that conceptions of the future as being in some way blocked by the past were limited to industrial, commercial, recreational, circulation, and residential land uses. There was discussion among futurist planners and architects, like members of CIAM, about zones of education and government, but these were not problematized, and were instead merely located in relation to the other newly conceived portions of the city. Since old educational structures were not obstructing the new vision, they could remain, providing a small island of stability amidst the upheaval for Ms. McMahon and her students. Those young students were the very future that socially justified public housing in the first place.

The Aliso Village Architects

27   The Great Depression had critically slowed construction work so that all participants in the building process were underemployed, including architects. The 1937 Housing Act, as much a jobs program as a housing policy, engaged talented designers nationwide. Some of Los Angeles's best architects had teamed up to design public housing, including Richard Neutra, Paul Williams, Lloyd Wright, Welton Becket, and Robert Alexander. The "Housing Group Architects" who designed Aliso Village were led by Ralph Flewelling, working with Lloyd Wright, George J. Adams, Lewis Eugene Wilson, and Eugene Weston, Jr.[19]

These architects had originally formed a group called the Utah Street Architects Association in 1934 to obtain—if not create—a commission for the Utah Street housing project under the PWA program. During 1934 and 1935, Wright visited Washington in secrecy and with great political machinations to obtain a PWA project for Los Angeles and the commission to design it for his team.[20] The same group, under the name Housing Architects Associated, worked together to design the first of the ten early LA housing developments, Ramona Gardens (Cal. 4-1), and slightly later the team designed Rancho San Pedro housing.[21] Such teams were carefully composed of members of the correct political party and with the necessary political ties. Most of these architects had been active in the Citizens' Housing Council of Los Angeles: Wright was a founding member, Wilson had been its vice president, Weston also had held office. The Citizens' Housing Council lobbied for low-income housing programs,

75　Cinco de Mayo celebration at Ramona Gardens public housing.

contributed to the defeat of amendments that would have weakened the 1937 Housing Bill (for example, one to limit the cost per dwelling unit to $3,500), and fought local anti-housing referenda.

Architectural practice during the thirties and forties was markedly different from today. Architects were lucky to get paid $1 an hour; they teamed up in loose joint ventures with other architects who had the appropriate political connections, resources, and skills. Lloyd Wright, for example, participated in three different joint ventures simultaneously, each with its own name and federal housing contract. The city housing authority, in order to spread its work among as many as possible of those seeking employment, hired associations of architects from several firms. When the Housing Group Architects received the Aliso Village contract, they struggled over setting up an office. This was a difficult, costly step, since they had not negotiated a start-up retainer. It appears that they did not open a joint office during design, but instead worked independently between group meetings. Then, according to Jean Whinnery, who was hired by Ralph Flewelling in 1940, they set up an office on the Aliso Village site to supervise construction.[22]

Judging from records of fees paid to various team members, Flewelling and Wright did the majority of the work. By early 1942, the total fee received was $98,000. The design, according to Whinnery, was a collaboration of the five architects involved, but working drawings were completed by Flewelling's office. Not long after construction began, Flewelling moved to Utah to undertake a large government commission he had recently received, at which point Wright assumed the leadership for Aliso Village. The contents of Wright's files indicate that he played a central role in the construction supervision phase of the project. By the end of construction, Wright was addressed as the Chief Architect, the title originally assigned to Flewelling.[23]

The Aliso Village Residents

Even though Mrs. Camareno and her neighbors in The Flats did not want anything to do with public housing, there were enough prospective residents to form
a long waiting list. Originally, the eligibility requirements were income below
$1,100 annually; U.S. citizenship; residency in Los Angeles County for one year;
and presently living under "bad housing" conditions. Once war broke out, ill-
housed defense workers earning $1 an hour or less were given priority. If you
were lucky enough to get one of these "modern, well constructed American
homes" (Los Angeles, Housing Authority, 1942), you would be outfitted with
an "electric refrigerator, gas range, gas water heater, gas radiator, window
shades, private bath and toilet, individual 'built-in' laundry tub, clotheslines,
parking lot as well as gas, electricity, and water."[24]

The project was one of the nation's first to be racially integrated, owing to
protests by the Citizens' Housing Council against the housing authority's segregation policy. Leonard Nadel documented life there in an unpublished book
featuring four families in residence, each of a different ethnic origin.[25] Nadel's
poetic photographic study of Aliso Village impressed the housing authority
enough that he began working with the agency. He recorded with particular
poignancy the slums of Los Angeles in the late forties and early fifties. His photographs argued for the construction of new, subsidized housing under the 1949
Housing Act.

76   Mrs. Carleton T. Taggart, resident of Aliso Village, learns to can. December 1948. Photographer: Leonard Nadel.

77   The four families featured in Leonard Nadel's monograph on Aliso Village. Photographer: Leonard Nadel.

Nadel's Aliso Village project championed the positive effects of subsidized housing on slums. In a draft of the text for the photo essay, Nadel wrote:

> Aliso Village stands out conspicuously just across the Los Angeles River on East First St. Slums surround it on every side . . . it had one of the worst slum records in Los Angeles. Bubonic Plague started near here in 1924 and took a toll of 31 lives and for years rats with Bubonic germs had infested the area.
>
> Today Aliso Village is an island in the slums. It has cut out and taken the place of the filth and rot and slum conditions that existed here previously. . . . Properly planned, there is available more space and room for more people living in Aliso Village today than lived in the slums that preceded it.

The faces in Nadel's monograph are hopeful, their stories idealized, and the direction of that idealization is telling: each family is hardworking, firmly located in the American dream, and appreciative of public housing as physical shelter and social community. There is a black family, a Mexican family, a white family, and an Asian family, depicting integration as the future of American communities and Aliso Village's modern architecture as the appropriate setting. The cooperative play school for preschool children was touted as "one of the finest examples of racial co-operation existing anywhere" (*Housing News*, November 1946, p. 1). At a time when government agents enforced segregation and interracial fraternizing signified communist leanings, the early residents of Aliso Village predicted a radically new society.

Modern Housing's Demise

29 Public housing did not realize the vision of modern housing, but it was part of the experiment. Modern housing had socialist, political roots that were taken for granted by socially oriented architects and planners. Technology would inevitably breed cooperative living, "good mass produced meals, in great apartment complexes where all the services were done for us" (Bauer, 1965, p. 52). Lewis Mumford believed that a fundamental communism lay in the emergent economic order of the 1930s. The problem of mass housing at the time of the New Deal inherently bred socialist utopian visions of a better city. The modernist manifestation—the aesthetic of public housing—was a function of the political and practical transformation new technology could bring to architecture (see Harries, 1997). Thus, it was not without grounds that the conservative real estate interests waged their red-baiting war on social housing, creating an inescapable trap for the advocates of public housing. Although some scholars of public housing have argued that housing activists were forced into the modernist aesthetic by real estate interests seeking to avoid market competition (e.g., Bratt, 1986), nothing could be further from the case.

Private builders had other gripes about public housing. Although Wright complained about the tight budget, Aliso Village was not inexpensively built according to construction standards at the time. Commercial builders who had been suffering financially during the Depression resented the added blow dealt by the federal government's War Production Board and War Housing Standards.

78　Baldwin Hills Village, soon after construction in 1942, showing the expansive open space that would grow into lush gardens. Photographer: "Dick" Whittington.

Rules, regulations, standards, and materials restrictions grated on the construction industry's members, but they were more irate that federally subsidized housing did not seem governed by the same rules, which strengthened their case about unfair competition. Builders found the deficiencies of socialist and communist regimes evident in the excesses of public housing agencies: "What private developer ever has been able to indulge in such a lavish mis-use of critical materials?"[26] Even representatives of the federal government recognized that the costs of construction had been too high.[27]

It was easy enough for private builders to make their financial argument against public housing, since they had some big residential projects of their own for comparison. In Los Angeles, one in particular stands out because of its superior design: Baldwin Hills Village (see for example *Arts and Architecture*, January 1942). Its 627 garden apartments were created by some of the same architects who worked in public housing.[28] Built on vacant land by a private developer in 1941 with FHA support, its land costs were one third those of Aliso Village. Baldwin Hills had seven dwelling units to the acre, compared to Aliso's nineteen, and twice the expenditure on site improvement (evident today in

Baldwin Hills' verdant landscape). Still, the total cost per unit of each is surprisingly comparable: $4,911 for Baldwin Hills Village, $4,401 for Aliso Village.[29] The commercial builders made their point: the most effective subsidy to stimulate housing production would go to the private sector.

The emergencies that instigated radical housing solutions like Aliso Village were replaced in the late 1940s by the most pressing housing shortage Los Angeles had ever experienced, as veterans returned from the war. Still laced with futurist ideals and unencumbered by the responsibilities of permanence, the veterans' housing solutions represented vast departures from tradition. As will be apparent in Rodger Young Village, technology, mass housing, integration, and socialist politics combined in ways that effectively doomed this form of housing. But it was also at Rodger Young Village that a formerly silent group of residents found its voice of protest.

Fugitive Places, Provisional City

> A bulldozer [is] poised to begin demolition work . . . to mark a new begin-
> ning for the dilapidated Pico-Aliso public housing project in Boyle Heights,
> a collection of nondescript World War II-era apartment buildings in one of
> the most crime ridden neighborhoods in Los Angeles. (Ramos, 1996)

More than a unique story of neighborhood housing, Aliso Village is an object
lesson about large-scale urban upheaval. The tale is not over, and the lesson
continues.

At the same time as Aliso Village was completed in 1942, Pico Gardens
opened just blocks to the south. Its 260 units were planned under the same appropriations bill and design thinking as Aliso Village. The Pico site had been
part of the original Utah Street project that Lloyd Wright had lobbied for in the
thirties, along with the intervening blocks. Unsurprisingly, then, when it was
time to select sites for the anticipated 10,000 units Los Angeles would build under the 1949 Housing Act, the intervening blocks were chosen. Over 300 units
of Aliso Apartments Extension were built in mid-rise towers. Now the public
housing chain was complete: Pico-Aliso consisted of three developments with
about 1,400 apartments. This mega development, planned according to the
ideas of modern housing, has not fared well. As in public housing nationwide,
skimpy operating budgets insured steady deterioration and an increasingly disadvantaged population served to stigmatize the neighborhood. Today, the three-

part development is riddled with problems characteristic of much public housing: gang warfare, drugs, inexorable poverty, unmaintained buildings. The past president of the residents' association told me that he was a good candidate for local leadership since he was a bachelor: gangs couldn't pressure him by threatening his family.[30]

Today, Aliso Village is physically and politically isolated, as is much of the early public housing, by its own initial ideals. Intended as an exemplary solution to the nation's affordable housing crisis, public housing has become one of the nation's most difficult problems to solve. Much of the early housing now falls under the jurisdiction of an office of the U.S. Department of Housing and Urban Development labeled Distressed and Troubled Housing. Contemporary solutions include demolishing such housing because it has decayed to such an extent that it is irreparable—a slum. Portions of Aliso Village's neighboring Pico-Aliso developments were demolished in 1997, to be replaced by one hundred fewer units in markedly suburban or New Urbanist imagery.[31] The housing authority staged a "Demolition Fiesta" to celebrate the end of the once visionary, now oppressive development. Many, though by no means all, of the residents seem relieved to see the place razed. Again social problems with economic roots are being redressed by utopian physical solutions. If gangs like AVK (for Aliso Village Killers) no longer have a home, then the problem will go away, or so this naive logic goes. Like overcrowding in the thirties, gangs are to be defeated by new buildings, only this time the buildings look backward to a nostalgic America.

Aliso Village presented to its low-income residents a new image of the neighborhood, and a new image of home. Planned all at once, built as a whole with various services, the Village's homes defied the American dream. They also embodied progressive ideas about community planning circulating at the time. The stripped-down modernism readily associated with the "projects," initially taken as a futurist symbol of efficiency and scientific rationality, has now come to stand for the failure of public housing. Modern housing, Bauer claimed, would be protected from blight by its clearly bounded site plan, but in fact the effect was more the opposite. Isolated in all ways from the rest of the city, Aliso Village awaits reincarnation by currently prevailing utopians, just like the adjoining Pico-Aliso. At the time of this writing, the enthusiasm for demolition has extended to Aliso Village, where the ramadas that had architecturally distinguished the buildings were removed to enhance surveillance of gang activity. It will not be long before it is entirely razed.

Given the federal government's adoption of nostalgic architectural imagery (Cuomo, 1997), the next upheaval will bring a thematic suburbia into the urban core. A postmodern housing scheme, with hipped roofs, stoops, and wood siding will replace much of the now-maligned modernist boxes of the

79   Ramadas at Aliso Village were demolished in 1998 as a means to reduce crime. Photographer: Beth Holden.

area's three developments. This represents a reversal of the cooperative, socialist ideals embodied by modern housing schemes, into a privatized sphere with
little or no public realm (see Gottdiener, 1997). That the entire area deteriorated
as a whole, lending weight to the argument of redevelopment as a whole, was
possible because of its original large scale. The seemingly permanent Aliso Village housing proved fragile and impermanent. In the next case study, what
began as a temporary yet immense upheaval persisted far past its hour of destruction. Together, the two examples demonstrate the perversion of permanence under conditions of recurrent large-scale upheaval.

Temporary Abode, Industrial Aesthetic: Rodger Young Village

IV

A New Emergency Looms

I don't know exactly how
we are going to proceed,
because the legislation still
is in Congress, but I have
orders from Wilson Wyatt,
national housing director,
to move fast.
Louis M. Dreves, 1946

31 Despite a great deal of national discussion about effective strategies for postwar conversion, peacetime, when it came, began to unfold unpredictably. As Louis Dreves, recently appointed Director of the Construction Division of the Civilian Production Administration for the Southwest Region, put it, no one knew how to proceed but everyone realized that whatever it was would have to be done fast.[1] It could not be done fast enough, as his boss Wilson Wyatt found out. He was forced to resign just one year later, in 1947, when all his expediting had only produced 35,000 of the one million housing units needed (see *California Eagle*, 1947). In Los Angeles, throngs of veterans came to set up housekeeping after being discharged. They had served their country well, they had won the war, and now they would begin their lives of prosperity. They deserved it.

Very soon it became evident that a new emergency was taking hold for the hopeful young warriors: there was no place to live. Or better put, there was *still* no place to live. Defense industry cities like Los Angeles had managed the war worker housing crunch inadequately. The wartime emergency had led to a series of temporary housing solutions. That emergency had followed on the heels of the housing crisis during the Depression, when foreclosures threatened middle-class homeownership at its roots. One manifestation of those serial emergencies were the slums, taken to be a crisis in their own right.

In each of these emergencies, a temporary collective mentality was formed or presumed, thus creating a momentary "public" and notions about the public

80, 81 *Rodger Young News,* masthead logo.

interest and public use. Defense worker housing was in the national interest, which enabled both the appropriation of federal funds and the expropriation of private property. Eminent domain is based on the presumption of a public good that serves the interests of the American people; only with the uncontested compliance of the population would such policies stand. It is in the period covered by this chapter—1946–1954, the lifespan of Rodger Young Village veterans' housing—that outspoken opposition to housing policy became organized and effective.

Inherent to the idea of emergency is its temporal abbreviation: emergencies are short-lived, requiring extreme but provisional measures. One can set aside the law in an emergency, because it is expedient for the moment, until "things return to normal." The "normal," however, is itself emergent and unknown. Thus, proclaiming an emergency as well as its end are political actions in search of empirical corroboration.

In an urban emergency, shifting notions of the public interest feed modern tendencies to upheaval. If blighted neighborhoods have reached crisis stage, get rid of them. If the defense industry or veterans need housing, slap up as much as possible in short order. If there are no sites, clear a place in the park. A sense of public duty surrounded each of these emergencies, and a broad if provisional strategy was needed to address them. Later, when the emergency had passed, divergent long-term solutions would be debated. When a quick strike is needed, the state can step in with emergency measures and the funding to effect them. Private-sector complaints are muted by the public cry for temporary relief.

And temporary relief can adhere to different standards than those of permanent solutions. Construction regulations are loosened, property acquisition is eased, aesthetic standards are disregarded, social mores are suspended. Enter the Quonset hut and Rodger Young Village. Life after the war would not be the same, for the individual, for the household, or for the city. The future that had been coming was here. Why not live it beneath the shelter of a corrugated metal vault?

82 750 Quonset huts of evidence that "Los Angeles cares for its veterans."

83 Morton Schmidt gets his shoes shined as he waits in the FHA line for new homes, May 1945.

84   Rodger Young Quonset hut under construction. Photographer: Edwin Eichelberger.

85   Ruffled curtains and dollhouses of conventional construction imply a certain discomfort with the Quonset home. February 1950. Photographer: Otto Rothschild.

From War to Peace: The Uncertain Social and Technological Future of Los Angeles

During the war, homeplaces were radically transformed around the country, but nowhere as significantly as on the West Coast. On December 8, 1941, the day after Pearl Harbor, blackout and dim-out began in Los Angeles. There was a palpable terror in the city when, a few weeks later, a Union Oil tanker was sunk off the coast north of Los Angeles by a Japanese submarine. Defense industries like oil refineries and aircraft factories were camouflaged; streetlights and car headlights were masked; block captains disciplined neighbors who forgot to draw their blackout curtains at night; and everything was rationed, from tires to butter. This was not life as Angelenos had ever known it before.

In defense cities, an influx of war workers competing for housing caused shortages, price increases, and rent control regulation. Dr. Edith Elmer Wood (1941b), a national housing expert, claimed, "Hitler's best chance of world domination hangs on the continued failure of American defense housing to keep step with American industrial expansion." But Wood's argument for subsidized housing and rent freezes was not popular with the building industry. Even *Architectural Forum* felt it necessary to distance itself editorially from the views she expressed in its pages.

With America's entry into the war, federally assisted housing built under the 1937 housing act adopted new priorities. Dislocated residents of demolished neighborhoods who once had had top priority for the newly constructed public housing were displaced again, this time by war workers. In addition, public

86 Rooftops of aircraft plants like this one in Long Beach, California, were camouflaged to look like the surrounding suburban houses and streetscape.

housing was temporarily dissociated from slum clearance in an effort to build quickly as much housing as possible for defense workers. The emergency of the slums was overtaken by the emergency of the war's ill-housed labor force.

The Lanham Act (HR 4545), passed in October of 1940 as anxiety about the European war led to an American defense building, initiated what would become an immense national program of temporary and permanent war housing. In 1942, when the shortage of defense housing became critical, the Lanham Act was amended to speed the delivery of temporary units. Like earlier housing legislation, the Lanham Act was an employment program as well as a housing program. But Los Angeles real estate interests, not wanting any competition from the federal government, testified against the Lanham Act in Washington in its early years. In these hearings, the superior organization of labor interests, particularly the United Auto Workers, was abundantly clear to the builders. This helped kindle what would become a very powerful national real estate lobby.[2] The national defense housing acts eventually incorporated private-sector interests, so that the government was not getting into the housing business. "In the pressure of an emergency, the federal government should not begin to take on a landlord role that it could not easily shed, once the pressure was off. For every plan to build a unit, there must be matching plan to 'dispose' of it after the war" (*Journal of Housing*, 1955a, p. 152). Wartime housing legislation virtually insured vast urban upheaval and impermanence, for its goal was to provide large quantities of housing as quickly as possible during the war, and then return it to the private real estate market as fast as possible after the war. In all, the federal government provided almost a million units of housing that would have to be disposed of at war's end.

Under the Lanham Act, permanent, semipermanent, and temporary shelter was built during the war, ranging from the seminal project, Channel Heights by Richard Neutra, to the 2,000-unit Banning Homes, much of it in the port area. Some fine architects and designers were involved with defense housing across the country, including Louis Kahn, William Wurster, and Garrett Eckbo. War worker housing in Los Angeles was in short supply, but the conditions were not as extreme as in Richmond, California, or Detroit, Michigan, because LA entered the war with a better supply of housing, and in part because LA's eventual housing crisis was spread over an immense metropolitan region.

Still, from an architectural perspective, the pressure to house essential war workers bred an expedience in housing production that virtually eliminated traditional aesthetic preference. Priorities had shifted, and the aesthetic symbols of efficiency, technological advance, material resourcefulness, and alacrity counted for more than traditional associations of home. Not that residents liked the temporary trailers they might be lucky enough to snag, but, like victory gardens, they were a sign of the patriotism and sacrifice of a nation. Mostly, they were a roof over one's head.

The unusual conditions that prevailed at the home front throughout the war were understood as temporary. Still, such short-lived experiences can have lasting impact. The young men returning from war had been required to shed their personal identities in service of the troop; indeed, their very survival had depended on sublimating individuality for the collective. Those who fought were asked to leave their homes, leave the women with whom they shared them

87   These Wilmington Hall dormitories for war workers are shielded by barrage balloons, visible at left.

88   Richard Neutra's Channel Heights. Photographer: Julius Shulman.

or hoped to make them, and live with the insecurity that, if they were lucky enough to survive battle, their long absence might lead to broken homes. The story of social transformation of gender relations because of the war abroad and war industries in America is well known. There has also been illuminating discussion about the impact of these phenomena upon the home (see Hayden, 1984; Wright, 1981). Women working outside the home during the war expanded their social and economic claims beyond the house to the city and the workplace. Women's urban spatial patterns were elaborated in irreversible ways.

Simultaneously, there was a racial transformation that began in the war and later fueled the civil rights movement. When Pearl Harbor was bombed and all the Japanese living in the West were forced into internment camps, their emptied neighborhoods became prime sites for other ill-housed ethnic groups to find shelter. Little Tokyo in Los Angeles became known as Bronzeville, because of the number of African Americans who relocated there. Blacks experienced the most extreme discrimination, with only about 5 percent of all residential areas of the city open to them (Collins, 1980). Between 1940 and 1945, the white population of Los Angeles rose about 18 percent while the black population increased 109 percent (Ovnick, 1994, p. 264). The defense industries began to stop discriminating against nonwhite workers in 1943, but the restrictive covenants that allowed segregated neighborhoods were not outlawed for another 25 years, via laws like the Open Housing Act of 1968. The injustice of a segregated city became inescapably apparent on the heels of an integrated defense workplace.

89 Los Angeles mayor Fletcher Bowron speaks to a black war worker's family that has moved into Little Tokyo, emptied by the internment of Japanese residents. Photographer: Otto Rothschild.

During the war, African Americans at home were waging their own battles, under banners like that raised by the *Pittsburgh Courier* called the "Double V," meaning "victory over our enemies at home and victory over our enemies on the battlefields abroad" (see Crawford, 1995, p. 110). The Los Angeles housing authority had been one of the first in the nation to desegregate in 1942. This might have been wartime emergency behavior, but after the war veterans' housing was integrated as well. Of these, the emergency after the war was more threatening, because it lacked an explicit terminus. Now African-American, Hispanic, Jewish, Catholic, Asian, and WASP children would grow up together and live together—indefinitely?

The vast majority of veterans came back to the States with virtually nothing: women had taken their jobs (now that their patriotic duty had been fulfilled, women were being encouraged to leave the workplace, but this was not an entirely successful effort), jobs were in shorter supply now that the war effort was curtailed, their cash supplies were low, savings nil, and there was nowhere to live. By December of 1945, 200,000 LA residents had lost industrial jobs; simultaneously, 17,000 servicemen were in the city waiting for discharge clearance, another 14,000 were aboard ships in the harbor, and a full 90,000 more were expected before the month was over. At war's end it was estimated that Los Angeles would need 280,000 new units annually (Los Angeles, Housing Authority, 1945). Men who believed in a better life after the war found that the barracks had been more comfortable than what they had to settle for at home. If homeownership meant status and identity, then manhood itself was threatened for the so-called heroes fast becoming vagrants.[3]

But there was another force at work upon housing at the end of the war, a belief in the possibility of progress and science, in technology and change. The spectacular achievements in defense manufacturing might become models for what could happen to solve the incipient housing crisis. If Kaiser could build a Liberty Ship in five days and Willow Run in Detroit could build a B24 bomber every hour,[4] then couldn't the nation produce the estimated one million homes

90   The rainbow coalition of children at Rodger Young Village. Photographer Leonard Nadel called this image "Freedom Train."

per year that were going to be needed? Clearly, the old solutions would not be adequate when new solutions promised economy, efficiency, and convenience.

On one level, the postwar conditions produced tremendous public support for housing solutions of all kinds, since the vast majority of the population in defense production centers like LA knew about housing problems firsthand. At another level, threats through housing to racial dominance, gender-based authority, status, and identity, constructed the possibility of a forceful reaction, which was exactly what happened in the early 1950s.

If subdivided land came on the market, it was sold out within hours, with the new owners sometimes waiting years for construction materials to become available. Long lines greeted news of every type of available housing. Moreover, excessive demand had inflated land values, labor costs, and materials costs (see, for example, *Los Angeles Times*, 1947). People refurbished buses to be used as shelter, and there were squatters in old rail cars. Competing for housing became the subject matter of black comedy. A story went around that a man had been gruesomely murdered in his apartment. When a reporter arrived at the scene he asked the landlady, "Can I rent his apartment?" "I'm sorry," she replied, "it's already taken by that man there," pointing to the chief homicide officer.

Emergency veterans housing, undertaken by the Federal Public Housing Authority, had as its stated policy "to provide housing equally as good as that furnished to war workers. Comfortable but not luxurious housing will be provided."[5] The Lanham Act was amended in July of 1945 to allow the transfer of temporary wartime units to temporary veterans' housing. In July of 1946, when 811 surplus Quonset huts were to go on sale at Port Hueneme, over a thousand

91   "Ideal housing" in 1947.

92 The veterans' housing protest in MacArthur Park, 1947.

veterans camped out some three days in advance to buy for $295 "their little quonsets and sweat out the housing squeeze for a year or two" (Cravens, 1946). When rents might be as much as $200 a month for an equivalent amount of space, veterans sought out a 16-by-36-foot Quonset to disassemble and re-assemble—if only an available lot might be found. One GI and his wife and two children were living in a remote canyon in Monrovia, with no utilities, and two mules to get to work or the store, but with no chance of getting to school. Living in cars, buses, squatter-type housing, and doubled up, the veterans staged mass rallies to publicize their plight. On January 10, 1947, a multiracial coalition of 1,500 veterans camped out in MacArthur Park to protest the housing shortage, carrying signs that read "Fox holes in 1945—rat holes in 1947" (Parson, 1983). By June of 1947, the city of Los Angeles contained only 8,987 temporary dwelling units for veterans; for Los Angeles County as a whole, the total was 16,413.[6]

The private housing industry had been stifled throughout the war, not just by material shortages but also by labor shortages, building restrictions, and all manner of regulation. After the war, regulations were still tight as the government sought to avoid inflation. Real estate interests had found their common enemy during the war and had united as never before in order not to eliminate but to control government intervention in their domain. Only indirect subsidy would be tolerated, and that going to the middle and upper classes.

The patriotic fervor that abounded during the war had converted to the national pride of a victor, and public sentiment was overwhelmingly in support of finding housing remedies to the veterans' problem. State funds, under the 1946 Emergency Housing Appropriation Bill, would match local monies ten to one. Los Angeles mayor Fletcher Bowron and the city council were supportive, so the housing authority proposed a number of sites for immediate temporary housing for veterans (see fig. 9).[7] The largest of these was Rodger Young Village. Among LA's urban upheavals, there is no place of the scale of Rodger Young that was more evanescent.

Rodger Young Village: "Quonset Hut Community"

33 We left our apartment in Brooklyn, and in '43, '44, and '45, I traveled all though the South with my husband in the service. I remember when we were in North Carolina, we lived with some fairly ignorant tobacco farmers. They'd never seen a Jew. My husband was blonde; luckily, they thought all Jews were dark. I didn't know what Jim Crow was then, but it was a segregated army. I got a real education in the South. It was terrible. It changed my life.

My husband was discharged in Fort Ord. We still had the apartment in Brooklyn, but when I hit LA I knew I was never going back. It was 1946, we were hunting for an apartment and there were none to rent. We didn't have a car or a job or a refrigerator—nothing, so we rented a room on Arlington instead and started going door to door. One day, someone told us that the Housing Authority had housing, so my husband put in an application, and it happened almost immediately. I was so excited. We didn't have any money and this was only $35 *furnished;* there was nothing like that. When we first moved in, there were other families already there, but there was no market, or soda shop, so we went by bus to Grand Central Market for *cheap* food. I had my first child in the Village in 1948.

Pretty early on, we found ourselves with a right wing and a left wing in the Village because an issue came up that labeled people. Libby Burke and her husband [Sidney] lived in Rodger Young and he wrote for *People's*

World [the Communist newspaper]. Evidently, there was an active group of Communists in the Village. They were the ones that got things done, like child care, because they were capable leaders. The Knights of Columbus— they were the right, from the Catholic Church—organized to get Libby and her husband out. They called a meeting and said, "People who want Libby Burke to stay, go to this side of the room; those who want her to go, this side." We found ourselves on the left, with many friends.

We bought a house in Burbank and moved out in 1950, when we knew we were going to have to get out. When I asked why they were getting rid of the Village, they said it was for a golf course. It seemed so sad—here were all these good people who needed housing. I don't know whether there was a stigma about Quonset huts—you couldn't really see the Village from the road anyway. The controversy, I think, would have been the successful integration. What was so wonderful for blacks and Jews, was the total integration of all races. We made fast friends. It was a heart-warming experience.

Dorothy Sterling, 1997

93 Holidays at Dorothy Sterling's Quonset hut.

Modern, Attractive, Well-Built Homes that sell for $4,000 to $6,000!

Stran-Steel Homes establish entirely new standards of beauty, durability and comfort in the field of low-cost housing. Never before has the home owner been able to enjoy such modern styling, such spaciousness and distinction, for so small an investment!

Ease and speed of erection, permanency and economy are achieved through the use of Stran-Steel arch-rib framing. Your local builder furnishes collateral materials and does the construction work.

Several designs, the work of nationally known architects, are pictured on the following pages. An almost unlimited number of additional designs can be created by your own architect.

Number 1 THE *Brighton* 20' x 36'

As little as $35 a month PAYS FOR A PERMANENT, SMARTLY STYLED HOME *like this*

ELIGIBLE STRUCTURALLY FOR F.H.A. MORTGAGE INSURANCE

94   Text describes the Brighton shown here: "Never before has the home owner been able to enjoy such modern styling, such spaciousness and distinction, for so small an investment."

If housing aesthetics are indicative of a collective domestic utopia, then we must stop and take notice of the temporary veterans' housing built in 1946 as Rodger Young Village. Its 750 corrugated vaults, extruded and multiplied, occupied a portion of Griffith Park and a former airfield at the park's northeastern corner. The war-surplus Quonset huts were erected in record time: state funds were appropriated in February of 1946, and Rodger Young Village opened that April, just sixty days later. Each hut contained two units, so that 1,500 veterans' families, or about 5000 people, found temporary shelter (*Housing News*, 1946a, 1946b).

Quonset huts are a particularly interesting housing solution from an architectural standpoint. Initial postwar applications suggested by the manufacturers themselves were as chicken houses and greenhouses. By the end of the war, magazine ads showed a man ready to carry his bride over the hut's threshold, with copy that explained it as modern, beautiful, durable, and comfortable: "As little as $35 a month pays for a permanent, smartly styled home like this" (*Architectural Record,* 1947). Stran-Steel attempted to capitalize upon the modern, pragmatic aesthetic that seemed to have caught hold of the American dream during the war, marketing Quonsets as popular, affordable housing. Lacking almost entirely in residential symbolism, its various models, like the Brighton shown in figure 94, attached some wood siding or multipane windows to give the hut a more homey appeal (see Young, 1996).

In Rodger Young, at least, residents were not making an aesthetic choice when moving into the Village: there were 13,000 applicants at one point for only 1,500 units (Turpin, 1954). But much to the residents' and their observers' surprise, the huts became home, the homes became a community, and all too soon they would be dismantled.

Quonsets at War

Quonset huts were strongly associated with the Seabees, and with the resourcefulness and can-do spirit that had led to victory in the war. The Seabees' talent for ad hoc construction was much revered: "As American forces moved island by island across the Pacific, [the Seabees] proved to be the most gifted scroungers

95   Trellises and trikes convert Quonset huts into homes.

96 Uncrating the Quonsets. Photographer: Louis Clyde Stoumen.

of all. . . . There was something joyous in the surprising things they did with oil drums and Quonset huts that seemed then to open the door to industrial materials and forms used in unexpected ways" (Hine, 1989, p. 169). During the war, the Seabees constructed for the Navy bridges, roads, airstrips, and buildings out of thatch, scrap metal, and any other possible material. One type of structure used by the Navy and Army alike was the Quonset hut, developed in Quonset Point, Rhode Island, and refined by Stran-Steel Corporation into a simple, economic, compact, lightweight, and efficient system. In early 1941, the Navy had asked George A. Fuller and Company, a large New York construction firm, to consider the problem of troop housing that could be prefabricated in America, shipped anywhere, and set up quickly. In May of that year, after just eleven weeks, the firm's first shipment of huts left Rhode Island. It is estimated that 160,000 Quonset huts were produced during the war (Young, 1996).[8]

The basis for the Quonset was an I-shaped, nailable member bent into a continuous arch, so that wall and roof were one. These semicircular arches, set four feet apart, were assembled with ordinary bolts and typically anchored to a 3-to-4-inch concrete slab or grade beams, with finished plywood flooring. Between the arch sections, masonite was used to line the interior, followed by laid-in insulation precut to size, followed by pre-painted, corrugated, galvanized iron

97 Construction workers apply corrugated siding. Photographer: Edwin Eichelberger.

siding installed horizontally for the exterior sheathing. Windows, three to a side, were shipped with the system, as were all the tools necessary to build it. A 20-by-48-foot hut was shipped in a 450-cubic-foot crate, three to a truckload (see *Architectural Forum*, February 1944; Steidle, 1944). These half-cylinders of corrugated metal offered a simple and efficient construction system requiring the standard skills of construction laborers, so that a crew could assemble a hut in just hours.

These accommodations were temporary, emergency, and prefabricated—all features understood as commonplace during the war. Prefabrication itself was associated with impermanence, because of the precedent set by wartime housing (see Reed, 1995). For these reasons, the huts did not shock their prospective residents, so desperate for housing. The Quonset was proudly featured on the masthead of the *Rodger Young News,* a community paper written within the Village (see figs. 80, 81). Surrounding the modest hut in the image are the words "harmony, equality, democracy; community, home, nation."[9]

Quonsets in the Park
The city housing authority, with the mayor's blessing, proposed a part of Griffith Park for veterans' housing. Only one voice spoke against the proposal, that

of Van Griffith, son of the park's founder and defender of his father's intention that all the parkland be preserved for public use. Griffith did not see veterans' housing as a public use, and was furthermore afraid that the housing might not be as temporary as was intended. He took his case to court, where he was soundly defeated (see Eberts, 1996). There was general agreement, which the courts legitimated, that veterans' housing was in the public interest.

Unlike Aliso Village, Rodger Young supplanted 112 acres of relatively uninhabited land: most of the site had been a California National Air Guard airstrip. For temporary housing, the airstrip had numerous advantages. It fulfilled a common expectation that all kinds of defense-related technology would be converted to domestic uses. Parks were being utilized across the city for temporary purposes, both during and after the war. Because the site was public property, the time and costs associated with land acquisition were nonexistent. Already a level site, it required minimal grading. Lastly, the hangars were ready to convert to commercial and administrative uses, becoming a panoply of village services (see figs. 99, 101). If all these factors did not speed construction enough, standard regulations were suspended: "For the duration of the housing emergency all temporary veterans' housing projects—built and financed jointly by the city, state and Federal governments—will be exempt from the city's building code and zoning laws under an ordinance the City Council yesterday ordered drafted" (*Los Angeles Examiner*, 1946c).

Site preparation cost $1.7 million, of which the city paid 10 percent and the state paid 90 percent. The federal government provided the huts from war surplus, as they did for veterans' housing across the country, from Yale University to the huts of Port Hueneme. According to one journalist, Rodger Young Village was the largest and first temporary emergency veterans' housing project in the nation (Turpin, 1954).

The architects for the Village, William Allen and W. George Lutzi, had the task of organizing the site, since the architecture of the Quonset huts was a given. Lutzi had been published in architecture magazines for his design of a 196-unit private housing development (see *Arts and Architecture*, 1941). Could a Quonset hut qualify as architecture? Most definitely. Bruce Goff had built a Quonset chapel at Camp Parks Military Base in California in 1945 (Hine, 1989). In that same year, Robert Motherwell commissioned Pierre Charreau to design a painting studio from a Quonset hut in the Hamptons (see Brook, 1985; also Reed, 1995). But in the popular eye, a Quonset hut was less architecture than technology.

The site plan of Rodger Young was an efficient tessellation pattern between Riverside Drive and the Los Angeles River to the east and Crystal Springs Drive and Griffith Park to the west. One primary east-west road intersected an

98　Site work at Rodger Young Village in 1946. Photographer: Edwin Eichelberger.

99　Hangars for the shopping center, 1953.

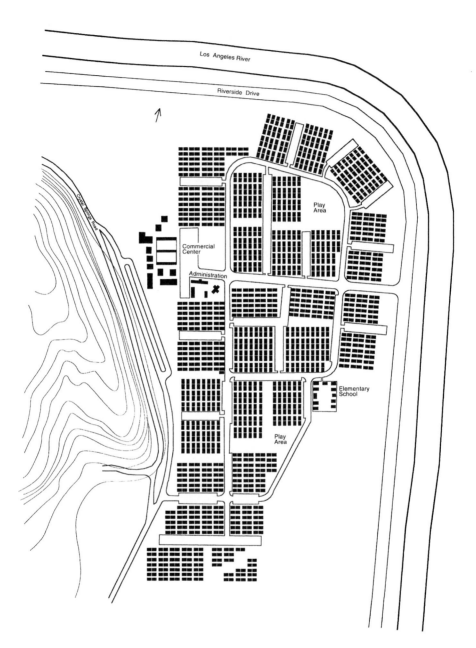

Los Angeles River

Riverside Drive

Play
Area

Commercial
Center

Administration

Elementary
School

Play
Area

100   Rodger Young Village site plan. Drawn by Sylvia Darr.

101   The shopping center included a baby shop, photo shop, dentist, dry goods and furniture, shoe repair, hobby shop, dry cleaners, message center, garden shop, laundry, gas station, garage, recreation hall, malt shop, barber, variety store, men's shop, jewelry shop, market, drug store, beauty shop, medical center, newsstand, and chapel. *Rodger Young News*.

102   Opening day dedication at Rodger Young Village.

internal loop road to link the Village Shopping Center, administration buildings, school, and play areas to the thirty different blocks each containing about 25 huts for 50 families.[10] Between the blocks were limited areas for cars. The huts in each block sat in parallel lines, equidistant one from the other, extending the Quonset huts' military imagery. Across the river was another world, of segregated Glendale, the Grand Central Airport, and Lockheed. Although some Villagers found jobs within Rodger Young itself, most working residents departed each day, leaving an army of young mothers in the huts. Practically everything they needed was in the Village Shopping Center, which housed some twenty-five separate establishments, including a chapel, a medical center, a gas station, a beauty shop, a recreation hall, and a malt shop. When added to the child care center, school, and library, services in the Village were more extensive than in most neighborhoods. This must have contributed to the sense of community and to the high degree of participation in all activities, from a resident-initiated newspaper to organized petitioning for the child care center, and eventually to protests over the Village's closure.

The grand opening was a glitzy affair put together by Frank Wilkinson, with stars and dignitaries and a huge American flag as the backdrop. The mother of the slain serviceman Rodger Young, whose heroic self-sacrifice was memorialized in the Village's name, appeared at the festivities for photo opportunities with mayor and movie star alike. In 1946, public opinion supporting the veterans played into the housing authority's publicity campaign. They tried to link the vast public support for veterans' housing with general support for low-rent housing, as the next federal legislation was taking shape in Washington.

Life in Rodger Young

For five months after serving in the Ninth Army in Europe, James Parkhill had been living with his wife and two children in a trailer behind the Hollywood Bowl. He was a sound technician who had found a job at the Bowl as a night watchman. On May 23, 1946, they became the first family to move into Rodger Young Village, at Hut Number 1087. They stayed to have another baby and save enough money to buy a house, moving out less than two years later (Turpin, 1954).

Each unit had two bedrooms, an icebox (not a refrigerator), and rented for about $30 unfurnished and $40 with furniture (Eberts, 1996). A common goal of the residents was to stay long enough to pay off debts and save $500 for a down payment on a house. During that time, their families grew. According to resident Mrs. Lucille Butts, wife of a veteran and operator of the baby shop, she did a booming business, with as many as 500 expectant mothers at one time ready to clothe the soon-to-be-born baby boomer generation. Those new babies

103   Move-in day.

would join their 2,750 brothers and sisters already living in the Village. The on-site school at Rodger Young, housed in another set of former airstrip buildings, was the largest of all nearby public schools (Turpin, 1954).

Residents recall the close proximity between families sharing a hut. Said resident Leota Fantl (now Smith-Flowers), "The joke went, if the child next door sneezed, you wiped your kid's nose." But noise was not the only way that families at Rodger Young shared in each other's lives: the Village was a political hotbed after the war. More than any other factor, the experiment with racial integration defined Rodger Young Village's brief lifespan. According to a resident survey in 1952, "approximately 48% of the people in the community are Caucasians; 28% Negroes; 20% Mexicans; the balance diversified Orientals and others" (Brown, 1952, p. 2). Black families lived in huts next to white families, and intimate lives intermingled in ways rare before the Village. Without explicitly intending it, interracial groups of black and white women would take the bus into town and stage impromptu civil rights demonstrations by trying to dine together at local restaurants.[11]

There was an active cell of the Communist Party at Rodger Young, the weight of which was exaggerated by the media. This was consistent with the opinion, often voiced, that Caucasians who were integrationists had to be Communists. Politics was neatly divided at the Village, between a conservative, primarily white Catholic group centered around the Knights of Columbus, and a progressive, multiracial group. The latter organized for better services in the Village such as heaters, garbage collection, and a larger recreation center, for keeping the Village open during the many bouts with scheduled closures and forced evictions, for fairness when a resident of color was accused of a crime. One of the hottest issues concerned child care facilities. Most of those on the proactive left knew that members of the Communist Party were at the helm, even though they themselves were not members. As one resident wrote:

> I was an idealistic person brought up in a religious house where the golden rule was the rule. I loved all the good things about this country—didn't like the bad things—went to work in an aircraft factory during the 2nd World War, gave six pints of blood to the Red Cross and overthrowing the government was the farthest thing from my mind but changing some things was definitely part of me.[12]

As this comment suggests, there was a general air of social change that residents breathed in Rodger Young Village, a part of which was socialist in nature. Suspected Communists received a public routing by the *Los Angeles Times,* which was vicious in its attacks on public housing and consistent in its bias for private real estate and downtown business interests (see Parson, 1983). The Burke case referred to in the opening quotation of this chapter was highly publicized. It was a particularly embarrassing incident for the housing authority, which was struggling against a socialist image. On October 23, 1946, the housing authority required all applicants for housing to take a loyalty oath, because of a "controversy that arose when it was discovered that Sidney Burke, non-veteran Communist newspaper editor, had been 'inadvertently' admitted to Rodger Young Village in Griffith Park, to which only veterans are eligible" (*Los Angeles Examiner,* 1946d).

Much social life seems to have taken place around children, of which there were legions, and around fundraisers, demonstrations, and community meetings. The *Rodger Young News* was produced for a brief period as a forum for the residents. Similar to a small town paper, it reported on community meetings, gave scores by Village teams (including for marble-shooting contests), advertised the price of turkey a la king ($.19) at the Village Market, announced when the egg man would deliver to your block, and included gossip columns. It also reported on the housing authority's intention to provide a library or install heaters, or the residents' effective demands to improve the recreation center for day care purposes. A series of Village-wide resident committees existed, including the most important Welfare Committee which had responsibility for "relief for hardship cases, meeting with the management, child-care, nursery activities, acquisition of better bus service, acquisition of telephones, etc." (*Rodger Young News*, January 3, 1947, p. 1). Resident management, like integration, was pioneered in Los Angeles public and veterans' housing.

The veterans' families who moved into Rodger Young did not voice any dismay at living in Quonset huts. Instead, they converted the industrial context with gardens, lace curtains, and tricycles. This does not mean that the huts were popular; most people had the "feeling that after the war Spam and Quonsets will enjoy the same degree of prestige" (Kempner, 1945, p. 118). As one journalist stated,

> The Quonset huts out on the rim of the city in Griffith Park are not mansions. They are humble dwellings, rows upon rows of them, each one just like the next. But the families who live in them have made them their homes, built trellises for plants, grown a few flowers, shrubs, vines. The homes are small, especially if there are six children to be housed with their parents in the two-bedroom homes, but to most of the families they are a haven and a shelter. (Simons, 1952, pp. 1, 3)

104   Years of tending turned Rodger Young Village into home for many families. Photographer: Leonard Nadel.

Retaining the Provisional

34

Rodger Young Village
Los Angeles 27 Calif.
March 8, 1952

Councilman Roybal
Dear Sir:

This is not only speaking for myself but for several families residing here in the Village that are in the same position I am.

I am the mother of six children and we are unable to buy our own place at the present. I thought I'd ease the situation a little by sending my oldest boy to Alaska with my sister-in-law, and another boy with my mother-in-law, but there are still four children in the family so nobody will rent us a place we can afford and in the place where they take children the rent is outrageous. So as far as we are concerned the emergency still exists very strongly, for us and most of the people here.

Sincerely,

Mrs. E. M. Trujillo[13]

Already by the late forties, when the first of several extensions had to be extracted for the Village from the Recreation and Parks Commission and from the city council, a new attitude prevailed about federally subsidized housing, an attitude that was bound up with the McCarthy-era criminalization of socialism and Communism.

Housing authority publications and public relations materials had undergone a transformation since the early forties. Instead of urging a moral duty to provide decent housing for every American, it now admonished the public to build assisted housing as a rational economic choice. The housing authority annual report of 1945 had opened with "A decent home, an American right"; by 1948 the report stated: "There's nothing sentimental about your pocketbook. Bad housing is bad business." While Rodger Young residents were fighting to save their Quonset huts in the late forties, the housing authority was touring thousands of Angelenos through the slums to show them how bad things had become in this otherwise invisible part of the city. They campaigned to guide public opinion toward the belief that low-cost housing was a public good. The housing authority was looking for support for 10,000 new units of family housing that would be appropriated once the new Taft-Ellender-Wagner Bill went through Congress. But public support for federally subsidized housing of any sort was dwindling, and the residents of Rodger Young Village felt the effect directly.

The closure of the Village was first threatened in 1948 when its original three-year lease was about to expire. After much public debate, the city housing authority finally prevailed with the argument that a housing emergency continued to exist—the emergency status being critical to the use of public lands. The Recreation and Parks Commission granted the Village a second three years of life which would extend from 1949 through 1952 (see *Housing News,* 1948b, p. 1; Eberts, 1996). At that point, about 6,200 veterans and their dependents lived in the Village, and there were over 3,500 veterans and servicemen on the waiting list even though no applications had been taken for months (*Housing News,* 1948b, p. 3; Baker, 1952).

On February 1, 1952, Rodger Young Village's permit expired, and the lease of parklands was not renewed by the Recreation and Parks Commission because they were "convinced that an emergency no longer exists" (*Los Angeles Examiner,* 1952a). Reaction to the order from the residents was described as "instantaneous and explosive." Said Mrs. Nancy Aaron, mother of four, "We don't know what to do. We'll have people living in cars and parks. I'm going to stay right here until they throw me out!" (Baker, 1952, p. 3). Downplayed in the *Examiner* and the *Times,* the scale of the protest was described in the African-American paper the *California Eagle* as involving nearly every household in the Village (Simons, 1952), and by the Communist paper *People's World* (1952b) as a "fiery" open-air rally that made anti-housing council members nervous.

Among the resident families, 60 percent were veterans of World War II, and the other 40 percent were the wives and children of men then fighting in the

105   Protesting the threat of demolition, Rodger Young residents stage a mass rally in 1952.

Korean War (Turpin, 1954). According to a survey reported in the sympathetic *Daily News,* 80 percent of the families in Rodger Young were in the lowest income group and 50 percent of the families belonged to racial minority groups. This prompted the editorial question, "Where are these poverty-ridden people to find decent housing at rentals they can afford to pay, and landlords who are not hostile to their children or their racial origins?" (*Daily News,* 1953). They would have qualified for the low-cost housing operated by the city's housing authority, but the existing 13,000 units were full.

   Residents organized a Community Emergency Committee chaired by resident Robert Brown. In their eviction protests, they were joined by Mayor Bowron, several city council members, and leaders from religious, labor, and veterans' organizations. In Bowron's speech to Village residents, against his own park department, he said, "I'm convinced that in Los Angeles there does not exist sufficient housing at rents within your income brackets. This city and every city in America owes an obligation to our veterans, and that obligation is decent housing at a fair price" (*Los Angeles Examiner,* 1952b). Bowron got his information from a thorough study by Rodger Young's Community Emergency Council, in which they found only a 2 percent vacancy rate in the city of Los Angeles (as of December 1951), and only 5 percent of those units rented for rates as low as the Village's. Brown and his group prepared a resolution to extend the temporary lease for two more years.[14]

For a month and a half, residents, veterans' groups, and their supporters protested Rodger Young's closure. At a city council meeting on February 18, 1952, representatives of residents and veterans' groups lobbied to keep the Quonsets operating. Hobart Keating, national commander of the Combat Veterans of America, stated, "There are more than 600 colored people in Rodger Young. I checked 250 vacancies in a paper and only two of them would rent to Negroes." Bob Brown added that 98 percent of the villagers have children. "It's appalling, but actually we're going to have to get rid of some of our kids in order to get rentals" (*People's World*, 1952a). This was exactly what Mrs. Trujillo had written to prohousing councilman Ed Roybal (quoted above), but even sending away two of her children had not helped her find housing for the other four. Under pressure, on March 19, 1952, the city council reversed the decision and voted to extend the Village's life until 1954. Finally, on October 27, the Recreation and Parks Commission authorized the extension of the lease, with the stipulation that no new tenants would be accepted after June 30, 1953, and that all residents would be gone on or before July 1, 1954 (*Los Angeles Examiner*, 1952d; Eberts, 1996).

Houses in most parts of the city were barred to blacks, Hispanics, and Asians, and homes in nonsegregated areas were often barred to children (*People's World*, 1953c). To protect these households, residents advocated the indefinite extension of both Rodger Young Village and its sister project, almost 1,500 units in army barracks called Basilone Homes in Pacoima. In July of 1953, residents again organized, this time as Save Rodger Young, to demand indefinite retention of the emergency project (*People's World*, 1953a). Mrs. Cora Anderson, a black resident of Rodger Young, told councilmen at a meeting in August 1953 about the tremendous need for private housing: "This is especially true in Glendale and Burbank where minority people like Negroes or Mexicans are not allowed to live." A Mrs. Jackson chimed in, needling anti–public housing Councilman Holland directly: "Would you speak to your buddies in that area, and see if we can get housing near Lockheed where most of us work?" (*People's World*, 1953b). But their efforts were of no avail. In *Southwest Builder and Contractor* (1954, p. 55), a notice can be found requesting bids for the "Sale and Removal of Quonset Huts"; precisely 106 huts and 19 administrative and commercial buildings were to be removed in this phase. There are no records of bids received or contracts awarded, but it is apparent that the housing authority expected that the low-bidding contractor would dismantle the Quonset huts and sell them for other uses. Although the Rodger Young Quonsets were taken down sooner than residents wished, they were left standing longer than the city intended.

The Recreation and Parks Commission took the position that only during emergency conditions was its mandate modified from providing park land for Los Angeles's citizens. Since it had neither the responsibility nor the jurisdiction to provide affordable housing, taxpayers would be justified in suing for failure to use park land for park purposes (Eberts, 1996). This was the position Van Griffith had been arguing all along. The Commission's general manager added that when the Quonset huts were removed, the land would provide golf and picnic facilities. In fact, by the time the Quonset huts were dismantled and carted off, the Riverside Freeway (Highway 5) had been platted right through Rodger Young Village, an undertaking with the kind of popular support that was given veterans' housing in the mid-forties. So, instead of becoming the parkland that both generations of Griffiths had fought to preserve, this particular piece of land went from airfield to temporary housing to freeway interchange and parking lots. So much for the public domain. Today, Quonset huts, some probably from the Village, can be found across the Los Angeles basin in industrial sections of towns, in school and city vehicle yards, and on college campuses.

Finding a Public, Calling Off an Emergency

35

The families of our community are particularly interested in the housing situation in Los Angeles. Rodger Young Village is indeed a haven for we who were living in stores, tents, autos, each resident could tell his own experiences with the housing shortage. But the Village is only a temporary project, to last a few short years, more than one of which is already gone.

We must prepare now for the time when our huts are abandoned. As it is, most of us are anxious to move into permanent quarters as soon as possible. Living in a Quonset is not the ideal post war home for veterans (*Rodger Young News*, 1947b).

Much of the debate surrounding the end of Rodger Young Village concerned whether there was still a housing emergency that would justify the use of park land for housing purposes. The emergencies that instigated radical housing solutions like Aliso Village and Rodger Young Village were officially terminated in the early fifties, a period explored in more depth in the next section. The sequential and linked housing emergencies of slums, defense workers, and veterans sparked some large-scale transformations of Los Angeles, as they did in many other American cities as well. Rodger Young outlived its own intended short lifespan: instead of three years, it was not dismantled until eight had passed. Despite the dimension of provisionality pervasive in Rodger Young, residents organized to protest its closure. As Eberts points out in his book on Grif-

106 Disabled American Veterans parade at Rodger Young Village. Photographer: Louis Clyde Stoumen.

fith Park (1996), residents may have stayed in the Village for only a short time but they firmly believed in fighting for its longevity.

Both Aliso Village and Rodger Young Village presented to their low-income residents a new image of the neighborhood, and a new image of home. Planned all at once, built as a whole, with various services, the Villages contained homes that defied the American stereotype and the American dream. They also embodied progressive ideas of the time about community planning. But Rodger Young was never seen as anything beyond a stopgap development, even by the most ardent housing supporters. In fact, the Quonset huts were themselves categorized as a kind of slum, in contrast to the desired solution of permanent public housing: "But if sub-standard housing is all that can be found for the evicted veterans' families, their condition will be no better than it was when they had to seek shelter in Quonset huts, and all that will have been accomplished is the substitution of private for public sub-standard housing" (*Daily News,* 1953). Perhaps the most telling is the comment of a resident to an unsympathetic council member during a public meeting: "There is not a person in Rodger Young who is there by choice. We can't find housing. If we can find housing, we can't afford it. If we could afford it, we wouldn't live in these cracker boxes" (*People's World,* 1953b).

Resident satisfaction with their Quonset huts must have declined over the eight years of their existence. Wear and tear would have something to contribute to the increasing problems, as would deferred maintenance, and the novelty of living in an ingenious wartime solution wore off. So why would residents critical of their housing fight so hard to save it? The Village was temporary not only in the sense that its demolition was planned from the start, but also in each resident's projected autobiography. Each family saw the Village as a stepping stone to its own permanent housing solution. But the latter was difficult to achieve. Since there was essentially no other affordable housing available, residents fought for the Quonset huts as the housing of last resort. The temporary nature of the structures had a mixed effect on the life inside. A three- to four-year stay was not significantly less than the typical stay in a "permanent" abode. And because the Village sprang from nowhere, all its original residents arrived together. Having veteran status in common meant a lot: they shared the war, their return, their young families, their desire to set up house. In this way Quonset life built a strong community, ready to fight again to save their homes, even though residents shared a vision of a better life beyond Rodger Young Village.

As for property and its associated rights, a central authority took over the portion of Griffith Park to make way for the veterans. As with Aliso Village, the property rights of the former occupants, whether the Griffith family or the residents of The Flats, were secondary to the crises confronting the city as a whole. Within Rodger Young Village, residents adopted a stance that was more communitarian than Lockean, in that they attempted to keep the Quonset huts in the public domain as interim, low-cost housing. It might be temporary housing for its individual residents, but they hoped it would be permanently available as temporary housing. Conversely, this tenor of socialism helped spark the national organization of the real estate industry, vitalize the forces of private builders in Los Angeles, and garner public opposition.

Mayor Bowron addressed the city council on August 8, 1949, to urge unanimous approval of 10,000 units of low-rent housing, arguing for the approval of these new units as a means to enable removing Rodger Young Village.[15] An entire section of his talk was devoted to "facts showing an emergency," which included the housing shortage, signs of an economic recession, increases in unemployment, blight, and competition for federal funds with other cities.

By the time Rodger Young was fully occupied, it featured a kind of resident activism that was not part of the Aliso Village story but is certainly part of one that soon followed: Chavez Ravine. Just as loyalty oaths became part of public housing applications, so tenant organizing grew more confident and sophisticated. Indeed, the two phenomena are related. The general air of social

107 Rodger Young Village at the edge of Griffith Park, with Glendale in the distance.

108 Rodger Young's site before construction, and after demolition. Photographer: Louis Clyde Stoumen.

IV Temporary Abode, Industrial Aesthetic: Rodger Young Village

change in the years after the war meant a regrouping on the part of the status quo. With the confident assertion of rights by veterans, tenants, and cross-racial collaborators, conservatives were sorely threatened. Outspoken opposition to the use of eminent domain, or to the closure of Rodger Young, were symptoms of a destabilized citizenry. If whites fraternized with blacks, how could racial dominance remain effective? If there was no agreement about the best interest of the public, how would those in power impress their programs upon the masses? Indeed, the very ideology of the nation needed shoring up. The Mc-Carthy era, with its loyalty oaths and un-American activities enforcers, met the threat of citizen protest head on.

Arthur Toy's family was the last to move out of Rodger Young Village, in February of 1954. They left the collective, integrated life of the Village for a suburban home at 10906 Orion Avenue in San Fernando (Turpin, 1954). He, like the other veterans, settled into the traditional American dream after a brief experiment with a radical alternative, now evaporated into thin air.

V

36 Rodger Young Village was closed in 1954, the same year that a new Housing Act passed in Congress. That Act provided enough federal mortgage insurance to entice lenders and entrepreneurs into urban redevelopment. It was the same year that the Supreme Court decided that property in any condition, good or bad, could be taken via eminent domain (Berman v. Parker; in Garvin, 1996). And it was the year after Los Angeles killed its public housing program.

In 1953, Mayor Bowron was voted out of office primarily because of his support for public housing, which, as subsequent chapters will reveal, had become the occasion of a McCarthy-era battle pitting socialism against private enterprise. Los Angeles had clamored for a piece of the new federal appropriations set forth by the 1954 Housing Act and, as with the previous case studies, initiated convulsive undertakings at various urban sites. The opposition to public housing was newly organized, and its participants not only utilized the authorized forums like public hearings but also took to the streets, the airwaves, and mimeograph machines. This period brings into new light ways that property, scale, and upheaval interact to shape urban form. At no time in recent history has politics played such a manifest role in the city's formal and particularly its residential destiny.

In terms of the American landscape, the decade following the war is usually characterized by agricultural land converted to seas of slab-on-grade, stick-built suburban tract homes. But this period also redefined the urban center. As

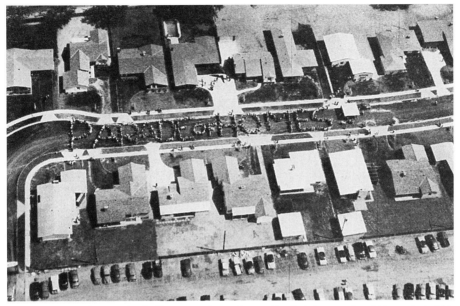

109 The "Parade of Homes" (spelled by construction workers and families) showcased model homes by individual builders on a simulated suburban street. From W. P. Atkinson et al., *Housing U.S.A. as Industry Leaders See It* (1954).

suburban development pushed past the periphery with federal support, regions of the already-built city were determined not worth saving and parts of a modern city were proposed. Real estate interests had grown more sophisticated in their organization and political lobbying, and more complex in terms of their interests. Commercial builders and community builders would find themselves essentially competing for federal dollars, but they did not fight over urban geography: the former claimed downtown while the latter worked the urban fringe. And they came together to fight any attempts by the public sector to develop vacant land. At least when slum clearance was part of the equation, the federal government was not adding to the overall supply of available housing units. In this next phase of upheaval, however, downtown real estate interests commandeered slum clearance as part of private development. By doing so, they created vacant land where none had previously existed and assembled large tracts of land that would have been too costly and too time-consuming to piece together without eminent domain.

Planners and housing progressives continued to advocate public-sector construction of housing in big, modernist projects. But the ground beneath their proposals was shifting rapidly. New directions for the physical form of the city corresponded to the political transformation of the nation, from the emergency mentality pervasive during the Depression and the war to an entrepreneurial orientation thereafter; from New Deal socialism to fervent privatization. With economic recovery, housing programs were losing those components tied to social need, even while effective lobbies were increasing the supports to the private building industry (see Abrams, 1946). Some of the last great battles in this urban political metamorphosis were fought in cities across America over the survival of public housing.

While many kinds of developments were seen as implicitly "Communist," from fluoridation of the water to interracial friendships, public housing stood as a direct assault to the American dream. Rather than federal subsidy of apartment renters, the opposition sought to reroute those subsidies to the home-building industry, in essence to create more homebuyers. Two places in Los Angeles, Westchester and Chavez Ravine, capture the poles of that debate. Westchester consisted of five square miles of relatively flat agricultural land that eventually became home to 50,000 people living in a sea of detached houses (see Applegate, 1989). The three hundred hilly acres at Chavez Ravine, by contrast, sheltered a poor Latino neighborhood that was violently destroyed to make way for public housing proposals, designed by Richard Neutra and Robert Alexander but never built.

110   The immense private housing development of Park La Brea, built in 1942, with towers visible at center and low-rise buildings to their left, in a 1954 photo. Photographer: "Dick" Whittington.

This section explores basic urban questions being debated after the war: How was the tremendous need for shelter to be met, and who were the people most in need of help? As the resources of the federal government were evaluated by policymakers and officials at the local, state, and national levels, the answers to these two questions would be unambiguous by the early 1950s: the construction industry, and white, middle-class homebuyers.

The issue of scale arose in myriad contexts during this defining phase of American urbanism and residential growth. Not only were massive federal funds contested and immense tracts of land transformed, but scale played into the ways that planners, architects, housers, real estate interests, and downtown business interests imagined that the city should be "fixed," which were layered over different notions of its critical problems. Among urban progressives, comprehensive urban interventions were thought to best lead to progress in the city: modern communities built on razed slums. Odd, lone voices offered incremental solutions involving building rehabilitation, historic preservation, or urban infill. These voices were overpowered by vociferous cries for progress by modernists—urban democrats advocating large-scale, rational growth (see Parson, 1993). But not only the urban democrats advocated large interventions; builders made the same case based on economies of scale. Progress or profits: both goals were best met by big solutions rather than small. Likewise, neither private nor public developers voiced concerns of conservation, so while the former paved over prime agricultural land and ecologically fragile terrain (see Davis, 1998), the latter had been pressured to build atop inner-city slums. Thus, the scale of projects in both public and private ventures was large, but the property to which each could claim development rights differed dramatically. The public sector, relegated to the inhabited urban communities of color, provoked upheavals with more immediate physical and social repercussions than did private market housing.

Together, public and private housing efforts reshaped the American city after the war, not in a coherent, planned manner but in surges and eruptions. Before analyzing the contrasting cases of Chavez Ravine and Westchester, I want to sketch the backdrop against which they should be viewed.

The Postwar National Housing Scene

37 Before the end of World War II, the Truman administration projected postwar housing needs and determined that the public housing program should be expanded. That expansion was written into the Taft-Ellender-Wagner Bill, introduced to wide legislative support in 1945. The following year it was stalled in committee, not reaching the Senate floor until 1948. It is remarkable that both parties had a pro–public housing platform in the 1948 elections, given the political shift that would occur so quickly thereafter. When the bill finally passed in 1949, there were hints of a troubled future. The most popular provisions of the 1949 Housing Act, which approved funding for 810,000 units of public housing nationwide, were slum clearance and supports to the private housing industry (Freedman, 1969). Title I, the urban renewal program, was to become the most influential part of the Act. Change was clearly coming, but none foresaw how bitter the struggles would be.

In the forties, housing was steeped in an industrial optimism. Americans widely assumed that just as the auto industry had converted to defense production to meet the demands of the war, so the energized young defense industry would convert to solve the postwar housing crisis. Industrialization would be the means to homeownership for everyone, as mass production brought the price of homes within range of all working persons. The house of the future would be produced like aircraft: on an assembly line, using advanced technology, with economy, efficiency, and high performance. These were modern dreams, in

111   The postwar demonstration house by Fritz Burns's Research Division, showing patio life of the future. Photographer: "Dick" Whittington.

terms of both production and aesthetics. Across the nation, there was a preoccupation with postwar housing that experimented with prefabrication, component assembly systems and materials. These experiments had begun during the war, when emergency housing like Quonset huts had been invented using quick, cheap building practices to create an *Existenzminimum*. Only with advanced strategies could the nation launch itself into the peacetime future as it had launched itself successfully into war. That future, if it were to overcome the tremendous housing shortage and eradicate substandard housing, would necessarily look different from prewar housing. At least, so architects, planners, and industrialists thought.

The "postwar house" was the topic of much rumination throughout the war. Magazines like *Architectural Forum* and *Arts and Architecture* published essays on it, builders laid out plans and model homes, prospective buyers flocked to department stores to survey its displayed components. At least in popular America, the house of the future looked a lot like the house of the past, except for some slick industrial designs for the kitchen and bathroom (see fig. 119). But in the professional journals and in housing research divisions, the postwar house would be modern in production, materials, and aesthetics.

The federal government, through the Federal Housing Administration and the Home Loan Bank System, propped up the market for postwar speculative homebuilders. At first, the federal effort seemed balanced by aid to Roosevelt's "one third of a nation" that was ill-housed; ultimately, it served the interests of lending institutions and the building industry (Abrams, 1946). According to Frieden and Sagalyn (1989), this shift in priorities occurred after World War II, when veterans returned to find good terms for homebuyers. Their family circumstances steered them toward the suburbs at just the same time that federal policy aimed to revive the construction industry. Housing construction jumped from about 300,000 units per year in the 1930s to 1 million in 1945, to 2 million in 1950. The rerouting of federal appropriations toward private builders and homeownership was accomplished by the increasingly organized real estate industry, whose national lobbies were spawned in Los Angeles with Fritz B. Burns at the helm.

On the other side of the housing battle, public housing advocates hoped to capitalize on the widespread, middle-class impact of the postwar housing shortage. The National Public Housing Conference, a lobbying group led by a clutch of effective women and men (including Dorothy Montgomery, Catherine Bauer, Lee Johnson, and Charles Abrams), along with the National Committee on Housing and the CIO Housing Committee, helped shape legislation and legislative opinion.

The uncertain public support for subsidizing low-income housing seemed to be stabilized by programs guaranteeing the removal of slum dwellings. Just why slum clearance had such broad support in the general public is not a simple question, but it was understood, especially in the late forties, as the housers' strongest card. It was played with a zeal that would be regretted in later years. Slum tours, data about disease rates and crime, and photographs depicting squalor were all part of the arsenal to defend public housing. Not until much later did it become obvious to the housing movement's progressives that slum clearance was a form of racial discrimination that had the opposite effect of its intentions: it actually made affordable housing more scarce.

The personal correspondence of Charles Abrams, a professor, lawyer, New York City housing authority administrator, and one of the nation's most articulate housing activists, makes visible the evolution of the progressives' policy. As early as 1945, for example, Abrams wrote: "We must recognize that housing is no longer public housing alone, and that public housing itself is no longer an isolable reform which can be separated from the larger problem of housing, planning, and urban redevelopment." He encouraged public housing advocates to broaden their sights, "taking up the fight for decent housing in every quarter," and avoiding the appearance that public housing was merely trying to get its "nose further under the government tent." He extended this view to demonstrate how coordinated legislation on public housing, urban redevelopment, rural housing, homeownership, and GI housing would not only better serve the public, but also "will be the most effective way of getting through public housing, for after the war when there will be a boom in building, public housing will stand no chance unless it is part of a comprehensive housing program."[1] Abrams, ever prescient, could also turn a cold eye to the past. Six years later, in 1951, he argued that slum clearance had been detrimental to the aims of affordable housing, as well as inhumane to the very people it had tried to serve.[2]

While housing activists worked diligently to create affordable housing in modern communities, the private housing sector was purchasing agricultural land at the city's edges to subdivide into the standard lots: deep, narrow pieces of property, each with its own street frontage and city services. Throughout the first three decades of the twentieth century, land had been purchased and subdivided long before any building was expected to commence. In a stinging article called "The Sad Story of American Housing" (1933), architect Henry Wright (who, it will be remembered, was instrumental in Hoover's housing conference on the matter of large-scale operations) enumerated the problems of such subdividing:

> This practice of speculative holding carries a triple menace. In the first place, it prevents the assembling, at a low price, of land needed by actual developers. In the second place, it has led our cities to the installation of expensive public services, far in advance of possible use; and what is more important, in the third place, the city plans are deprived of any real or definite objective in terms of a specific region to be used in a special way.

What Wright described in cases from Michigan, New York, and Illinois was exaggerated in Los Angeles. Viewed on maps, vast tracts of vacant land looked ready for builders and homebuyers to move in (see fig. 38). This was the case in Chavez Ravine, which corroborated Wright's predictions about land assembly when the housing authority battled large numbers of property owners in condemnation proceedings.

Just how the American housing scene would shape up depended, in great measure, on how federal policy was tailored, which hinged in part on effective lobbying. Within the immense sector with vested interests in housing economics, the real estate lobby was well organized at both local and national levels. As noted above, no group worked more effectively for urban planning and regulation of community building activities than realtors (Weiss, 1987). Prior to 1917,

112 The private development of Wyvernwood in 1939. Photographer: "Dick" Whittington.

when the nation's first real estate brokerage and sales licensing act was signed into law, there had been almost no means to regulate or standardize real estate practices. The older, more established realtors wanted to protect against "curbstoners," control various subdivision procedures, and coordinate activities like infrastructure at an urban scale. They saw subdivision regulations, zoning, land use planning, and the establishment of planning commissions as reforms that would operate in their own interest.

Prior to the war, there was still a separation between builders and subdividers. Realtors were regularly engaged in subdividing land for subsequent sales, but were rarely involved in construction. This was the domain of contractors, most of whom built very small numbers of houses primarily under contract with owners rather than on a speculative basis. With the advent of "operative builders" or "community builders" (Weiss, 1987) came the vertical integration of previously segregated tasks. This contributed to the growing strength and effectiveness of what was emerging as "the construction industry."

California was a national leader as realtors and homebuilders pursued the local and national projects of professionalization. In 1908, the National Association of Real Estate Boards was founded by nineteen local real estate boards and just one state association: California's. Indeed, Los Angeles established the first citywide Realty Board in 1903, the nation's first zoning law in 1908, and

113   Park La Brea in 1946. Private-sector housing built in 1942. Photographer: "Dick" Whittington.

the nation's first regional planning commission, the Los Angeles County Regional Planning Commission, in 1922 (Weiss, 1987). By 1929, 27 states had licensing procedures for real estate, and fly-by-night curbstoners were being regulated out of existence. A double purpose was served by these actions: first, planning and zoning would help preserve property values; second, licensure would help regulate the participation of realtors in the market.

It should come as no surprise that substantially before Levittown was constructed, planned communities were being built in Los Angeles. A few private-sector projects stand out as modern housing experiments, following Bauer's recommendations to varying degrees. Most interesting were the Radburn-like exploration at Baldwin Hills Village in 1941 (see fig. 78), the low rise–high rise combination at Park La Brea in 1942 (see figs. 110, 113), and the earlier garden apartments built at Wyvernwood in the 1930s (see fig. 112). Still, these were isolated experiments; nothing could match the construction of detached, single-family dwellings except the even greater demand for these homes. As the population of Los Angeles increased by nearly 50 percent between 1940 and 1950, homebuilders tried to keep up. The years between 1937 and 1941 had seen a building surge (Ovnick, 1994); then materials shortages and building restrictions led to a steep decline in housing starts during the war, bottoming out with a total ban on private residence building permits in 1944. Slowly, materials shortages waned, and by 1947 housing construction had picked up again: 32,000 dwellings were completed in the first five months of that year (compared to 35,000 during all of 1946).

Homebuilders recovering from the Depression relished the enormous pent-up demand generated by the war. Costs threatened to spiral out of control, as builders competed for the inadequate supplies of materials and labor while potential buyers competed for the woefully inadequate supply of houses. In 1945, the federal Office of Price Administration was setting maximum rents, while the War Productions Board assigned materials and labor priorities to war worker housing. The problems continued after the war was over; in 1946, the federal government set ceiling prices on new homes, existing homes, and building lots as a means to assure affordable housing for veterans. Houses were limited in square footage, and regulated materials like lumber, pipes, and gypsum board were released to builders who offered their houses exclusively to veterans for the first 30 days (Ovnick, 1994).

After the war, the tremendous housing shortage in LA led the United States Employment Service to warn people to postpone moving to southern California, where there was no acute labor shortage and "an extremely critical housing shortage" (Ovnick, 1994, p. 276). New construction was hampered by price controls and materials shortages. In January 1946, the federal government sought to stimulate housing production, particularly for low-cost veteran housing, giving priority on regulated materials (like lumber, pipes, gypsum board, and bathtubs) to builders who built houses selling for less than $10,000 or renting at no more than $80 per month. By April of the same year, this price ceiling was lowered to $7,000 for the LA area (Ovnick, 1994).

In a 1950 address before the National Association of Home Builders in Houston, Housing and Home Finance Administrator Raymond M. Foley admonished his audience:

> As I have told you many times, you operative builders are not the whole building industry. You are mistaken when you let that be assumed. You do not control your costs, or your supplies, or the services you need. You compete for them among yourselves and with other construction interests. Soon you will compete for them with the defense demands of America. So long as there is unlimited competition for limited supplies, costs will rise, prices will rise, but the market for houses will tend to shrink, even with unlimited credit to support it.[3]

Private real estate interests, including homebuilders, landlords, and lenders, fought hard to retain and even strengthen federal supports to the homebuilding

114 Construction as industry at a Marlow-Burns housing development in 1943. Photographer: "Dick" Whittington.

industry. Simultaneously, they worked to reduce regulation and to direct the government participation in housing production that had begun in the Depression. After long years of zealous government regulations, real estate interests drew upon their national organizations to cohesively shape American public policy on the housing industry. Builders and landlords, frustrated by federal interference (and with little public recognition of the benefits their own industry reaped from it),[4] strengthened their national lobbying. It should be made clear that the real estate interests did not oppose federal participation in their industry: they sought federal assistance insofar as it could create more or better buyers (e.g., through mortgage guarantees, extending credit, and lending programs) while simultaneously keeping government as far as possible from construction itself. Federal stimulation of demand was advantageous; federal participation in supply was not.

From another quarter of the construction industry, organized labor had strongly supported public housing. Labor's interests were not only in the construction jobs but also in the affordable housing needed by its members. Once the war was over, labor found these interests better met by the private sector.

By the 1948 election, slum clearance, then associated with subsidized housing construction, had wide popular support. With the resurgence of private homebuilding, builders grew wary of the bonds between slum clearance and the public provision of housing. It would be in their best interest to keep the government out of construction, and therefore out of demolition as well. Residential (in contrast to commercial) real estate interests thus developed an alternative strategy to slum clearance: gentrification and code enforcement in run-down neighborhoods. Across the country, groups like the Build America Better Council of the National Association of Real Estate Boards, and ACTION (American Council to Improve Our Neighborhoods), were formed to promote private real estate solutions to the deteriorating housing stock. The Build America Better Council lobbied for the enforcement of ordinances on housing standards, a drive supported by real estate boards in 154 cities and 38 states as of June 1953.[5] Building inspectors were to report substandard conditions, which property owners would then be required to redress. Without armies of inspectors and enforcers, however, this strategy had little impact. In fact, incremental solutions like rehabilitation by individual property owners were difficult to effect, in the face of large-scale urban upheavals. Not until the historic preservation movement took root in the sixties was an encompassing and utopian ideology formulated for saving deteriorating neighborhoods.

It is ironic by present standards that real estate interests were the first to promote rehabilitation of older housing, while progressives were still advocating slum clearance. When older stock was improved, gentrification followed, since real estate interests did not support rent control. Effectively, more low-income families were displaced to other deteriorated housing stock—giving effect to the metaphor of slum as spreading cancer.

Two Men in the Los Angeles Picture

38 While housers like Charles Abrams, Catherine Bauer, Lee Johnson, Mary Simkhovich, Edith Elmer Wood, and Dorothy Montgomery were strategizing to keep public housing on the national agenda (where women were at the heart of the movement), Congressman Augustus Hawkins worked diligently on the legislation. The first black assemblyman in Sacramento, and then the first black Congressman from California, he put through most of the major public housing ordinances. None of it would have been possible without scores of local activists working in every major city in the United States. In Los Angeles, Frank Wilkinson was in a class of his own. Having graduated from UCLA in 1936, Wilkinson set off on a pilgrimage that would change his life. Traveling through the Middle East, Europe, and North Africa, he observed enough poverty and religious rivalry that he abandoned his plans to become a Methodist minister, committing his life instead to improving the social welfare of others. Upon returning to LA, he was startled to discover his own hometown's slums, which he set about revealing to the rest of the city. He joined forces with Monsignor Thomas J. O'Dwyer, head of the Catholic church's programs for hospitals and charities and president of the influential citizens' advisory group called the Citizens' Housing Council. The council was one of the forces instrumental in developing the first ten public housing sites in LA under the 1937 Housing Act. Its members included most of the important players in LA's housing scene, including architects like Lloyd Wright and Eugene Weston. Frank Wilkinson became its secretary.

115 Frank Wilkinson speaks for the Citizens' Housing Council in 1952, with Monsignor O'Dwyer at right. Photographer: Leonard Nadel.

When the early public housing developments were ready for occupancy, Wilkinson and his fellow housers learned that the housing authority intended to racially segregate the new developments. Since the council's mission had as much to do with integration as it did with housing, Wilkinson, O'Dwyer, labor leader Neal Haggerty, Jesse Terry, a leader in the black community, and other members of the council staged what Wilkinson characterized as a "Quaker-like witness" to protest segregation in the very first public housing projects in LA when they opened. Wilkinson's stormy and significant years with the City Housing Authority (now called the Housing Authority of the City of Los Angeles) began as a result of that protest: its then executive director, Howard L. Holtzendorff, panicked, according to Wilkinson, who was recruited right off the picket line to become manager of Hacienda Village's integration experiment. Later he became Holtzendorff's special assistant. In that broad role, Wilkinson was instrumental in selecting sites for future housing projects, acting as liaison with the architects designing housing, leading the public relations campaign seeking support for public housing, and mediating between resident management groups and tenant activists and the authority. In 1945 he toured the major urban housing authorities in the United States, and from 1945 through 1950 he toured Angelenos by the thousands through their own city's slums. When there were grievances among residents, some of whom were affiliated with the Communist Party, Wilkinson negotiated for the housing authority. A victim of the red-baiting of the McCarthy era (see section VII), Wilkinson was belatedly honored with a special citation from the mayor and city council of Los Angeles in 1995. He used the occasion to remind citizens of the city's loss. "It so happens that 43 years ago, in September of 1952, a nationwide political witchhunt cost the people of Los Angeles an unprecedented opportunity to rid the city of slums and to provide new homes for thousands of our most segregated barrios and ghettoes."[6]

In the opposing political camp was a remarkably effective player: Fritz B. Burns, born in 1899 to a Catholic family in Minneapolis. Burns left college to lead a team of traveling real estate salesmen, curbstoners par excellence, selling lots in twenty different states; he was just 21 years old when he and his crew arrived in LA in 1920. Within two years, he was selling lots worth over $2,000,000 annually for the Dickinson and Gillespie Corporation (Maher, 1952a, 1952b). With uncharacteristically bad timing, Burns bought the company's Los Angeles office in 1929. Still, he managed to stay afloat through the Depression, unlike so many builders at the time who went bankrupt. His talent at sales and at running a sales force became legendary, with his armies of salesmen doing calisthenics in unison as prospective buyers lined up for the spectacle of an opening day. From Glendale and Alhambra to Palisades del Rey in West Los Angeles, Burns sold lots at a record pace, building his own fortune and reputation as he built LA. He once said he could have retired in 1930, when he was 30, if it weren't for 1929.[7]

Burns eventually grew to be one of southern California's largest builders. Burns, like Henry J. Kaiser with whom he founded Kaiser Community Homes in May of 1945, was not a hardline real estate conservative. Big operators like Kaiser and Burns could not afford to be so blatantly ideological. He admitted that government intervention might be necessary to curb inflation in times of tremendous demand for housing; he built a "Home of Tomorrow," a suburban house with relatively open plan outfitted with futuristic gadgets; he was called a "leading advocate of low-cost housing" (Maher, 1952a, p. 49). In his national role among realtors, he became a "blight expert" and "slum clearance authority," according to news reports during 1953 and 1954, when he toured over 50 cities giving over 150 speeches about how to "outlaw slums."[8] His stance on slums and low-income housing was fashioned to keep government out of housing construction. Burns developed over 20,000 homes in southern California alone during his lifetime, making about 10 percent profit on each house, but he was much more than a builder. Over fifty years he played local and national political roles, for a time heading LA's Committee Against Socialist Housing (CASH)[9] and helping, through the National Association of Real Estate Boards, to put redevelopment policy in place through the 1954 Housing Act. The first head of the National Association of Home Builders, Burns also led a number of national real estate initiatives, including the Build America Better Council and Rebuild America. These were largely intended to put a more positive face on building industry opposition to public housing (Freedman, 1959).

Burns was among the leaders in Los Angeles of realtors advocating a greater municipal role in planning and federal role in financial stabilization (e.g., insured mortgages), while simultaneously battling the public taking of land for slum clearance through eminent domain and the federal construction of public housing. In his view, private enterprise could provide all the houses the nation needed, and as it did so, older houses would be left vacant for the lower income groups. Gathering vast citywide support, Burns helped Los Angeles to shut down housing subsidies except those to private interests.

116   Fritz Burns kneels to shake hands with the first families to move into Kaiser Community Homes, 1947. Photographer: "Dick" Whittington.

By what mechanisms, financial and institutional, would affordable housing for the masses be produced? As a postwar urbanism took shape, there were two opposing models. The first, manifest in public housing projects like Aliso Village, was supremely embodied in the plans for Chavez Ravine. The second was the private real estate industry's alternative of planned communities, exemplified by Westchester. These two models illuminate the directions taken and obstructed in the American city's residential landscape.

39 Like organized labor, architects had been supportive of public housing before its demise. The Citizens' Housing Council had extensive participation from architects, as did other progressive housing lobbies such as the National Public Housing Conference. While there was genuine political and social concern for the ill-housed, architects themselves experienced very high unemployment during the Depression. Thus, any housing program was simultaneously, even primarily, an employment program for all those involved in building, including architects. After the war, as the demand for new building rose, so did the demand for architectural services. Architects' support for federally subsidized housing waned as the profession attempted to wedge itself into the explosive homebuilding being undertaken by the private sector. Although architects had hardly bothered before with the small house as an architectural problem, it became a central interest during the war, particularly for modern architects.

There was a sense that postwar housing, with its new materials, new systems of production, and new building technologies, would require architects' expertise. *Architectural Forum* ran a series of articles on the postwar house (January–April 1944) claiming that the prewar house would not be good enough for the postwar buyer, who would have enough money and the desire for better quality. Architects, and modernists in particular, would be at the center of this new housing production, because they best understood industrial production, new materials and building systems, and "design in terms of merchandising; [not] . . . fancy trim and doodads over the front door" (January 1944).

The magazine foresaw that the most important social change would be the woman's move to work outside the home. Compared to prewar precedent, the new house would have to be efficient and practical; it would have three bedrooms, two baths, a pitched roof, more glass (picture windows, glass walls), more storage, prefabricated elements, more and better-designed appliances, controlled ventilation (to "produce a dustless interior"), and superior space organization. Moreover, the homebuilding business was rightly predicted to become the neighborhood-building business.

In contrast to *Architectural Forum*, which spoke for the middle of the architectural profession, *Arts and Architecture* was a voice for the avant-garde. A supremely Californian publication, the magazine considered arts, film, sculpture, and architecture in social and aesthetic terrain under the strong editorial hand of John Entenza. In its August 1943 issue, *Arts and Architecture* announced the winners of a national competition, "designs for postwar living," with Richard Neutra, Sumner Spaulding, Gregory Ain, John Leon Rex, and Charles Eames as jurors. The competition was to design a small, modern worker's family house, a "house for postwar living that can really be built when the war is over." First prize went to Saarinen and Lundquist, second to I. M. Pei and Duhart, third to Raphael Soriano. Nearly all the entries to this competition were planned neighborhood schemes, rather than single house plans. Most schemes used some kind of module system of construction, incorporating the materials plywood, steel, concrete, and glass. This new attention to the small house had its flaws. Eames commented, "There seemed to be too much 'architecture' in both the solutions and the jury, and values became mixed up with the ego of a specialized profession." Ain made the astute observation that the romance with prefabrication had turned it into an end in itself, not unlike tradition before it. "But we need no reiteration of the inevitability of prefabrication: we do need plans worth prefabricating" (*Arts and Architecture*, August 1943).

This competition was the precis, as it turned out, to the Case Study House program, for which the magazine would become famous. In January of 1945, *Arts and Architecture* announced the program and its first eight architects.[10] The goals of the program were to rethink the single-family house in relation to its context, but primarily on its own terms. "It is to be clearly understood that every consideration will be given to new materials and new techniques in house construction. . . . The house must be capable of duplication and in no sense be an individual 'performance'" (*Arts and Architecture*, January 1945). Esther McCoy, in her seminal review of the Case Study House program, describes the propitious beginnings:

New plastics made the translucent house a possibility; arc welding gave to steel joints a fineness that was to gain the material admission inside the house; synthetic resins, stronger than natural ones, could weatherproof lightweight building panels; new aircraft glues made a variety of laminates a reality. . . . Fresh approaches to plan, to form, to structure lay on paper ready to be tested. The day of the architect was in sight. (McCoy, 1977, p. 8)

These houses were intended to lead popular builders away from traditional so-lutions, demonstrating that new experiments in "a good living environment" could be readily built, affordable, repeatable. All such experiments after the war, in spite of great expectations, were restricted by limited availability of materials, poor quality of the same, and regulations set by the government (such as a max-imum of 1,100 square feet of enclosed living space when the first Case Study House was built).

McCoy argues that the Case Study House program was a success because so many of its features reappear in what she calls "contractor-designed houses" (1977, p. 19). She specifically attributes the pioneering of the servantless kitchen to the Case Study houses. This comment suggests why the Case Study program did not have greater impact, namely the mismatch of market and marketer. These intentionally affordable houses were designed for someone from the up-per middle class, someone once assisted by household staff but now servantless. Of course, the vast market for houses consisted of those who never had nor would have servants. Actually, many had never owned a house before. Perhaps the most telling of these images of the new, postwar life was Ralph Rapson's drawing of the typical family's morning goodbyes: as the husband flies off to the future in his personal helicopter, his premodern wife hangs laundry on the line. The gender bias encapsulates a wider double standard: the culture was ready to move recklessly into the future if it could also hold doggedly onto symbols of do-mestic tradition. Perhaps the workplace would be revolutionized, but the home and its social foundations were to remain static. In fact, Rapson's sketch captures a nostalgia for prewar domesticity, before women left home for the wage-labor marketplace. Perhaps this is what McCoy's contractor-designers understood and managed to capture in their own building solutions, which were more af-fordable than helicopters, and aimed at the woman who found the image of a Bendix washer more appealing than wet laundry.

While 368,554 people visited the first six houses completed in the Case Study program between 1946 and 1948 (McCoy, 1977), there was an experi-mental house in the mid-Wilshire district that attracted far more visitors, all of whom paid admission fees to boot (which were donated to charities). Built for

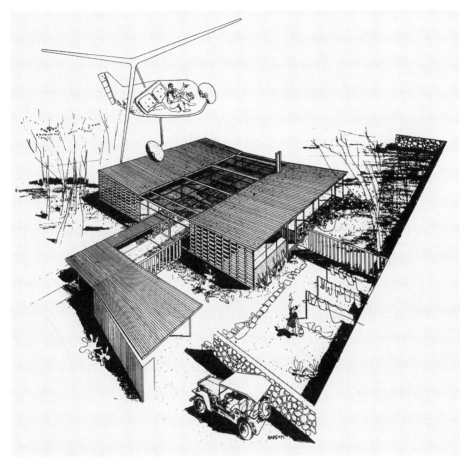

117 Ralph Rapson's Greenbelt House.

none other than Fritz B. Burns, the Postwar House was designed by William Wurdeman and Welton Becket, with the landscape designed by Garrett Eckbo. Both Becket and Eckbo had been involved in the public housing program. Like the first Case Studies, Burns's house opened in 1946 to star-studded galas and enormous crowds, and *House Beautiful* in May of 1946 gave it a 42-page spread. It was such a success that Burns repeated the experiment in 1951 with the Home of Tomorrow, again designed by Becket and Eckbo.[11] These houses were surprisingly tame, given their titular promise. Furnished by the distinctly middle-class Barker Brothers Company, the Home of Tomorrow was advertised as containing antiques as well as modern furniture. Its main "futuristic" components were programmatic, with relatively minor architectural implication. Living was to occur equally indoors and outdoors; sliding glass doors opened onto the patio's "barbeque kitchen," which had radiant heat through the entire slab (see fig. 111). Every room was considered a living room, which seems to

118 Crowds waiting to tour Burns's Postwar House when it opened in 1946. Photographer: "Dick" Whittington.

have meant that one could dine in almost every room in the house: there was no formal dining room, but eating areas in the living room, family room ("really an informal hideaway just off the kitchen borrowed from grandmother's keeping room"), kitchen, and patio. Like Rapson's Case Study House, the Postwar House had a helicopter landing pad. Function played large, so the kitchen and bathrooms received the most attention. It was not a kitchen for lace curtains, but an industrialized workroom outfitted with domesticated machinery, with undercounter refrigerators, a central cooking island, and automatic dishwasher (see Forty, 1986). Perhaps the only room of the house that had been designed in high style was the bathroom, straight "from the drawing board of Henry Dreyfuss, industrial designer." It too was conceived as an interior decorating problem, but it was conceived as a single unit rather than a furnishing arrangement. "In this room, of lucite, tile, china, and glass every convenience is at hand from built in stocking dryer to wall radio." [12] (A stocking dryer was the future for the wife, the helipad for the husband.) Moreover, this 2,400-square-foot house had only two bedrooms. The future was planned for small families needing a lot more square footage than most could afford, and with plenty of leisure time.

The house itself was not intended to shock anyone into the future, but to gradually ease them into shopping at Bullocks and Barker Brothers, buying products already on the market, and into donating money to Burns's favorite Catholic charities. The modern influence is apparent in Becket's architecture, which is relatively unadorned (though expressive in terms of materials like wood and stone) and highly functional. What Burns got right was the way middle Americans would enter into the future: in bits and pieces, from automatic dishwashers to built-in bedside phones and armrests.

In the Fritz Burns house, as in the experience of most Americans, modern living was likely to be defined in an additive way—in the purchase of new appliances, in the remodeling of an old house, in gradual additions to the small, boxy house that was virtually all that was available to most people immediately after the war. While the Case Study architects were concerned with creating a new technology of the house, most people simply wanted to add new technology to the house. (Hine, 1989, p. 173)

119   Sleek modern lines and the pop-up dishwasher characterized the Postwar House's efficient kitchen. Photographer: "Dick" Whittington.

120 Henry Dreyfuss's molded bath in the Postwar House, 1946. Photographer: "Dick" Whittington.

121 A postwar image of leisure and convenience. Photographer: "Dick" Whittington.

But perhaps the Case Study House program was not that distant from the contractor-builders it intended to influence. As mentioned earlier, Kaiser's Housing Division took a more radical stance than any Case Study House in its admittedly exploratory (and unbuilt) studies of new building technologies. This was very much a function of the changes within the building industry and of the availability of materials in the 1940s. Kaiser, unlike Entenza, controlled the means of production: he owned or leased factories that would produce every major building material he would need; he built his own factory to preassemble housing components. Recognizing the potential of plastics, his Housing Division developed an all-plastic house, styled in the modern idiom because it was the appropriate form for such new materials.[13] While slowed by the nationwide materials restrictions, Kaiser overcame them more effectively than any other homebuilder. Thus, he could imagine putting an all-aluminum house into production, whereas such a house would have been pure fantasy for a Case Study project. It was far more likely that such a house would emanate from the aircraft industry than from architectural inspiration. Combining both in 1946, Edward Larabee Barnes and Henry Dreyfuss conducted housing experiments with prefabricated aluminum-clad panels for Consolidated Vultee Aircraft in Los Angeles. The panels actually went into production on a factory line, but only two Vultee houses were ever produced (Reed, 1995).

The Case Study houses had to be conservative: in order to have their intended impact upon the building industry, they had to experiment in ways that were not too far removed from current practices. Spaulding and Rex's plywood modules and Thornton Abell's work with concrete block are modest experiments. "The problem of the architect is to walk a tight rope between experimentation and prudence," as Abell put it (McCoy, 1977, p. 45). Wurster put the architect's position in an even more conservative frame: "Where the individual custom-tailored house is desired, and at the same time the dollar must be stretched, there is as yet no system that competes with stud construction on a cost basis" (McCoy, 1977, p. 51).

As it turned out, Kaiser's researchers determined that Wurster's pronouncement was nearly true even when mass production and standardized plans were part of the calculation. The Case Study program was, in the end, a romantic view of the future, rather than one that grappled with tough technological changes. Its achievements were in the domain of planning: an openness to the outdoors, or a modern, free plan. Builders, after examining the economies that could be produced, returned to wooden stud construction out of purely pragmatic considerations and affixed the minimalist's romantic image to the exterior. The primary difference between the architects' and the builders' romanticism was that the former was directed toward the future, the latter toward the past.

122   Conceptual rendering of Henry J. Kaiser's All-Plastic House. Henry J. Kaiser Papers.

And counter to *Architectural Forum*'s prediction that the American public would demand a better house than the 1939 Cape Cod house, it turned out that few buyers had the luxury of exercising such demands, if indeed they wished to. First, many more households with lower incomes were entering the housing market than before the war. Second, industrial production and prefabrication never had the widespread impact on housing that was predicted, even in the case of Kaiser Community Homes, as we shall see. Prefabrication, and the modern forms that went with it, had only minor implications for housing production. Last, the buyer might have been willing to give up doodads, but postwar taste ran much more in line with Cape Cod than with aircraft manufacture, much to the modernists' dismay.

While both the Case Study houses and public housing exhibited modernist aesthetics, hardly a modern house was built in the land of private real estate development. Eichler Homes probably incorporated modernist principles better than any other mass-produced housing, in their relatively open plan, large areas of glazing, and strong connections between indoors and outdoors. Kaiser and Burns's houses were advertised as "homes that are 'right out in front' in Modern Architectural Design" (see Hise, 1995, p. 172) but actually had little modern to recommend them. The architects within Kaiser's and Burns's organizations were buried and rarely named. Burns's longtime associate, William Hannon, told me that architects were needed mainly to "make the windows line up" on the elevations and draw up the plans.[14] Indeed, architecture was not important in the contractor-designed house; features were. This remains the credo of developers who add on "amenities" to boxes of standard construction.

Forum's harangue to builders rings empty today:

> Before the war he [the architect] would have given his eye teeth to have
> worked for you, but after the war it will be a little different. The best of the
> modern architects will have been signed up—by the big merchant builders,
> by the manufacturers new to the field, by the prefabricators. Many have
> been commissioned already. And for these men, the 1939 house will not
> be the answer. (January–April 1944)

Joseph Hudnut put the postwar houses in slightly different terms: "We are right
to love the machine, but we must not permit it to extinguish the fire on our
hearth" (Hudnut, 1949, p. 109). But technology did not reshape either the practice of builders or that of architects. Architects lost the bid to design houses
for the masses, as contractors proceeded with stock plans augmented by trim.
Then architects lost their bid to plan housing in the rational city as well, since
unpopular public housing developments were turned back and downtown redevelopment interests promoted commercial buildings rather than residential.
Large-scale residential upheavals would erupt without benefit of architect all
around the city boundaries, while large downtown public housing was about to
meet its end.

Convulsive Suburbia: Westchester

VI

The Story of Westchester

There was a Marlow-Burns sales office out here, and I kept going to see them. I haunted the place, really. You see, during the war, no one could get into Westchester unless you were a defense worker. Finally, when Tract 13440 was getting ready to open, they gave me a call. It was on January 4, 1946, and there were little flags all over to show the different lots. By 10 am, they were all gone. We picked out the odd lot, a wide, reverse-key lot, and got it for $1750. The others were selling for around $1500. As soon as we bought the property, we went looking for plans. I knew some architects who had books of plans: we paid $10 a copy and another $10 to modify them to suit our needs and our lot. My father-in-law had been working with some builders named Pittman Brothers, so we went with them. Because of the materials shortages, we couldn't get water and power out here so we didn't start construction until '48. All the while, Marlow-Burns was putting in the streets, curbs, sewers and the like.

. . . In my wife's and my family, we were the first ones to own a home—my parents and her parents rented. We thought we were in heaven when we got our house. . . . They built a few multiples out here, but they weren't too popular. Everyone wanted their own home. We were all the same when Westchester started: we were all the same age, with young children, looking for houses when there were none to be had.

William Goss[1]

123   Fritz B. Burns and Henry J. Kaiser announcing their goal to construct 10,000 houses annually, 1946. Photographer: "Dick" Whittington.

As affordable housing advocates worked to meet their objectives in the urban core, the private housing industry had no such commitment to the city, nor any requirement to clear the slums. In fact, federal policy was pushing decentralization through FHA programs and thus accelerating blight (Abrams, 1946). Homebuilders concentrated on undeveloped, agricultural land at the urban edges. Had public housing successfully uncoupled itself from slum clearance and moved some of its operations to the periphery's less expensive land, the program might have had a different fate. Instead, subdividers and community builders were the ones to provide America's best shot at homeownership for the masses. This was far from a perfect solution, since it was not affordable for the poor, risky for those with moderate incomes, and not available to people of color because of racial restrictions. Moreover, suburban residential development rested heavily on various types of federal subsidy, even while touted as private enterprise's retort to government housing. Federal policy thus led American cities into spatial decentralization: development of the periphery went hand in hand with a disjointed approach to revitalizing the urban core. The geographic choices carried other implications for private and public construction undertakings: sites were abundant for private developers but scarce for public hous-

124 Westchester in 1949. Photographer: "Dick" Whittington.

ing; development costs were lower on the edges of town than in the center city, to which public projects were restricted; racial segregation was easy to maintain in newly built, peripheral zones. Moreover, whole neighborhoods could be started from scratch, with new streets, and sites designated for schools, churches, and stores to accompany the new homes. This community, however, was effected as the market demanded. Services that modern housing advocates incorporated in the initial plans were nonexistent when new homeowners moved into the subdivisions.

Far from the gritty scenes of the downtown slums, in West Los Angeles near the sea—and most importantly, near defense-related industry—Westchester began to develop in 1941 on a five-square-mile piece of property. At that time the three thousand acres contained just seventeen houses, along with barley, beans, hogs, and oil (Boynoff, 1948a). Howard Drollinger, a longtime commercial developer in the area, remembered that the Westchester property was owned by three entities: Superior Oil Company owned about half the area, L.A. Extension Company owned about a third, and the rest belonged to Security Bank which held it in trust. Those agencies, demonstrating an unusual degree of cooperation, selected Frank Ayres to create a master plan for all three land-

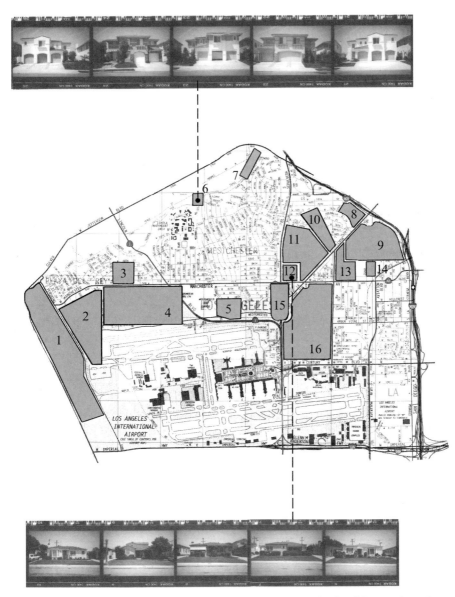

125   This map of Westchester shows some of the independent housing tracts developed there. At the top is a 1990s development called the Kentwood Collection (6); at the bottom is one of the first Marlow-Burns tracts from the early 1940s, much the same today (12). Photographer: Dana Cuff. Layout by Ken Gutierrez.

holders and to act as the subdivision agent. Most of the parcels had between 50 and 200 lots for housing and an occasional "spot corner," earmarked for restricted businesses like gas stations, dry cleaners, and other community-based service or retail. In two areas, namely Kentwood and the Westchester Business District, Ayres was the exclusive agent, but for the rest he acted as the agent for the landowners, selling to builders and real estate subdividers.[2] Four large homebuilders took most of Westchester's area in that first round of development: Nowell, Ayres, Marlow-Burns, and Farrar. Together, they built 3,230 dwellings for 10,000 defense workers and their families in the four years between 1941 and 1944 (Hise, 1997). The increment of development was not the house but the tract, with 10 to 50 acres of houses built all at once. Where all the houses were constructed by a single builder, they also aged together, in some cases creating large parcels of land ripe for later redevelopment. The convulsive pattern of urban transformation is thus evident in suburbia as well as in the urban core.

The master plan was simple: there would be one major business center with a few additional commercial operations at intersections throughout the area. Several major boulevards would take the majority of the traffic past Westchester, secondary streets would surround superblocks, and the residential areas would be protected and isolated from them. This pattern is perhaps the one most characteristic of Westchester today. A grid of internal streets is lined with houses, all of which face into the neighborhood. The neighborhood streets are connected only at distant intervals to the main thoroughfares. This produces superblocks of secluded communities and major streets lined with a cacophony of backyard fences. Because of this, many parts of Westchester feel uninhabited to the commuter. According to Drollinger, who began working for Frank Ayres and Son just after the war, this organization was protected by a narrow strip of land about three feet wide between the rear property lines and the sidewalk which was maintained by the landholders so that no additional points of access to the boulevards could be made. On occasion, a public sidewalk sneaks between lots to link the inside of the neighborhood with the outside commercial district. This model of isolation was lauded by city planners in 1942, who called Westchester the "model residential community of the decade" (*Daily News*, May 8, 1942). The same model would be criticized by urban designers in the 1990s wishing to reestablish the interconnections characteristic of a traditional neighborhood and its commercial enterprises (see for example Krieger, 1991).

It was not long before the plan's shortcomings made themselves clear, since by 1948 there were nearly 25,000 people living where none had lived just seven years earlier (Boynoff, 1948a). William Hannon, chief of operations at Marlow-Burns and Burns's right-hand man in Westchester homebuilding since 1937, described it this way: "Every tract we went into, we wanted schools and churches because that created value. We never made churches and schools pay full price. We didn't go in for parks."[3] In spite of the idea that schools added value to their subdivisions, Westchester's developers had not systematically planned for them nor were they giving sites away. By contrast, Levitt and Sons donated land for various community purposes, including parks, schools, recreation facilities, and churches. At Westchester, the tremendous need for housing permitted other needs to go unattended. By 1948, most of the adults were between the ages of 30 and 34 and they had produced an abundance of offspring. Less than half the children had reached school age and already the three elementary schools were overtaxed, running three half-day sessions of kindergarten in the morning and the same again in the afternoon. There were no playgrounds or parks, no schools at all in Westchester for older children, and the library was located in a small shack. With profit driving Westchester's development and little community planning required by the city, much had to be done to make Westchester livable once the war was over.

Westchester represented the way suburban homebuilding would mushroom after the war. Despite some attempts at planning such communities, much was unforeseen. Because these communities were inhabited more or less at one time, the residents moved into new phases together: first there were not enough playgrounds and elementary schools for their young children; then as those children grew older there were not enough ball fields and high schools. As the kids left home, the supply of elementary schools exceeded demand, forcing some to close or convert into community centers (see Applegate, 1989). Because convulsive communities erupt all at once, they are particularly ill-balanced and lack the diversification that permits problems in other neighborhoods to be absorbed. The legacy of convulsive change is propagated by the conditions of initial upheaval. Predictably enough, the Westchester community continues to experience violent upheaval today.

126 Westchester streets like this one that border inward-looking neighborhoods appear abandoned. Photographer: Dana Cuff.

Building Westchester

41 In 1941, Congress passed Title VI of the Housing Act, which gave homebuilders good loan terms as an incentive to build small, low-cost housing in industrial, defense production areas. The next year, the National Housing Agency restricted housing construction in Los Angeles County to an area south of Manchester and Firestone boulevards, and the War Productions Board banned all nonessential construction (Hise, 1997). Westchester was in the building area, proximate to four major aircraft production industries. Beginning in 1940, the first lots sold and model homes were opened in a part of Westchester called Westport Heights developed by the Nowell Building Company. Advertised as an "FHA Approved Tract, Building and Racial Restrictions," it was a 25-minute drive from downtown, minutes away from four aircraft manufacturers, and the regular Pacific Electric Train would take you anywhere in the city. Two- and three-bedroom homes were offered at $4,300–$5,600, with payments of just $33 a month. For the buyers, Westport Heights (like the rest of Westchester development to follow) was an unusual commodity: when you bought the lot, it might come with the house, the lawn, a sprinkler system, and even blinds. Darrell and Gertrude Ratzlaff were some of the first buyers in Westchester, making a $250 down payment on $4,800 for lot #58 at 8406 Vicksburg in August of 1940. For an extra $117.30, the house was to be built as they custom-ordered, with such features as a tile wainscot, a wood mantle, and six additional venetian blinds.[4] Hannon explained that the houses were outfitted with whatever the

127 Shopping for home builders. From W. P. Atkinson et al., *Housing U.S.A. as Industry Leaders See It* (1954).

FHA was willing to finance at the time, and this changed over the years. "The homes in Westchester had what FHA would loan on. At one time, you couldn't put in carpets or a washer. It was all handled by the banks, and you had to have FHA approval on every loan."[5]

By June of 1942, 700 homes had been built by four separate building companies, which together offered a multitude of exhibit homes for prospective buyers to peruse. One of those builders was the Marlow-Burns Development Company, formed in 1938. Burns had been eyeing this vast tract of rather idyllic agricultural land since his early Palisades del Rey land sales for Dickinson and Gillespie. Burns himself lived in a lavish Spanish-style house there. From its office on Manchester Boulevard, the Marlow-Burns Development Company proceeded to subdivide the land and construct, with J. Paul Campbell as builder and Bill Hannon running operations, "Homes at Wholesale."[6] Fred Marlow, the finance expert, was the FHA's first regional director on the West Coast. His FHA experience was invaluable, since no one understood the programs when they began and it was Marlow who instructed banks and builders alike about the ins and outs.

Since his arrival in Los Angeles, Fritz Burns had led homebuilders through the evolution from high-powered salesmen of buildable lots, to constructors of ready-built homes, to complete community builders and modern-day real estate developers. Westchester was not Burns's first community building achievement, nor his last. While Westchester now presents to the outsider a relatively static appearance of like suburban tract homes, its initial buyers (like its present residents) saw things differently. Prospective homebuyers could view seventeen models from Nowell, nine from Marlow-Burns, along with thirty-eight others, many of them fully furnished. Hannon explained that models were located in different areas so that homeseekers could picture life in each of the different subdivision tracts. The previous system of marketing houses was the "Parade of Homes," in which an array of builders would each display one house along a makeshift street (see fig. 127). From this mock neighborhood, buyers would select a builder to devise a partially customized, one-off house for a lot purchased at another time in another location. While some tracts in Westchester were still sold as lots only, most came with houses built by the "operative builder" or developer-builder. This was modern marketing, and economies of scale brought down prices, if simultaneously increasing repetition. The threat of domestic monotony, at least in the neighborhood, was of grave concern to architects, builders, and manufacturers.

The Marlow-Burns houses were flavored: Ranch, Cape Cod, and Suburban model homes staked out the aesthetic possibilities for the thousands of

128   The most basic of the early Westchester homes. Photographer: "Dick" Whittington.

129 Staging a move-in day for publicity purposes exaggerated the instant-community phenomenon. Here Fritz Burns stands on the stage with appliances to give away. Photographer: "Dick" Whittington.

home seekers coming to Westchester. According to William Hannon, the plans of these houses were essentially identical, because Burns and he had honed them to perfection. They knew the best location for each light switch, door swing, cupboard, and window—designed for convenience, and wherever possible to make small houses seem larger. The architects involved were "mainly there to draw it up, since we told them just where everything should go. And also to make the windows line up and look nice from the outside."[7]

Defense workers moved in, situated neatly between Douglas, Hughes, Northrup, and North American (see fig. 4). On move-in day in 1942, families arrived in unison with their moving vans, ready to disgorge an instant community, which must have pleased Burns greatly. This was a publicity event, staged by Marlow-Burns and a popular magazine which had erected towers to photograph the activity. Lunch pails and lawn mowers at the ready, Westchester residents took to their new surroundings, finding the same heterogeneity as Levittowners did later (Gans, 1982). If the population was homogeneous in terms of race, it was relatively diverse socioeconomically, according to both the 1940 and 1950 censuses, divided among operatives and laborers, professionals,

130   Ad for the original Cape Cod model.

131   The Cape Cod in 1998, over fifty years old and still much the same. Photographer: Dana Cuff.

132   Trotting through the Marlow-Burns Toluca Wood tract in 1942. Photographer: "Dick" Whittington.

craftsmen, and proprietors and managers (Hise, 1997). The minute distinctions between houses barely perceptible to the outsider were the same significant differences that had led each homeowner to select a particular model as her or his own. While some of these houses have been remodeled, many others remain virtually untouched.

Burns's houses for Westchester had originated in two prior LA developments, Westside Village and Toluca Wood, and never varied much from that efficient prototype. A tight, 800-square-foot plan of two bedrooms and one bath sold for just under $3,000 in 1939, and by the early forties at Westchester for just under $4,000.[8] Burns, the consummate salesman, knew his customers' desires: no flat roofs and no blacks allowed.[9] Institutionalized racism went hand in hand with traditional residential aesthetics as surely as public housing's modernism symbolized socialism. But a few shutters and gables barely masked a functional box that was in many ways modern. Compact, thin-skinned, with open fenestration, Burns's house was frank, unadorned, and ready for mass production. What ornament it had was as efficient as possible in getting across a "style": a wooden porch on the Rancho model ($3,890), shutters and false dormers on the Cape Cod ($3,890), trellises on the Suburban ($4,790), with other features on the Defender, the Victory Home, and the Harmony Home. Burns kept tabs on buyers' preferences and altered new product accordingly. The Burns houses commanded a certain respect; when one came on the market, the newspaper ad bragged it was "Fritz Burns built."[10]

Sales Meets Manufacturing

It was probably his marketing savvy in popular housing that attracted Henry J. Kaiser to Fritz Burns. Burns, like most American industrialists, expected defense production to convert to domestic purposes, with housing construction a prime target. Still, Burns knew that houses should not look like planes if they were to appeal to the general public. Kaiser had built defense housing out of desperation to serve his manufacturing facilities across the country, including Vanport City, Oregon, for shipbuilders, at the Willow Run bomber plant in Michigan, and in Fontana, outside Los Angeles. In 1943, Vanport City was a radical boomtown for 40,000 people, designed, built, and occupied in ten short months. It was racially integrated, complete with schools, child care 24 hour a day, seven days a week, as well as cooked food services, so that mothers with small children could work round the clock on Kaiser's ships (Hayden, 1984).

Kaiser was not shy of innovation if it served some purpose or if it would turn a profit. Kaiser's Housing Division, under the direction of H. V. "Lindy" Lindbergh, researched building materials and efficiencies. When Kaiser teamed up with Burns, that Housing Division took Burns's Toluca Wood house and studied every aspect of its production.[11] Kaiser was ready to innovate upon Burns's more traditional formula if it made economic sense. With the stick frame, site-built Toluca Wood house as a baseline, under Lindbergh Kaiser's research arm invented an all-aluminum house and an all-plastic house, the latter being at least fifty years ahead of its time. The all-plastic house was a modern

133 A Rube Goldberg-like contraption to meet Kaiser's construction goals.

paragon, with one entire wall glazed, flat roofs, and relatively open plan (see fig. 122). Its design, according to the authors of an internal report, was necessarily modern because of the materials. At another point, Lindbergh worked with George M. Wolff, the Vanport City architect, to develop the "Kaiser Cottage" or expandable house, a 20-by-24-foot unit that could be marketed through Sears Roebuck. When shown the drawings, Burns "was very impressed and believes we are on the right track with this small, yet livable dwelling."[12] Had any of these experimental houses fared better in the financial analysis, Kaiser and Burns next would have been required to reform FHA guidelines. They just might have been the men to do it.

The idea of a Burns-Kaiser partnership for homebuilding had been brewing for a couple of years when Kaiser Community Homes was announced in May of 1945, with Kaiser as chairman of the board, Burns as president, and Marlow as head of the land development division. H. V. Lindbergh headed the housing division. The plan was to build 10,000 houses a year for starters. "Our 1946 goals are: two houses a day in January—three a day in February—10 a day in March—30 a day in April . . .". Not so long before, Kaiser shipyards had built a Victory ship in days; turning out houses was something Kaiser believed

134 Kaiser's shipbuilding experience was a foundation for his homebuilding enterprise. Photographer: "Dick" Whittington.

he could easily master. "Mr. Burns says the Kaiser houses will take 45 days to build. Mr. Kaiser says that Mr. Burns is a conservative, but will learn in time that one-half that long will be almost too long."[13] Burns's optimism paled next to Kaiser's.

Kaiser's wartime shipbuilding positioned Kaiser Steel for exactly the transformation everyone in industry as well as architecture envisioned: wartime production would convert to and transform domestic industries, utilizing advanced technology, new materials, and prefabrication (see fig. 133). Futurist zeal exceeded the modernist tendencies, though the two were hitched. Their association was apparent in the modern, flat-roofed prototypes Kaiser tested in his aluminum and plastic houses. But critics claimed that Kaiser homes would have to be better built than Kaiser ships, which "fell apart" and which were a way for Kaiser to get into "buck-passing to the government."[14] While some studies showed that an all-aluminum house would lead to slight savings over conventional wood frame construction, the Kaiser-Burns team investigated instead innovations in production. Only small savings could be squeezed from Toluca Wood, but those savings would become significant if mass quantities of housing were produced, leading Kaiser and Burns to focus on setting up factories for prefab-

135   A Kaiser Community Homes tract opens in Westchester with model homes in 1947. Photographer: "Dick" Whittington.

rication in major urban centers where large demand was assured. The recipe for upheaval was now set: large-scale manufacturing technology producing large numbers of housing units that would have to be built in whole communities.

They wanted to build entire communities, as Burns was already doing in Westchester and Kaiser in Fontana. This was rhetoric they might have adopted from the most progressive housing advocates of the time. That would mean 200-plus houses at a crack, along with health facilities (like Kaiser-Permanente), schools, recreation, and business. Kaiser Community Homes would concentrate its southern California resources on Westchester. Homes were to sell for under $5,000, with $150 down and monthly payments of $30, and would be built with steel frames (Kaiser Steel, inciting the lumber industry's wrath), gypsum wall board (Kaiser had leased the Standard Gypsum Company), stucco exterior (Kaiser's own Permanente Cement Company), and a prefabricated mechanical core, called the mechanical heart of the house. Comprised of kitchen, bath, and heating unit, the heart was to incorporate a dishwasher developed by Kaiser (see fig. 119) with other elements supplied by independent producers.[15] Eight months later, by January of 1946, production of Kaiser Community Homes was one house a day—far short of the thirty needed to meet an annual goal of 10,000. Escalating construction costs had pushed the sales price to $8,000. As it turned out, residential construction was more a part of Burns's world than Kaiser's. Mass production was complicated by uncontrollable supply factors, the most significant being materials shortages and land costs, since property values soared after the war. Nevertheless, Kaiser Community Homes was producing twenty houses a day by 1947—which Kaiser described as "a pitiful showing." In spite of Kaiser's disappointment, Kaiser Community Homes was the world's largest homebuilder at the time. When asked to speak about the housing crisis before the California State Joint Legislative Housing Committee in 1947, Kaiser summed up his experience thus:

> The Kaiser organization started worrying years ago about today's housing emergency. In 1943 we started an analysis of the housing problem of California and of the West Coast. In 1945 we formed the Kaiser Community Homes organization to build low-cost homes in five communities for re-

136   Manufacturing Kaiser Community Homes in 1946. Two production lines are visible, making interior partition walls. Photographer: "Dick" Whittington.

turning veterans. As far as building homes is concerned, we have been doing everything possible to solve this situation.

But I want to leave you with one fundamental thought. . . . You cannot get low-cost homes—and in volume—until you increase the flow of basic materials and until these materials are in surplus. Basic materials. That's the answer. Then you will get the homes.[16]

Kaiser Community Homes made houses out of prefabricated components assembled offsite in an old aircraft subassembly plant near Westchester. Plumbing and cabinetry were preassembled in complete banks to be trucked to the building site. They also prefabricated interior partitions, ceilings, floors, and exterior wall panels of plywood bonded to framing with a synthetic resin. Kaiser Homes's primary innovation over conventional building was not prefabrication, but the particular use of plywood. Plywood panels, "utilizing 'stressed skin' principles common to aircraft manufacturing, are strong and durable."[17] To make this claim, the builders performed various tests to assure the panels' strength, some of which were rather bizarre (see fig. 139). In fact, the factory assembly was only a small step away from Marlow-Burns's earlier preassembled building components, visible in a construction photo taken in 1943 (fig. 140), three years before the production lines at Westchester. Many politicians dropped by for photo opportunities and to show their support for such peacetime conversion, but the operation was never the success it promised, and after several years the lines came to a halt. Still, they had built a lot of houses.

The Kaiser homes were more expensive than had been hoped: house and lot sold for $8,650 for the three-bedroom model (the one in greatest demand). Both the two-bedroom and the three-bedroom plans were efficient to the point of being cramped. To keep sales prices down, square footage and amenities were minimal. With slight variation, these plans were being replicated at the edges of

139   Kaiser Community Homes plywood tests, 1946. Shooting plywood was intended to demonstrate the material's strength and safety for residential construction. Photographer: "Dick" Whittington.

140   A Marlow-Burns yard in 1943, with prefabricated framed wall sections being loaded on a truck to be taken to the building site. Photographer: "Dick" Whittington.

141   The removal of the wall between dining room and kitchen created a perceptually larger space in a very small house. Photographer: "Dick" Whittington.

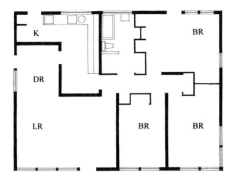

142   Standard three-bedroom plan for Kaiser Community Homes. Tulay Atak.

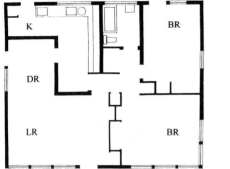
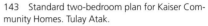

143   Standard two-bedroom plan for Kaiser Community Homes. Tulay Atak.

144   The standard two-bedroom plan for Levittown placed the living room at the rear. Tulay Atak.

most American cities. Levittown houses may have had a fireplace and washing machine; Kaiser Homes had a distinct dining area and more conventional room arrangement.[18] A family needed $615 down to settle into this Westchester subdivision, with monthly payments of $55 for 24 years (*Washington Times Herald,* March 23, 1947). The price of homes rose from $4,300 in 1941 to an average of $13,000 by 1948, permitting every Westchester resident to participate in the land speculation that had founded their community. Still, Westchester remained a "middle of the middle class" neighborhood, affordable to families with a single wage earner in a midlevel blue collar or service sector job (Boynoff, 1948b). The architecture of Westchester was the architecture of suburbia: efficiently planned houses of prepackaged stylistic affect, moderated by the economical ornament mentioned above. Burns went on to build other LA area communities, most notably Panorama City (a Kaiser Community Homes project).

Although mixed land use was something to be avoided in such developments, Westchester was a large enough community to tolerate carefully located commercial zoning. Most of the commercial property was restricted to the Westchester Central Business District, along Sepulveda just north of the airport. There a three-block stretch of shops and offices front along the street with expansive parking behind. Building the commercial core was no easy task, particularly because of wartime restrictions. One Ella Drollinger built the first store in Westchester, starting in 1940 and finally opening as a Jim Dandy Market in 1944. To do this, she had to send a representative to Washington to seek special dispensation, since all construction was limited to defense housing. Her market, it was argued, was essential to the war workers of Westchester. She won that approval, but still she had no fixtures for the market until she rounded them up from other stores that had gone out of business.[19] Ella persisted, and her son, Howard Drollinger, Jr., has continued the tradition of commercial development in Westchester, now operating as the largest commercial landowner in the area. Drollinger experienced success just after the war, as the area grew into a viable commercial district complete with major department stores, large chain stores, and theaters. Then, in the sixties, two events led to a downturn: first, airport expansion removed about 3,000 homes and their 10,000 occupants, who constituted the demographic base for the stores, and second, the Fox Hills Mall, a regional shopping mall, was completed. This second event was replicated across the country, as malls sucked away department stores and theaters from downtown retail districts in every city. Westchester's downtown has never recovered: vacant stores and "For Lease" signs line Sepulveda; some of the occupied stores have blocked their street entries so that their only entrance is at the rear, facing the parking. The theaters have closed, converted, and closed again.

"Westchester Business Center
H. B. Drollinger Co., Realtors
8921 S. Sepulveda Boulevard, Los
Taken January, 1964."

145   The Westchester Business Center in 1961, showing airport at upper right.

The Airport at Westchester Today

43   In the process of urban growth, the very places that came into existence through upheaval are subjected to later convulsions. Tracts of homes all built inexpensively and quickly decline together where circumstances thwart investment by individual homeowners. At Westchester, Fritz Burns continued to study airports in all their aspects to determine the changing impacts of Los Angeles International on his real estate developments. With consultations from Howard Hughes about increasing noise levels, danger, and aircraft developments, it was determined that housing at the end of the runways would have to be demolished (see Hamilton 1995), housing originally built as an extension of Burns's early Playa del Rey housing before the airport's presence grew intolerable. The ghosts are still there in the form of curbs and occasional street signs, but all the houses were removed. Soon the airport began to take land outright. By 1952, the Los Angeles International Airport had become one of the three largest in the United States, and could accommodate any airplane in operation (*Los Angeles Examiner,* 1952c). Expansion plans for parking lots, runways, traffic management, and related office development were effected during the fifties, sixties, and thereafter. Residential areas that had been built just ten to twenty years before were targeted for demolition. The first Homes at Wholesale tract was an early victim (see fig. 125).

      Only in old aerial photographs and tract maps can the Marlow-Burns subdivision be located. Airport parking paved over land where families bought a

146   John Stagnaro and Jack Macintosh shoot the breeze with Jemima Lugibihl in 1999 in front of a Marlow-Burns home built in 1942. Photographer: Dana Cuff.

little bit of the American dream in the forties. When John Stagnaro and Jack Macintosh bought their homes from Marlow and Burns in 1942, they came to work in the aircraft industry just like all their neighbors. Their children grew up and moved away, leaving an aging neighborhood behind. Now when they look down toward the end of their street, they remember the homes taken by the airport expansion. They wonder, in the short breaks between deafening landings of 747s, whether their own neighborhood is safe. An engineer takes decibel readings at the corner to determine whether any kind of noise abatement might be effective. It seems unlikely.

The airport expansion was swift and shocking, like the earlier upheavals cited in this book. Residents recall the eerie impact of the expansion. "It was weird. One day we went to school and half the kids were just gone. Their houses were all torn down. Somehow things never seemed the same after that in Westchester."[20] There were eminent domain proceedings, appraisals, and unsatisfactory settlements. "No one wanted to move when the airport expansion started. I think the people who made their deals early on were better off than the ones who stayed to fight. The people who sold out got more money than the ones who went to court," reflected Westchester resident Bill Goss. And so goes

147   The Rancho in 1942.

the story of convulsive transformation. As at Russian Flats or Chavez Ravine, so in parts of Westchester big moves wipe out big parts of the city, especially those moves sponsored by the state.

Just one part of Westchester's business district has been revitalized, where Drollinger followed his mother's model and built a market. Some residents of the area say he has done too little, too late. If he continues his revitalization, the "main street" planning of Westchester will disappear. Reversing the parking diagram to the 1990s model, the new Ralph's strings small retail establishments past a sea of parking, to the market at the rear of the site. Elsewhere, on Manchester Boulevard, the local high school is filled with faces of every ethnic hue, coming from all parts of the city by bus, since there are no longer enough area students to fill the school. The remaining homes that Fritz Burns built seem depressed, threatened by further airport intrusions, discouraging investment and generating the kind of blight that Burns himself thought should be outlawed. A flyer at the local Submarine Sandwich shop implores neighbors to come to a meeting to register their opinions about the next proposed airport expansion.

148   The Rancho in 1999. Photographer: Dana Cuff.

Driving through much of Westchester today is like driving through Levit-town. The original homogeneity has been overgrown by vegetation and over-built by home improvement projects. Still, there's an air of sameness and consistency despite the intervening fifty-odd years. Unlike Le Corbusier's Pessac, which was so transformed by its occupants as to be almost unrecognizable, at Westchester the residents did not intend to change the fundamental way things looked. Building setbacks, the scale and massing of the original houses, the sin-gle-use zoning, and trees that have grown in unison for decades, all give the place a particular feel.

There are exceptions to this sameness. In the Kentwood section of town, hulking 3,000-square-foot houses have burst out of their original 850-square-foot boxes, overwhelming their own parentage as well as neighbors. Just a few blocks over, on Dunbarton, Andover, and Altamor Drive, the street trees are small and the lawns look like they were rolled off the backs of gardeners' trucks yesterday. This is the Kentwood Collection (see fig. 125), a new subdivision of three dozen gargantuan tract houses on lots scaled for those little, original boxes, with virtually no yard, three-car garage, and home security system in place. All you need to buy one of these $600,000 homes is 480 times the down payment of $250 that the Ratzlaffs paid in 1940. Venetian blinds are still included.

But those sections of town that have been little altered over the fifty years look something like The Flats must have looked to outsiders in the 1930s. There, the 800-square-foot Marlow-Burns houses and Kaiser homes, built to such great demand, stand in various states of disrepair. Still, a diverse group of resi-dents occupy the houses, some undertaking modest home improvement projects, others running makeshift businesses from overstuffed garages. On Veterans Day, there are a lot of flags flying here. You could buy one of these houses for as little as $150,000,[21] which in other parts of Los Angeles wouldn't get you a studio condominium. That fact will not escape the airport planners. Could this be the fate of the new houses on Dunbarton, some fifty years hence, when Loyola University decides to push its eastern boundary out a bit further? Will the three-car garages have been converted into illegal, income-generating apartments by then? Not if the Kentwood Home Guardians have anything to say about it, who seem to have named their community organization well.

It's probably not so difficult to imagine for Adelle Wexler, past president of the Home Guardians, and her fellow Kentwood residents. They spent a good deal of energy between the mid-eighties and nineties negotiating with the developers of the enormous project expected to rise out of the adjacent wetlands. Wexler's bluffside home surveys open fields that are poised to become Playa Vista, which has all the trappings of those large-scale operations advocated at the 1931 Hoover conference: a large block of land is developed in one continuous operation; it can be comprehensively planned and efficiently designed; it protects property values; and it permits affordable housing. But not much: as of 1999, 417 units out of more than 10,000 were to be affordable. Hoover's conferees had met to encourage private development of low-cost housing, with a clear underlying message: where the market failed, government would step in. Public housing was the key federal program to redress private homebuilding's inability to serve the city's lowest income groups. But somewhere between Westchester's inception and Playa Vista, public housing effectively died, while large-scale operations, the determining power of private property, and upheaval remained. The story of Chavez Ravine elaborates this crucial period in urban development history.

Chavez Ravine and the End of Public Housing

VII

And 10,000 More: Remaking Chavez Ravine

While 'Slum Clearance' and 'sub-standard' are merely words to cover up the *diabolical plot,* this is the Housing Authority program that Mayor Bowron quotes as being FREE, knowing full well, also, that under his *appointed Commissar,* they are actually *routing people* from Elysian Park Chavez Ravine and other selected areas, out of their privately owned *homes* (although these people *hold title of contract* for life *to* their homes) in order that the *land* be cleared to set up *Socialistic Tenement Housing.*

Catarino Esparza, President, City Center District Improvement Association[1]

44 While Fritz Burns was giving lectures about revitalizing dilapidated buildings through private means, Frank Wilkinson was herding politicians and powerful citizens through the most deteriorated neighborhoods of Los Angeles as visceral proof that new housing had to be built. Wilkinson believed that awareness of the deplorable conditions in the slums would insure support for affordable housing programs. He was following the Rosenman method, named after the head of the National Housing Committee who made slum tours a strategic part of pro-housing lobbying across the nation.

In the late 1940s, housing was still easily defined as a crisis in Los Angeles. Veterans were inadequately housed and there were desperately poor areas of makeshift housing. Some of this part of LA was documented by capable photographers like Otto Rothschild, Louis Stoumen, and Leonard Nadel. Nadel's slum photographs, commissioned by the Housing Authority, are remarkable works of art, anthropology, and propaganda, portraying the worst of sub-standard housing inhabited by a submerged (usually white) middle class—the "deserving poor." These were not unlike the Depression-era Farm Security Administration images of Walker Evans, Dorthea Lange, and company, which illustrated the need for federal supports for the rural poor.

By the late forties, housing activists were building creative linkages between slum clearance for downtown redevelopment and public housing. In 1948, Mayor Bowron appointed the city's first five commissioners to the Com-

149   Surveying the field at Chavez Ravine. Photographer: Leonard Nadel.

munity Redevelopment Agency, under the authority of the state Community Redevelopment Act, passed by the legislature in 1945. The intent was to clear
slums in both urban and rural areas, to create sites to be leased or sold to private interests for commercial or residential construction. It was required that
"any and all people displaced in the process be offered safe, sanitary housing at
a price within their means." In Los Angeles, the lack of decent affordable housing for the displaced slum residents was a "major stumbling block." It was easy
then to make the case that downtown Los Angeles—Bunker Hill, for example—
could not be redeveloped unless public housing legislation passed. "However,
with the advent of the new Congress and the expected early passage of a low-
rent housing program, it is reasonable to expect that this problem will be eased
to some degree. If so, mid-town Los Angeles can look forward to an early, and
much-needed face-lifting" (*Housing News*, 1948a, p. 4).

When the 1949 Federal Housing Act passed, it promoted an early version
of redevelopment and provided for new public housing as well. While real estate
interests were pursuing the implications of redevelopment, housing advocates
initiated 10,000 more units of low-rent housing across Los Angeles.[2] Like nearly
all large U.S. cities, Los Angeles had established its public housing program, even

if it was not as robust as some others; by 1952, there were 7.5 public housing units in Los Angeles per 1,000 persons, compared to 18.5 per thousand in Boston and 14.2 per thousand in New York.[3] Southern California housing advocates hoped the 1949 appropriations would make up some of this difference.

Public housing advocates took the opportunity of the widespread postwar housing crisis to initiate an extensive new series of projects. Wilkinson, accompanied by Simon Eisner and Joe Solons of the Health Department, spent a month in 1945 conducting an "eye survey" of substandard housing in Los Angeles, looking for possible sites to develop. According to Wilkinson, "We were always thinking about sites."[4] They knew that a large appropriation would be coming when a federal housing act was finally passed. Wilkinson was supposed to have all the sites selected before that time. At least a year before the 1949 Act, he, Eisner, and Solons had settled on eleven different sites, mostly located in the vicinity of downtown, stretching from Chavez Ravine at the north to Jordan Downs in Watts (see fig. 9).

Like The Flats, the Chavez Ravine area had been determined to be a slum by a finding that most of its dwellings were substandard. Descriptions of Chavez Ravine tell another story, such as that by Leo Politi (1966), artist and historian, written after the last homes there were demolished:

> Chavez Ravine grew into a village with a grocery store, a school, and so forth. In its last years it had about two thousand families. It was a happy community where everyone knew and helped one another. At night there were lighted bonfires, and people gathered around and sang songs.
>
> Many houses had some sort of domesticated animals such as sheep, cows, goats, pigs, chickens and peacocks.
>
> In many ways, Chavez Ravine was living a life all its own. Horse drawn plows were still in use, and the hillsides were planted with corn and sugar cane.
>
> There were religious processions in the village, one during Lent, another on December 12th commemorating the Madonna of Guadalupe. . . . Though all this reminded one of a village in Mexico, nonetheless this was old Los Angeles with a charm all its own, a Los Angeles we will never see again.

Photographs best describe Chavez Ravine just as demolition was threatened, since English news reports at the time fluttered between paternalistic racism and romanticization of rural poverty. On August 20, 1951, the *Los Angeles Times* ran photos and a long article about "the passing of Chavez Ravine." Long opposed to any kind of public housing, the *Times* sympathized with the families

150   Looking north up Paducah Street in Chavez Ravine with the homes that would be demolished, surrounded by Elysian Park at the top.

151   Rural frontier in the 1950s at Chavez Ravine.

152 Joe Spennoza, his wife, and four children lived in this one-room home on Brooks Street in Chavez Ravine with no plumbing, no gas, and no toilet. Photographer: Leonard Nadel.

who were being removed from what it portrayed as a quaint Mexican village, quoting residents in privatized, patriotic rhetoric that served the *Times*'s agenda: "We built our homes here, not the government. We don't want to live somewhere else. Taking away our homes takes our incentive to be good American citizens" (*Los Angeles Times*, 1951a, p. 2). Somewhere between 970 and 1,800 households with about 3,300 inhabitants were to be removed, depending on the estimate. According to a housing authority document dated June 13, 1951, the Elysian Park Heights site comprised 254.4 acres with 972 dwelling units. In a survey of dwelling conditions, it reported that 87 percent had one or more basic deficiencies, 64 percent had two or more, and 14 percent of the dwellings were "standard homes."[5] A basic deficiency, in this case, involved major structural deterioration or lack of sanitary facilities.

News reports indicated that a full third of the families refused to sell, forcing the city housing authority into extensive condemnation proceedings. Wilkinson tried to lessen the opposition of the *Times* by taking Chandler's son to the Chavez Ravine site. Wilkinson believed anyone could see that it was an ideal site: there was no land that large within 40 miles of town.[6] The effort must

153   Homes of Chavez Ravine in 1948. Photographer: Leonard Nadel.

have been wasted, since the *Times* continued its steady campaign against Elysian Park Heights in particular and public housing in general. Perhaps Chandler saw the point all too clearly but preferred another land use.

Housing advocates had prepared well for the expected 10,000 units; LA was the first city in the nation to apply for and be granted federal funds from the 1949 Housing Act. But big dreams needed a lot of elbow room. Scale was the defining factor at Chavez Ravine, and there, as at Aliso Village, it unleashed large-scale destruction. With 10,000 units to come, the housing authority needed to find some big sites in order to avoid splitting its building efforts into dozens of smaller sites. The 254 acres of Chavez Ravine, renamed Elysian Park Heights, would absorb 3,360 units, a full third of the total.[7] This and one other large site (an extension at Rose Hills to a hundred units of existing public housing) were to account for half of the total between them.[8] In the end, these extra-large projects would not only be canceled but would bring down public housing across LA.

It was indeed a beautiful site, with rolling hills and distant vistas, nestled into a wild city park. All this made it easy to imagine the utopia to come. Indeed,

154   Chavez Ravine with armory just visible at left.

it had been taken as a "site" of civic interest for many years, when planners considered locating a world's fair there in 1938 and again a few years later. Like
Aliso Village, Chavez Ravine's ultimate development was preceded by earlier
attempts which, while they failed to build their proposed projects, effectively
paved the way for later undertakings in more ways than one. (As we shall see,
this pattern also describes Playa Vista's development.) It may have been the
world's fair campaigns that drew Burns's attention to the Ravine, where he and
a partner named Weingard[9] (the developer of Lakeside) bought a large piece of
land. These for-profit developers would, in the final analysis, be instrumental in
the Ravine's outcome. In addition, the Navy–Marine Corps Armory was built
there as another indication that Chavez Ravine had a public purpose in the city.
But what about all those families living mainly at the top of the Ravine?

   The scale of the homes was small, in some cases extra-small. Strewn along
dirt roads, stepping down the hillsides, ad hoc houses leaned into the fences of
more substantial bungalows, next to churches, stores, and school. That description of the houses stemmed from one well-publicized photo (see fig. 155)
taken of an atypical part of the Ravine. Unlike most of the homes, which followed western suburban patterns of a single house facing the street on a single
lot, in this zone dozens of small dwellings are scattered across the hillside, just

below the reservoir. Some sit directly in the roadway easement, others are strung precariously along steep footpaths.[10] This image provided evidence that Chavez Ravine was like no other part of the city. As propaganda, it argued for slum clearance. Yet, as such photographs attest, the rural quality of this community held a certain attraction to the outsider and resident alike.

Chavez Ravine was named after Julian Chavez, who arrived in LA from New Mexico in the 1830s and soon thereafter succeeded in gaining title to the land. Chavez Ravine's settlement origins are spotty, but in the *Times* a well-known, liberal attorney named Marshall Stimson is credited as the first speculator and houser. It was he

> who moved about 200 Mexican families, then living in the Los Angeles River bottom, into the area about 1913.
>
> Today he says "I sold them homesites. They had to buy to have pride of ownership, but the price was cheap. They had good air and they raised their children.
>
> "I resent this talk of slum clearance. These humble homes are not the finest but the same health standards do not apply where there is plenty of free air as compared with crowded tenements downtown." (*Los Angeles Times*, August 20, 1951, p. 2)

Perhaps even more than in The Flats, the people of Chavez Ravine appear to have constituted a stable community. There was the strong presence of the Catholic church, a number of neighborhood commercial enterprises, and a fine community school, Palo Verde Elementary. The residents had organized successfully in years past to demand city services like sewage and street paving, and against the threat to health of a local brickworks. These previous debates helped residents organize against the public housing development proposed. They were joined in the battle against the 10,000-unit program by a number of odd bedfellows. Some of the most vocal were the middle-class homeowners' organization near the Rose Hills site, CASH (Citizens Against Socialist Housing), the Chamber of Commerce, and the Home Builders Association, not to mention the *Times* (see Hines, 1982a; Freedman, 1959).

Of the eleven sites under consideration, Chavez Ravine was receiving far the most attention from the housing authority in terms of architecture and funding. As of May 1, 1952, over $3 million had been paid to owners of site property at Elysian Park Heights, while at Rose Hills, where a development of similar magnitude was proposed, only about $600,000 had been spent by the same date. Clearly, it was Chavez Ravine that had to be stopped, from the point of view of public housing opponents.[11]

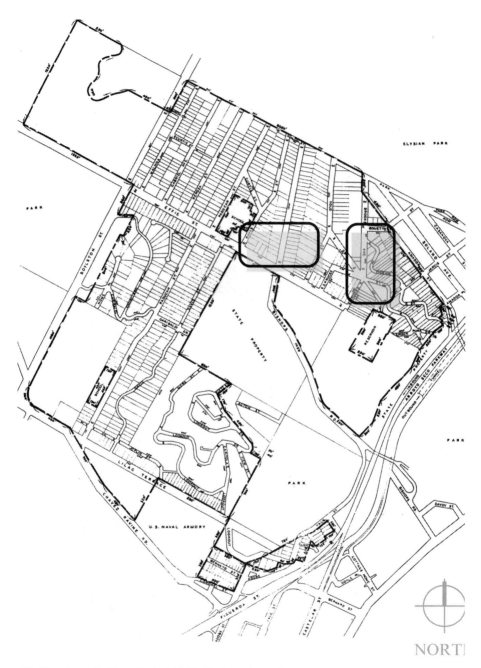

NORT[

155   Views located in Chavez Ravine's hillside. The lower photo of houses on Spruce and Phoenix streets was an anomaly, but was widely shown as a typical condition. Ken Gutierrez.

Utopian Plans

45 Because Chavez Ravine was going to be the centerpiece of the housing authority's new developments, the executive director, Howard Holtzendorff, enlisted architect Robert E. Alexander, then head of the Los Angeles City Planning Commission. Alexander in turn invited Richard Neutra to collaborate on the immense project. Alexander was well connected in the Los Angeles political scene and had been part of the team that designed the much-touted Baldwin Hills Village, a fine example of the benefits comprehensive planning held for housing and neighborhoods. Neutra had participated in associations of architects that designed early public housing at Hacienda Village and Pueblo del Rio, and had recently completed 600 units of the best defense production housing in Los Angeles at Channel Heights, another hillside site.

Together with Simon Eisner, who worked as the chief site planner, Alexander and Neutra used the garage in Neutra's home as their studio for Chavez Ravine. They concocted a scheme of high-rise and low-rise housing, situated in a Radburnian plan where only local traffic entered the site. The landscape was to be designed by Garrett Eckbo, a noted midcentury modernist. One of the primary hurdles for the designers and planners was the rugged terrain: grading, soil conditions, and siting of buildings were all problematic. Eisner was the one who dealt most specifically with issues of the terrain, but the constant changes made in the site plan were a visible reminder of unresolved topography. Eisner was critical of Neutra and Alexander's preliminary scheme: "Bob and Richard had

156   Channel Heights war worker housing by Richard Neutra. Photographer: Leonard Nadel.

drawn a very sketchy plan where they had disposed of—and that's probably the best language I can use—some 3,360 units on the site. It was a flat piece of paper with a flat land layout with a whole bunch of matchsticks scattered around there in some kind of pattern that didn't really add up to anything, didn't relate to anything." Eisner insisted they get good topographic information on the site. Early on, he advised an immense cut-and-fill scheme whereby thirty to forty feet would be cut from the hilltops and used to fill the valley floor. This later proved

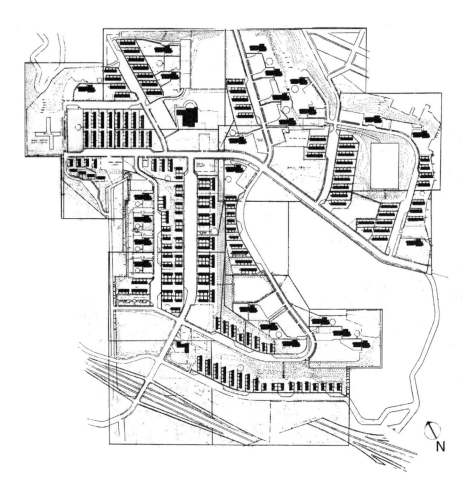

N

157   Elysian Park Heights site plan. Reworked by Ken Gutierrez.

infeasible, instigating the reworking particularly of the lowest, southern portion
of the site. As the project developed, Eisner's respect for Neutra grew: "[Neutra]
would go down in the valley and look up at the site, and he would picture how
these buildings would be sited on the hill and make them monuments, literally,
part of the landscape. He did a beautiful job, and his sketching was fabulous"
(Eisner, 1992, p. 67).

The project began with a scheme for 24 thirteen-story towers with 1,016
units and 163 low-rise residential buildings containing 2,542 units, for a total
of just under 3,600 apartments. The plan also included a great community
building with indoor and outdoor theaters, two schools on over 15 acres, nu-

merous playgrounds, nurseries, and four church sites (Los Angeles, Housing Authority, 1951). 17,000 people were to occupy the site in the plan's first incarnation, paying rents averaging $35 a month.

Architectural historian Thomas Hines (1982b) suggests that Neutra was reworking his Rush City utopian thought at Elysian Park Heights. Rush City depicted a rationalist modern utopia of high-speed transportation through the geometrically organized city. Technically clean, with ordered slabs of housing in green space along traffic corridors, Rush City transferred with relative ease to the Chavez Ravine site. What appears overly rigid in the site plan would have been greatly mollified by the site's topography. Much as at Channel Heights, Neutra placed buildings on a regular grid that would have been perceptually broken by changes in elevation. Indeed, site sections show a careful attention to the immediate relations between housing units from one building to another. Neutra gave extensive consideration to the sight lines from one apartment to the next, and to the interface between the private space of the house and semipublic space for domestic activities like laundry and play. He used changes in elevation to effect the desired degree of privacy and interchange.

In the drawings in Neutra's archives, it is the low-rise, garden apartments that receive most of his design attention. These dwellings are simple structures well conceived in plan and section, if less so in elevation studies. Each unit has access to the ground and to its own private garden space. Interior studies are populated with families, showing flexible inhabitation with modern furnishings. The Elysian Park scheme included an early example of designing for dis-

158   Site perspective of Elysian Park Heights.

abilities: several buildings along the primary axis were intended for residents with special needs.

At the terminus of the primary axis up from the freeways, climbing through the site toward its northeastern quarter, stood a stunning community building. Able to open itself up to the outdoors via movable walls, the building was carved into the hillside, creating natural amphitheaters, entries on two levels, and sheltered gathering places. It contained over 33,000 square feet for cultural and recreational facilities.

Although the towers were only a part of the first scheme, the rest being two- and three-story garden apartments, it was the towers that generated the most controversy. Independently, Clarence Stein and Catherine Bauer expressed their grave opposition to Elysian Park Heights plans, primarily on the basis of density and high-rise living. "[Stein] asked me straightforwardly how I could justify in my own mind working on a project which was going to take people who are accustomed to living on the ground, having their gardens, having chickens and their little animals in their yards, having space around them, having flowers, to have these people living in these twenty-four thirteen-story-high buildings" (Eisner, 1992, p. 70). Editorials and interviews proclaimed that towers were no place for kids or the poor; a police captain was quoted as saying that apartment skyscrapers for lower-income families would be bad for "juvenile control" (*Herald Express*, 1952). The specter of poor families boxed in high-rise housing fueled protests about the proposed development, even though the high-rises at Chavez Ravine were never intended for families. Households with

159   Typical garden apartments of Elysian Park Heights.

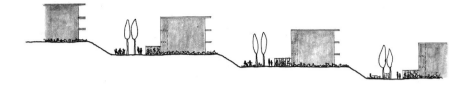

160   Site section of Elysian Park Heights showing how garden apartments utilized the slope to create privacy, views, and public promenades. Tulay Atak.

children were to be located in the larger three-, four-, and five-bedroom units in the low-rise buildings. Opposition to the towers reflected displaced concern about the overall scale of the project, and also strategic campaigning on the part of anti–public housing interests. In the face of increasing public objection, density was reduced to about 2,800 units, and eventually all the high-rise buildings were eliminated. In an interoffice memo from October of 1952, Neutra's progress report to the housing authority stated that three-story buildings would replace all the elevator towers, substantially reducing the number of units from 3,350 to 2,000.[12]

Richard Neutra and Robert Alexander were content initially to include high-rise solutions in the Chavez Ravine proposals. Alexander was planning the same for Bunker Hill, where he devised the matrix of apartment blocks first intended for this downtown renewal project (described in chapter 48). Redevelopment caught architects in the camp of what Parson (1993) calls the pro-growth democrats who backed modernist progress. Theirs were rational visions of urban growth, sanitized and sleek. In terms of the site planning, Neutra's allegiance to CIAM and its principles is abundantly apparent. But the rational utopian plan of land use and zoning did not impede his development of architecturally humane spaces.

Still, there was a lot of convincing to do: Neutra invited to his home Mrs. Slavin, the principal of Palo Verde Elementary School, to argue the project's merits. The school, according to Eisner, was one of LA's most interesting multicultural institutions, with festivals that brought together Mexican, Chinese, and Filipino traditions. Eisner was at the meeting between Neutra and Slavin:

> I sat there and listened to him explain what he was going to do for the local residents, how he was going to do these wonderful things. I sat there thinking in the back of my mind of those twenty-four thirteen-story buildings and didn't know whether to choke or what. But that was one of the

161   Palo Verde Elementary School fiesta in 1951. Photographer: Leonard Nadel.

interesting parts. He actually convinced this woman that he was going to actually save the culture of these people in that valley, but again, that never happened. (Eisner, 1992, pp. 66–67)

Correspondence between the architects and the housing authority indicate constant downscaling for political reasons. Wilkinson and Ignacio Lopez held numerous meetings with Chavez Ravine residents to explain the project and offer priority status to those who wanted to move in.[13] These promises, like those to residents of The Flats, turned out to be empty.

In the financial woes of the housing authority's political demise, Neutra and Alexander were caught with over $40,000 in unpaid bills. In 1953, Neutra despaired in a letter to Howard Holtzendorff:

[Consider] our imponderable investment, three years of our prominent and sensitive profession lives. . . . Nobody contemplates this at the moment, but it is very well possible that it will kill me if it is later contemplated [to hire other architects to replace us] and done and we have signed away our natural right of protest. Sure, we want to keep out of bankruptcy which threatens at this moment, after having worked so long with all dedication.[14]

While some of the financial matters were resolved, Neutra never had another opportunity to fashion his biggest utopian dreams.

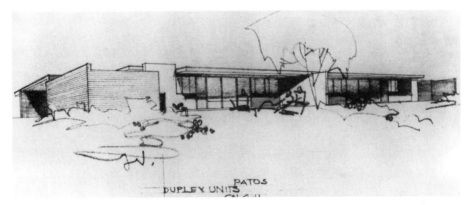

162   Duplex units at Elysian Park Heights, early 1950s.

163   Proposed administration building at Elysian Park Heights, early 1950s.

Political Enemies

46 The battle over Chavez Ravine was about more than public housing, but public housing crystallized the oppositions. There were at least three principal skirmishes waged over this development. First, there was the problem between the *Los Angeles Times* and Mayor Bowron. According to Alexander (1989), "The *LA Times* had become increasingly disenchanted with Mayor Bowron who after the elections no longer took orders from across the street. As I see it, the *Times* used the Public Housing issue to get rid of Bowron." Second was a heated-up competition for federal funds between downtown commercial real estate interests and suburban residential builders. And third, there were strong reactions from private-sector builders against direct public-sector engagement in housing construction. This had been an issue in previous cases I examined, but with Chavez Ravine came decisive action.

The 1949 Housing Act had crystallized the real estate industry's opposition to direct federal intervention in housing, while subsidies to lenders had become institutionalized. Builders had envied the UAW's lobbying organization six years earlier in debates on public housing, but by 1949 their own machine was well oiled. President Harry Truman lamented: "I have been shocked in recent days at the extraordinary propaganda campaign that has been unleashed against this bill by the real estate lobby. I do not recall ever having witnessed a more deliberate campaign of misrepresentation and distortion against legislation of such crucial importance to the public welfare."[15] The opposition to Chavez

Ravine's development became front page news, as builders worked against the construction of 10,000 new units of public housing and residents tried to save their homes, or at least get a fair price for them. Fritz Burns and his organization, the Committee Against Socialist Housing (with its pointed acronym CASH), and other real estate groups were funding one battle after another to get the government out of the housing business (Freedman, 1959). The builder-developers were now experienced and well organized. Having won anti–public housing battles in 1948 and 1950, they pulled out the same political strategies, campaign managers, and funding networks in 1952.[16] In a referendum on June 3 of that year, voters rejected by a 60 percent majority the city's contract with the federal government to build more public housing. At this time, the building industry's recovery gave its constituents confidence, as well as cash for campaign contributions. There was a lot of "contributing" that was not quite seemly. It appears that the city council, which in 1949 had unanimously supported the 10,000 new units of public housing, was bribed into taking a stand against it. It was discovered, for example, by city officials after his death that council member Ed Davenport had received some $50,000 in bribes from the real estate lobby to round out the mere $7,500 he received in councilman's salary (see Parson, 1999).

Fritz Burns and Frank Wilkinson debated on the radio the question of whether public housing had improved or worsened the lives of its residents (Wilkinson, 1965). To further entangle matters, Fritz Burns was part-owner of a sizable piece of property in the Chavez Ravine development site.[17] He was also a staunch Catholic, a primary contributor to church causes, and a good friend of the archbishop. Burns's pointed efforts to stop public housing must have caused a fair amount of difficulty in the archdiocese, since its Monsignor O'Dwyer was one of LA's most fervent housing activists and Wilkinson's closest ally. In the end, the Catholic church appears to have sided with Burns.

Frank Wilkinson, now the "Public Information Director" for the housing authority, served in a variety of capacities. When the residents of Rodger Young Village, organized by an active cell of the Communist Party, protested for better garbage service, it was Wilkinson that the authority sent out to negotiate peace. When a black resident of public housing was a victim of police brutality, Wilkinson was asked to quell the brewing riot. And it was Wilkinson who was sent by the housing authority to convince a small but effective number of Communists in Chavez Ravine to support the public housing project. In many ways, Wilkinson ran interference between the housing authority administration and the social, if not socialist, life of its tenants. This would soon be used against him. The chief of police put together a dossier on Wilkinson and nine other housing authority employees, accusing them of subversive affiliations. He delivered it to

164 CASH (Citizens Against Socialist Housing) members present their case to the Chamber of Commerce in 1952. Photographer: Leonard Nadel.

Mayor Bowron. A friend of Wilkinson's family, Bowron's best was to disassociate himself and stand back.

Another of Wilkinson's jobs was to be an expert witness in eminent domain proceedings, testifying as to why a condemnation was justified. Weeks into such proceedings for Chavez Ravine, on August 28, 1952, the lawyers for one set of property owners brought out the police chief's dossier and asked Wilkinson to list all political affiliations since his college days. Wilkinson believes that Fritz Burns was one of the owners of that property. Although he had often signed the loyalty oaths required of housing authority employees (and tenants), this time Wilkinson protested the question as irrelevant. Judge Otto Emme let the question stand, and the housing authority lawyer accompanying Wilkinson would not come to his defense, afraid to be caught in the noose that all immediately saw tightening on Wilkinson. Councilman Davenport led the city council in adopting a resolution to bring the House Un-American Activities Committee to investigate the housing authority (Parson, 1999; Wilkinson, 1965).

Wilkinson was forever changed by the events of that day. The executive director and board of the housing authority turned their backs on him and the other employees accused of being Communists. Indeed, according to Wilkinson, board members pulled him aside to beg him not to implicate them in the scandal. On August 29, Wilkinson was out of a job; soon after, his wife lost her teaching position; his children's applications to summer camp were denied. Much later, he was offered his first job after being fired from the housing authority, as part of the night cleaning crew for a business owned by sympathetic Quakers, on the condition that he come and go in darkness. By stark contrast, in 1952 Fritz Burns was named "Builder of the Year" in recognition of "activities in Southland building and for his anti–public housing leadership."[18]

Frank Wilkinson was betrayed by all those who had depended on him, most particularly the housing authority itself. The Catholic Church sent O'Dwyer on a sabbatical of sorts, probably to protect him and the church from red-baiting. Wilkinson never again saw O'Dwyer, with whom he had worked every day for more than a decade. Refusing to plead the Fifth Amendment (the right to avoid self-incrimination) before the House Un-American Activities Committee, Wilkinson instead claimed that the First (the right of free speech and assembly) was at stake. Eventually he was tried and sent to jail for this stand, one of the last such victims of the McCarthy period.

After he was finally released, long court battles gained Wilkinson the right to see his FBI files, which comprised 130,000 pages.[19] The FBI began its surveillance in 1942, when Wilkinson first displayed integrationist leanings during

165   Mayor Bowron testifies at a hearing on public housing (at far right) before the House UnAmerican Activities Committee in 1953.

the Citizens' Housing Council protest against racial segregation in public housing. He has spent the rest of his life defending First Amendment principles through his organization, the National Committee Against Repressive Legislation. The demise of public housing at Chavez Ravine also produced an extraordinary new contortion in the fight over those 300 acres.

A Dodger Victory

Saw Mayor Norris Poulson
dining jovially last Friday
night at the Red Barn in the
Valley with Fritz Burns, the
builder.
Leslie Claypool, *Los
Angeles Daily News,*
December 2, 1953
(Freedman, 1959, p. 282)

47 In 1952, the California Supreme Court had ruled that the city council could not cancel its agreement to build public housing, and that the upcoming public referendum on public housing would have no legally binding effect. Nevertheless, in June of that year, the majority of voters sided with the city council. The Supreme Court had no say over mayoral elections, however, and when the electorate voted Bowron out in 1953, they gave his successor, Norris Poulson, the opportunity to strike some new deals. The housing authority by this stage was substantially weakened and sought a compromise that would permit as many housing units to be built as possible.

A newsletter for the Washington-based National Housing Conference reported that Mayor Poulson, members of the Los Angeles city council, and representatives of the housing authority had met with Congressional and housing officials to negotiate the termination of the city's public housing program. The following was agreed upon:

> Those projects now under construction will be permitted to go ahead. The two large projects, where land has been acquired and cleared, will be stopped. The Federal Government will release the city and the housing authority from its contract. Proceeds from the sale of the land will reduce the Federal loss. The local authority will handle land disposition, and is given one year to dispose of it for a public purpose. If that fails, it will go under

the hammer to the highest bidder. The PHA [Public Housing Administration] has approximately $7,000,000 invested in these properties. It is hoped that enough will be returned from the land to reduce the Federal loss to some $5,000,000. Instead of 10,000 units under the Housing Act of 1949, Los Angeles will go forward with 4,300.

The Los Angeles decision set a dangerous precedent, for many other cities were trying to abrogate contracts.

> While negotiations were going on here Fritz Burns, Los Angeles builder and leading opponent of public housing was, with friends, hovering in the background [in Washington, D.C.]. Washington officialdom is happy over the settlement. So is Congressman John Phillips (R., Calif.) who was chairman of the House Conferees, as he managed to stop the national program and bail Los Angeles out at the same time. Los Angeles home builders are delighted, as are their colleagues in opposition to the program. The LOS ANGELES TIMES scores a great victory, and who cares about the families who stay in the slums or the taxpayers who cough up $5,000,000 to make a few people so very happy?[20]

Fritz Burns was not just an LA builder but a national player; that much is obvious. Moreover, he seems to have been present at each key moment in the upheaval at Chavez Ravine. California was leading the anti–public housing war, with Congressman Phillips at the head (see Freedman, 1959). In 1953, Burns was named to an advisory committee to the Federal Housing Administration. His ties to Eisenhower were direct, as indicated by his participation in an "off record" breakfast with the President when he came to Los Angeles in January of 1954. The political tide had definitively turned against the social appropriations of the New Deal programs; though it was just such federal help that had allowed the real estate industry to recover after the Depression, they used their recovered strength against public housing.

What to do with the Chavez Ravine land, now cleared of all but the last, litigating holdouts? Once it became obvious that no housing would be built on the site, the housing authority deeded the land to the city for park and recreational uses. Some accused the real estate interests of plotting the whole course of events so that they might spring upon the site, now cleared and ready for construction (Donovan, 1952). But this was not to be. By a strange series of machinations, Chavez Ravine would be virtually given away as a site for a professional baseball stadium. A recent standoff between Walter O'Malley, owner of the Brooklyn Dodgers, and New York's powerful parks commissioner, Robert

Moses, had left O'Malley with no acceptable replacement in the New York area for the Dodgers' Ebbets Field. Mayor Poulson met with O'Malley at the time of the 1956 World Series and proposed he send his engineers to evaluate the Chavez Ravine site (Henderson, 1980).[21] By his own account, Poulson was willing to do virtually anything to get the Dodgers to Los Angeles and to that site: "To save the day for the Dodgers and their legion of backers, there were strings that quietly had to be pulled. As mayor of Los Angeles at the time, I pulled them. And I have no regrets, even though the fallout doubtless cost me the last election" (Poulson, 1962, p. 15). The *Los Angeles Times* was fully behind the Dodger deal, as was the *Herald Examiner*. Burns, with ever-lengthening reach, seems to have had a hand in bringing the Dodgers to LA: O'Malley's son later said they could never have accomplished it without Burns.[22]

There was an outcry, primarily from Chavez Ravine residents still in the throes of eminent domain proceedings, that Chavez Ravine was to be maintained in public use. Without a public use, eminent domain could not continue. The city and O'Malley argued that various public recreational facilities would be built with the ballpark. Though these proposals varied from report to report, they variously included a zoo, park, golf course, or playgrounds. Officially, at the time of a public referendum on the plan, the plans included a 40-acre youth recreational area, which the Dodgers would maintain for 20 years.[23] Two serious legal challenges were waged: one by former residents of Chavez Ravine, one on the basis of the public use clause (Henderson, 1980). The Citizens Committee to Save Chavez Ravine for the People formed to campaign against turning the area over to the Dodgers. In spite of those efforts, voters in June of 1958 narrowly supported the city's contract with the Dodgers. The Dodgers got 315 acres along with $4.7 million worth of site grading and roads, in exchange for the 9-acre Wrigley Field that O'Malley had purchased in 1957 in another part of Los Angeles (Parson, 1993). Opening finally in 1962 and causing the worst traffic jam in the city's history, Dodger Stadium gave back to the city the 40-acre park and about $2,000,000 in annual taxes by 1972 (Henderson, 1980).

Even as Chavez Ravine technically slipped away from the public realm, eminent domain evictions continued. Though the *Times* supported the Dodger deal, the *News-Herald and Journal* decried it as an "utterly fantastic giveaway of the taxpayers' land and millions of dollars of their money . . . supported with all the power of the city's executive machinery" (Asa, 1959). Legal battles waged to stop the Dodger deal were based primarily, and ironically, on the terms of eminent domain. Land had been taken from private property owners for public purposes, for which a privately held baseball stadium did not qualify. But, as I described in section II, eminent domain in the United States had evolved to have

166   Anti-housing group protests against public housing in 1952.

167   Chavez Ravine with Dodger Stadium under construction at upper left.

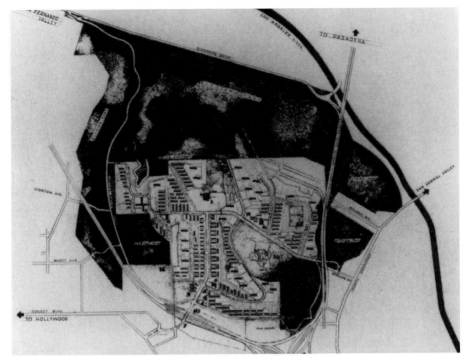

168   Site plan showing park wrapping around Elysian Park Heights public housing.

a very loose construction of public use. Eventually, the California Supreme Court ruled that O'Malley's contract with the city was legal. The U.S. Supreme Court dismissed a final appeal in 1959.

That left only the final evictions of remaining families from the Ravine. One extended family, the Arechigas, were offered $10,050 for land they claimed was worth $17,500 (see Poulson, 1966). It was one thing when the city wanted their land for public housing, but it was difficult to understand why the Dodgers shouldn't pay a fair price (Henderson, 1980). On what became known as Black Friday, May 9, 1959, the last residents were forcibly removed from their homes. The women of the Arechiga family resisted eviction; one was carried out kicking and screaming and another was sentenced to 30 days in jail (*Los Angeles Times,* 1959; Parson, 1993). In dismay, Mr. Arechiga watched as his home of thirty-six years was bulldozed while his wife threw stones at the evictors (Henderson, 1980).[24]

The publicity and violence of Chavez Ravine's takeover remains part of LA's Latino heritage. Indeed, recent real estate activity in the area remains mindful of the Chavez Ravine history. Large developers holding land that extends from Aliso Village north to Dodger Stadium advise their consultants to tread quietly through Solano, a working-class Latino neighborhood adjacent to Chavez Ravine that watched as their neighbors' homes were destroyed. Since then, residents have vigorously opposed threats to their own neighborhood to avoid the same fate.

Next, Bunker Hill

48 In 1954, the same year that Rodger Young Village was closed, a year after public housing was soundly beaten back at Chavez Ravine, Los Angeles's city council approved redevelopment plans for Bunker Hill. About 10,000 residents would be displaced, the same number that would have been housed in the final schemes for Chavez Ravine. This was no coincidence; it was the plan: "There are 7,000 substandard dwelling units in the Bunker Hill area. Elysian Park Heights will provide the legally-required homes for families of low income living in Bunker Hill when the Community Redevelopment Agency begins its redevelopment of that area."[25] The Bunker Hill dwellers were mostly poor people of color, many elderly, who lived in once-grand old Victorians, now subdivided and dilapidated. As Donald Parson notes in his essay of 1993, it was ironic that the enemies of "creeping socialism" were extremely vocal when federal subsidy crept into affordable housing, but silent about the subsidy to private real estate investors at Bunker Hill, or to Dodger Stadium at Chavez Ravine. The end of public housing signaled the effective dislodging of slum clearance from housing construction for the poor, and its reassignment to support downtown business interests.

It was the housing authority's executive director, Howard Holtzendorff, who had approached Simon Eisner, then with the city planning department, to become the first employee—acting director—of a redevelopment agency for the city of Los Angeles. In 1949, Eisner had grand plans for redevelopment: "LA has

60 square miles of blighted area, and we were going to tackle that thing whole-sale. . . . I was naïve and thought that once you had a federal law and lots of money, you could do anything" (Eisner, 1992, p. 57). Six months later, a discouraged Eisner left the redevelopment agency to join Alexander and Neutra as the site planner for Chavez Ravine.

In its initial formation, the redevelopment agency showed its biases: its officers were involved in real estate, big retail, and construction. Eisner recalled that before one member would act on any decision, "he would call people at the realty board to find out if they would approve his actions" (Eisner, 1992, p. 58). Eisner remarked, "Here again, you see the influence of the downtown business people and again, the reconstruction of the central area" (p. 57). According to Eisner, it was at this time that the city council realized that redevelopment need not be a housing program but could be used as an opportunity to "acquire land and reconstruct the economic value of it, write down the costs and make it available to private enterprise to do private work . . . giving private enterprise a great big plum" (p. 61).

Urban redevelopment, in fact, had demonstrated just how effectively a housing program could undermine affordable housing. Early public housing efforts were relatively neutral; by Abrams's calculations (1946), the 1937 Housing Act built 170,000 dwellings nationwide for low-income families but demolished 142,583 of the same. In Los Angeles, 3,468 were demolished in conjunction with the first ten public housing sites, which contained nearly 3,500 units (Los Angeles, Housing Authority, 1955, p. 44). But later redevelopment had the potential to eviscerate the city of its low-income housing; Abrams's multifaceted analysis demonstrated its overwhelming benefit to the real estate industry rather than to home seekers. Indeed, the promise or specter of redevelopment, depending on one's perspective, underlies all postwar urban housing.

The Housing Act of 1949, and its Title I provision in particular, created the urban renewal program. This act made redevelopment economically feasible via subsidies to reduce site costs to developers. In cities across the country, this sparked new actions targeting blight; condemnations, demolition, and site preparation followed. Politically pushed by groups like the Central Business District Council of the Urban Land Institute, downtown businessmen and real estate interests got their wish to replace low-income neighborhoods with everything from office buildings to convention centers (Weiss, 1980).

Soon after the 1949 Housing Act passed, it became clear that still further incentives would be needed to entice lenders into the renewal areas. In 1954, the Housing Act was amended and a generous mortgage insurance program (the FHA 220 program) initiated a new, widespread wave of construction. Historians like Alex Garvin (1996), who advocate private-sector development, see these programs as among the innovative cures to urban ills. Critics like Abrams, and more recently Boyer (1973), argue that government supports should have aided the broadest tier at the bottom of the social pyramid, but instead lined the pockets of for-profit real estate speculators. By 1967, urban renewal had demolished about 400,000 residential units, rebuilding fewer than 11,000 units on those sites (Weiss, 1980).

The urban renewal programs basically reduced or removed the up-front costs and risks to developers: site assembly and acquisition, costs to relocate a site's residents, demolition and site clearance, site grading, and infrastructure. The FHA had done approximately the same thing for homebuilders since the war. These tasks were not only costly but extremely time-consuming (a risk in its own right). Urban renewal meant that the risk would be shouldered by local authorities via federal mandate, or in other words by the taxpayers.

While downtown commercial interests favored these developments, however, private residential builders often did not. As public opinion had turned against low-rent housing, Fritz Burns extended his efforts to campaign against federal subsidies for slum clearance. Burns wanted to convince the public and policymakers that slum clearance could be done without tax dollars, since he saw slum clearance as the public-sector foot in the door to housing construction. Although Burns's Build America Better Council had helped shape national urban redevelopment policy, he eventually opposed urban renewal in the celebrated case of Bunker Hill. The ubiquitous Burns owned property there too. In order to demonstrate effective private solutions to blight, he and his son Patrick remodeled a rundown house on Bunker Hill, converting it into two apartments. Many news clippings noted the tremendous increase in rents they gained, with an implicit argument against federal subsidy of slum clearance. A 1952 *Times* story, headlined "Slum Clearance Report Jostles Housing Advocates," reported the head of the city's Building and Safety Department's conclusion that "90% of the city's so-called substandard housing units can be rehabilitated by enforcing present health and building laws" (*Los Angeles Times*, 1952). This had sure taxpayer appeal. In the paradoxical political climate to follow, housing advocates formed "Citizens for Slum Clearance" and the pro-business, anti-housing *Times* put a photo on its front page of residents locking out appraisers coming to condemn their homes for new public housing (August 20, 1952).

The Bunker Hill neighborhood sat adjacent to the central business district, nearly surrounding City Hall. It would be transformed from a collection of multifamily affordable dwellings to a commercial extension of downtown. According to Alexander (1989), Bunker Hill had been targeted for slum clearance very early in the thirties under the Public Works Administration's housing program. As in other such cases, the area had been primed to become a site long before its

169 Fritz B. Burns, with hands outstretched, argues against public housing in 1952. Examiner Photos.

actual transformation. In the redevelopment agency's initial proposal, known as the Babcock report (Babcock, 1951), some $35 million in federal redevelopment funds would demolish Bunker Hill's slums and rebuild a series of high-rise apartment buildings. Supported by downtown business interests, the proposal was opposed by residential builders within the real estate industry, a split in political-financial interests that in part defines the political economy of the contemporary city. Eventually, Alexander designed and built just one residential tower in the first phase of Bunker Hill's upheaval.

In the Babcock report, the proposed apartment density would have located 170 families to the acre, compared to the 39.6 families to the acre at Park La Brea, or 22 per acre proposed at Elysian Park Heights.[26] Now, strange bedfellows: progressive councilman Ed Roybal and the housing authority were on the same side as Fritz Burns, all suggesting that Bunker Hill as outlined in the Babcock report was an extreme case of residential development. The housing authority used it to show that private multistory housing was feasible, undermining arguments against high-rise housing in public housing. The building lobby's root concern was not density but the use of vacant land for new, federal construction. Of the eleven sites for which the authority proposed new public housing, three involved significant amounts of unused vacant land.[27]

When the housing authority and its supporters defended the use of vacant land for new public housing, it did so with three rationales. First, these were still slum clearance projects under the equivalent elimination provision. Slums in industrial areas were not suitable for new housing, but could be redeveloped appropriately as industrial sites, and those units demolished counted toward one-for-one elimination so that public housing could be built on vacant land. Second, in areas like West Los Angeles, "there are not concentrated slum areas" but scattered, substandard dwellings "blighting otherwise standard residential neighborhoods." If new public housing was built, deteriorated housing could be condemned and families relocated into new low-rent housing. Lastly, vacant land developed as affordable housing would generate much-needed civic revenue, paid by the city housing authority as "Payments in Lieu of Taxes."[28]

The policies of urban renewal temporally restructured real estate development, yielding very specific political possibilities. First, given the long time periods involved, local opposition could have an impact. Second, local agencies and political powers could modify initial plans over the duration of the project. Any lingering ideas about constructing affordable housing could be slowly excised. Because there were few of the regular financial imperatives to move projects quickly to completion, low-rent residential parts of cities were demolished and then remained inactive for years. During that time, all kinds of political machinations operated upon the project. In Los Angeles, public housing at Chavez Ravine became Dodger Stadium; the apartments planned for Bunker Hill became office towers.

Convulsive City, Urban Krill

49

When the [1937 Housing Act] started out, it was hailed by housers all over the country as a slum clearance law. This was the impetus that got it going. By the time that it got through Congress, it was no longer a humanitarian law, it was a property law. This is not unlike the Constitution of the United States, as far as that goes. By the time that Congress got through with it, the question became: is the property distressed? What can we do to improve the value of the property? Not what can we do to help the people. (Alexander, 1989, p. 546)

According to Robert Alexander, historically significant architecture was demolished along with tenements at Bunker Hill, based on early plans to excavate the entire hill from the city. Large pieces of fine-grained residential areas—lots of individual houses—were consumed by the whale-sized, state-subsidized utopias, from Aliso Village to Elysian Park Heights at Chavez Ravine. Only the state could confer the right to demolish so much in the name of the public good. The small buildings demolished merited little interest, and good intentions were hardly bothered by the significance their sum might hold. Their sum was not valued. In the inner-city cases, the pieces were never seen as a coherent grouping because the slum meant chaos. Unified utopian visions were to take their place. But those visions did not win over the hearts and pocketbooks of middle America, as Catherine Bauer analyzed in an incisive article in 1953. Even Alexander, strangely enough, criticized his and Neutra's proposed design, saying it was probably better that Elysian Park Heights was never built (Alexander, 1989).

Indeed, the modernist aesthetic of public housing had become the emblem of its own inadequacy—as decent housing, as urban salvation, as a solution to poverty. Instead, the nation elected to transform nature into the garden city, buying up houses on recently converted agricultural land at the urban fringe. These were not, however, typical suburban developments as we now think of them, for these wartime and early postwar subdivisions were not bedroom communities but were specifically located near jobs and industrial areas (Hise, 1997). The recipe for developing property, however, was fundamentally the same as for later suburban subdivisions, including some form of federal support: housing development led an area's growth; once populated, it attracted commercial and retail development as well. Then it would be up to the residents, through political means, to gather the public infrastructure of schools, parks, transportation, playgrounds, and cultural institutions.

Chavez Ravine and Westchester are linked not only by federal subsidy but by upheaval instigated by public institutions. The Homes at Wholesale demolished to make way for the airport were similar to the homes at Chavez Ravine and The Flats: inexpensive, small, rather thin constructions occupied by people of commensurately slim economic means. Indeed, few if any homeplaces in the urban landscape are stable. Even as we imagine our homes as our most protected form of property, our rights in them are limited and our security elusive.

While Westchester demonstrates the practices and efficacy of realtors beginning in the 1940s, its success parallels the decline in public housing epitomized at Chavez Ravine and the rise of urban renewal for downtown business interests. Though eminent domain would be used in urban redevelopment projects through the 1960s, never again would property seizures be justified on the basis of eradicating slums while simultaneously replenishing the affordable residential stock with public housing. The political defeat of the public housing program at Chavez Ravine left urban revitalization in the hands of developers who had already mastered the art of framing public policy and obtaining funds to further their own work. This legacy is still apparent in practices of urban development today, as confirmed by the final case study, Playa Vista.

In the battle over housing, *Southwest Builder and Contractor,* the region's principal forum for news across the building industry,[29] remained relatively silent on the issue. On occasion it expressed an anti-socialist, anti-Communist view, but never in direct relation to the housing debate. Clearly, the various members of the building industry had something to gain from federal programs, even if it might be ideologically distasteful. Not until April of 1952 do the editors argue that public housing is directly tied to delinquency; a month later they take a far stronger position: "Exaggeration, equivocation, and even prevarication have become, it seems, an accepted part of every political campaign. But seldom have there been such heavy doses of them as are being fed to the people of Los Angeles by the proponents of socialized housing in that city" (1952c, p. 7). By this point, construction costs for residential builders were declining, materials were more readily available, and private industry had a strong case to make for edging the government out of construction.

By 1954, public housing as it had been known was ended. According to the newsletter of the National Housing Conference,

> This morning, the Senate-House Conferees on the Independent Offices Appropriation Bill for fiscal year 1954, tied the noose on the low-rent public housing program. They agreed on a program for this fiscal year of 20,000 unit starts to be made from *existing* loans and annual contributions contracts. *No* new loan and annual contributions contracts may be entered into. In other words the program is in the process of liquidation. It is stopped dead in its tracks. It marks a complete victory on the Washington front for the opponents of low-rent housing. It marks a disastrous defeat for those families, living in slums, who believed their Government in 1949 when the Congress adopted a housing policy of a decent home for every American family.[30]

Besides ending public housing, the Chavez Ravine case proved the efficacy of referendum politics. Public opinion was politically maneuvered by powerful influence and deep pockets with an urban agenda on the part of groups like CASH, the downtown business lobby, or the *Los Angeles Times,* and then recorded through votes. The anti–public housing vote of 1952 and Proposition B of 1958, the baseball referendum, were effective determinants in Chavez Ravine.

The stories of both Chavez Ravine and Westchester reflect the larger narratives of the book. Each was an upheaval of large scale that radically transformed one place into another, via a totalizing utopia. Each proposed new housing in a whole community package, with shops, schools, and residents preconceived. The upheavals varied in terms of contestation: while Chavez Ravine sparked confrontations that undid mayors, council members, city employees, and homeowners, Westchester came about with no such protest. It fit the standing model of urban transformation, and no one cried for the displaced beans and hogs. But Westchester is a major player in a contention that followed, due to its geographic proximity to Playa Vista.

The stories of Chavez Ravine and Westchester epitomize urban political ideology shaped during World War II. Architecture, property rights, and economics intertwined to unleash each convulsion. The architecture envisioned at Chavez Ravine by Neutra and Alexander was modern and utopian; this helped the opposition, as it gathered support for the view that public housing was anti-American. What actually got built at Chavez Ravine was conventional to the utmost degree.[31] At Chavez Ravine, as at Riverside South in New York or the Pruitt-Igoe site in St. Louis, the upheaval was so raucous as to produce wholly incongruous, unexpected outcomes. Perhaps the American city was less prepared for the striking future it had conjured than it was for the war that set the city in motion. The city would erupt, inevitably, rapidly, repeatedly, and as it did so it would wipe out the past just as it refused to lay out the future. The sense of the provisional pervades this period of the city's growth. Chavez Ravine stands as a transitional project: it targeted an older, poorer neighborhood of color for demolition, which rose up against its fate; it targeted an underdeveloped site preserved by its physical characteristics, in this case, rugged topography. Playa Vista, the last case we will examine in depth, also resisted development because of its environmental qualities, in that case a wetlands. The frontier of urban convulsions has shifted, but to no less politicized terrain: from slums to environmentally sensitive ground.

Large-scale convulsions like Chavez Ravine (or Playa Vista, as we shall see) are so disruptive and unstable that they can morph, midstream, into a wholly other form than the one intended. When the Elysian Park Heights plan was rejected, it left no more trace than the Chavez Ravine inhabitants who had been displaced. Dodger Stadium appeared from another quarter, its rocky prehistory illegible in its final form. The forces of modern urban transformation were powerfully present throughout: large scale, property rights, and upheaval. Murals in the city record what the environment itself obscures, as do memorial texts by all the major participants. Chavez Ravine's contested ground remains a contested history, a problem not of forgetting but of remembering in such a way that the spatially victorious do not overwhelm the record. And Chavez Ravine, with Dodger Stadium, is primed to undergo a new upheaval in the coming decade.

VIII

Political Evolution of
Property and Voice

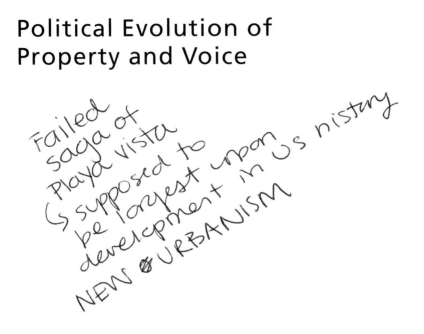

Failed saga of Playa Vista
(s supposed to be largest urban development in US history
NEW URBANISM

50 When Proposition 10 on the California state ballot passed in November of 1950, it symbolized a new, more restricted relationship between local and state politics, between property rights and policy, between homeowners and those in need of housing. This proposition, sponsored by the real estate lobby (or lobbies, as Marcuse [1995] reminds us), required a referendum in every county or city to approve, by a majority of qualified voting electors, any "low rent housing project by the State, or any county, city, district authority, or other state public body." Thereafter, no state action to promote the construction of affordable housing was possible without the local approval of voters. Until this point in time, the state could effectively redesign the provision of low-income housing, converting slums into public housing projects. With Prop 10 in California, slums could still be razed but new low-rent housing could not replace the old without great political effort. This surely assisted the transformation of slum clearance from a tool for affordable housing to one for commercial redevelopment in the urban renewal programs of the fifties and sixties.[1]

In this instance, what was billed as a victory for property owners and taxpayers was in fact one for commercial real estate interests and residential builders. Commercial real estate benefited from having massive federal urban renewal funds rerouted in their direction (and away from low-income housing). Residential builders benefited from the removing of federal agencies from low-cost housing production, a goal they had long sought in order to reduce competition for entry-level housing. More importantly, it helped shift policy toward financial supports for the private housing market.

In the evolution of participatory planning in urban development and architecture, it is not always clear who benefits from increased citizen participation, as the example of Prop 10 demonstrates. It is clear, however, that housing is made less affordable by the process and less of that housing is actually constructed (see Frieden, 1979). In his analysis of group opposition to public housing, political scientist Leonard Freedman draws some general conclusions for public policy. Most relevantly, he notes that "if those opposing a program cannot prevent its being passed into law, they will try to write into the law provisions that multiply the number of points at which decisions on its implementation must be made" (1959, p. 394). This strategy has proven particularly effective, since it appears to serve public interest even while predominantly benefiting organized opposition, the latter structured to operate more effectively within the legislative context. Thus well-funded, special interest lobbies fare better under this multiple-decision-point strategy than local citizen interest groups (Freedman, 1959, p. 395).

In the thirties and forties, when a new conception of the city was being formulated in the United States, slums and blight were contrasted with planning. Only with "completely designed communities" would the benefits of community spirit be realized.[2] This thinking on the part of American housing and planning advocates like the Regional Planning Association of America had its international roots in the Congrès Internationaux d'Architecture Moderne, or CIAM, which held its first gathering in 1928. The "functional city," as formulated by CIAM members, treated five general urban components, at least four of which could be properly and separately zoned: housing, commerce, recreation, transportation. (The fifth, regularly overlooked by adherents and analysts, was that of historic buildings.) This doctrine was clearly articulated in CIAM's Athens Charter of 1933 (see Frampton, 1980), and the significant role of historical structures and regional context was further emphasized at the next congress in 1937. A successful theorizing of the extant city, however, was never produced in conjunction with the rational new urban ideal—and a very large ideal that was. It is ironic that what I have been calling large-scale upheavals in Los Angeles are truly dwarfed by CIAM undertakings like Costa and Niemeyer's Brasília or Le Corbusier's Chandigarh.

Anthropologist James Holston, in his study of Brasília (1989), notes that the motivation of modernist planning is the wish to create a new social order. An unwanted present condition is to be transformed by means of a physically embodied utopian future (see also Holston, 1998). He adds a tentative insight: "This ideology of planning is utopian, not because it is critical of the present or because it has as its objective the disruption of taken-for-granted norms. . . . Rather, it is utopian because its notion of alternative futures is based on absent causes and its methods on a theory of total decontextualization" (Holston, 1989, p. 41). Thus, without any cultural impetus save the master plan itself, modern housing and the modern city can be invented in the hopes that it will produce its own social milieu, its own proper occupants. Frank Lloyd Wright made the same claims in a sense, for he believed that the true problem of American housing was that Americans did not know how they *ought* to live (see Kruft, 1994).

Modern housing corroborates Holston's description. It exploited new technology for a rather nebulous vision of a future modern society. Modern housing advocates surely saw the problems in the inner city, but these were not their primary interest; they adopted the critique of existing slum conditions out of necessity. Thus, negative present conditions supply the political motivation for the plan, which serves to ground the vacancy of the future. In America after the turn of the century, and particularly in Los Angeles, the slums—an unwanted present—were exaggerated and conceptually extended, in order to make their eradication compulsory. To clean up the blight required the creation of a new community, where a new society could be envisioned.

This architectural and planning leap toward the future cannot, of course, be made without recourse to the past. This sets up a "utopian paradox,"[3] in which a kind of perverted exaggeration of the unwanted present is created by the very process that aims to eradicate it. Public housing, as it evolved, has become just that perversion of the blight it sought to cure. In that sense, the provisional city is constantly reconstructing itself as provisional and in upheaval.

When the modernist planners put forward ideas about modern communities, state authority was at the ready, joining as general partner in the remaking of cities. This stands in contrast to the work of private builders, with whom the state participated as a silent partner, in no less helpful but far less utopian a manner. In the final analysis, this was the genius of private builders as well as their tether. It remains to be seen whether the not-so-new but ever more explicit public-private undertakings, such as Playa Vista, hold a different future for their communities.

Utopian planning has at its root centralized state authority: "the apparatus of the modern state as the supreme planning power" (Holston, 1998). This feeds the large-scale urge of utopia to be all-encompassing and comprehensive. Public housing developments in America are a prime example of such modern planning, but this study also raises the issue of modern community planning in the context of the commercial builder. Within a capitalist economy where real estate is imagined as one more commodity, the market determines what can be built where, and for whom. When Henry Kaiser's Housing Division rejected the modern-styled aluminum house or the all-plastic house, they did so for purely economic reasons. However, on the Kaiser drawing boards were stick-built modernist houses to be located alongside the ridge-roofed Defender and the beshuttered Cape Cod. These economical modernist plans never saw the light of day either, for reasons of popular taste embodied in FHA regulation. As salesman-par-excellence Fritz Burns instructed, flat roofs ranked with Negro families among marketing dangers to be avoided at all costs. So Westchester, and for the most part Playa Vista, were planned with market assumptions in mind. This made not for social or architectural utopia, but for slight economic advantage over other options. Like the kind of innovation described as "reductionist," the Kaiser-Burns communities were not unlike what Burns had built in many other locations, except for being somewhat less plagued by crosstown traffic, slightly better equipped, more ready for move-in, and with better loan terms. Compared to vernacular traditions of house building which make almost invisible incremental changes generation after generation, Kaiser and Burns leapt forward in a radical way. But compared to the non-market-driven, utopian planning of the modern housing advocates, the private builders were regressive.

The private building enterprise, of course, is now not at all private, but solidly backed by the same apparatus of the modern state that fed public housing. Significantly, however, rather than acting as a supreme planning power by improving conditions in the physical realm, in private development the state improves conditions in the socioeconomic realm. The state does not make better cities, but better buyers. This is a utopia for private builders, to be sure.

Managed through the Department of Housing and Urban Development, there are about a million units of public housing left in the United States. Much of this housing was built in the 1940s, on sites that have since become prime urban property. These old, large public housing developments are blamed for the poor conditions of their surrounding neighborhoods. Federal loans to local authorities are now paid off, cuts in operating budgets have left them in grave disrepair, a very poor, disadvantaged population is in residence, public opinion is extremely unfavorable, and real estate prices are attractively high. All this has led former HUD secretary Henry Cisneros and his successor, Andrew Cuomo, to champion what is called the HOPE VI Program, by which older, low-density developments are "revitalized" to create mixed-income communities. Sometimes this means tearing everything down, as in the case of Normont Terrace in Los Angeles (see fig. 19). Or in the case of Pico-Aliso, it can mean targeted demolition and rehabilitation, with some new construction.

Just as architectural modernism came to stand for early public housing ideology, the replacement housing at the end of the twentieth century would

170 New public housing, made to look like a bit of suburbia, was built in downtown Los Angeles in 1999 to re-place the demolished units of Pico-Aliso public housing. Photographer: Beth Holden.

have its distinct architectural character. According to Cuomo, the government has adopted the practices identified with New Urbanism:

> We stress New Urbanist principles because we've seen that they work. Developments that use these principles are planned with the human ele-ment in mind. They offer a mix of houses, townhouses, apartments, and businesses, and are more cohesive than suburban subdivisions. Streets flow with the community, rather than ending in cul-de-sacs or dead ends. Houses present their faces to the neighborhood rather than being set back and isolated. There are sidewalks that people actually use. By design, these communities make it easier for people to interact with neighbors and also walk to shops and—ideally—jobs. (Cuomo, 1997, pp. 47, 49)

There is good political thinking in such a decision. Though Cuomo argues for traditional town planning over the suburban model, it simultaneously flies di-rectly in the face of the much-criticized modernism it will replace. Rather than projecting the optimism of a new and better future, as did modernism, the neo-traditional principles of New Urbanism would have us believe that small towns, pedestrians, mixed use, and vernacular architectural traditions should never have been discarded. The popular desire for these traditional elements of cities has spread the promotion of New Urbanism, because it helps public- and private-sector builders make it through the public trials that any development will suffer prior to construction. This is a retro utopia, and its multifarious contradictions will become apparent in the following discussion.

I have endeavored in the preceding chapters to document the emergence of development strategies that characterize modern American urbanism. In order to bring that historical view to contemporary relevance, I offer one final case, that of Playa Vista: 1,087 acres at the southwestern edge of Los Angeles.[4] The politics of planning at Playa Vista bear witness to the remarkable changes that have transpired since Aliso Village and Elysian Park Heights were planned. Yet architecture, urban design, community politics, planning policy, and environmental preservation participate in the making of the contemporary city in ways that are linked to the earlier period, even though they may at first be unrecognizable.

The Playa Vista Saga

51 Some ten miles north of the site where Playa Vista remained in crysalis stage, a round red sticker was visible on each of the lampposts and parking meters on Lincoln Boulevard: "Boycott DreamWorks. Save the Ballona Wetlands," referring to the primary occupant and environmental feature of Playa Vista, respectively. Twenty years after its inception, Playa Vista remained in the planning stage, and the opposition, while sporadically appeased, may never be quelled. In November of 1998 DreamWorks SKG, the powerhouse creative firm of Hollywood and Disney heroes, signed a long-negotiated agreement to locate in Playa Vista, which seemed to cinch the entire development venture. Not necessarily. Some eighty different opposition groups, national and local, combined to form the Citizens United to Save All of Ballona, permitting DreamWorks its 60 acres but proposing that the other 1,030 acres become a public park and nature preserve (Gibson, 1999).[5] In 1999, DreamWorks pulled out. Legal environmental challenges ongoing at the time of this writing, the departure of key players, new development teams, and changing political and economic climates have extended the perpetual limbo that has characterized the immense project for over two decades. All these comings and goings have transpired in the harsh light of extensive media coverage, encouraging various interest groups to leap back into the fray whenever there was energy and an opening. If Playa Vista proceeds as planned, it will be the New Urbanists' biggest experiment. It will house 30,000

171   Playa Vista's site, looking west with Hughes buildings in the foreground.

residents and 21,000 workers, comprising the largest urban development in U.S. history at a total of $6–8 billion in development costs (Gibson, 1999).

Playa Vista was designed as a set of mixed-use, pedestrian-oriented "villages," with high-density, low-rise and mid-rise development. It puts a priority on the public realm: a full 50 percent of the site is dedicated to some form of open space (Katz, 1994). This calculation includes the marina, the bluffs, the concrete flood control channel, and the wetlands. The design imagery derives from local vernacular or regionalist architectural tradition, but it also stands in contradistinction to the suburbs. Peter Katz, in one of the first books to attempt a comprehensive survey of this form of urban design, says the New Urbanism "addresses many of the ills of our current sprawl development pattern while returning to a cherished American icon: that of a compact, close-knit community" (1994, p. ix).

General Description

There are several different development zones in the current Playa Vista site plan, labeled A through D (see fig. 172). Zone A, at the northwest corner of Ballona Creek and Lincoln Boulevard, is planned as an extension of the adjacent marina. Zone B abuts the wetlands that are to be conserved, and includes a relatively small amount of housing and retail, as does Zone C. Zone D is the largest zone, extending east below the bluffs from Lincoln and comprising perhaps two-

172 Playa Vista development areas: A includes the marina, B the wetlands. Area D was the first to begin development.

thirds of the intended construction. Here site grading was initiated in the late nineties along with demolition of most of the Hughes industrial buildings. In it is the commercial zone, called the "village center," and the majority of the mixed-use residential and retail, along with all the office and hotel development. Small pockets of parkland are distributed throughout the residential areas (see fig. 173, middle) to go with the preserved wetlands and the linear open space at the base of the bluffs. Some of the open space is to be developed for recreational uses, including bike trails, a wetlands interpretation center, and playing fields.

As is apparent in the site plan, the overall area is organized around traditional neighborhood blocks, with a predominant north-south orientation to take in views to the bluffs. It was the designers' intention to counter typical, broad-brush land use plans with a fine-grained, block-by-block study of building types. Street sections have been designed, as have typological buildings, so that developers purchasing parts of the master-planned Playa Vista will have more than zoning and building envelops to guide them. It is not at all clear, to the designers or to the public, however, whether there will be any mechanism besides good faith to insure adherence to the master plan.

Nowhere is there serious debate recorded about how that "compact, close-knit community" might work out in relation to Playa Vista, or just how close and compact a development the size of Playa Vista could be. What happens when the 80 acres of Seaside, the seminal New Urbanist development in Florida,

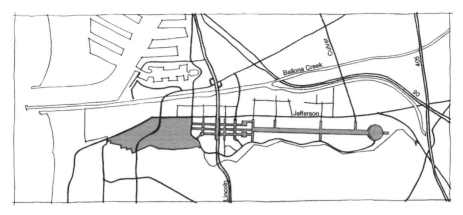

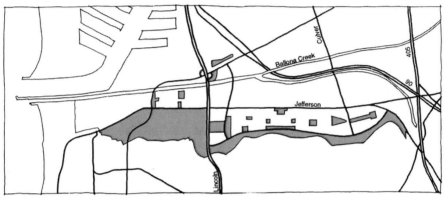

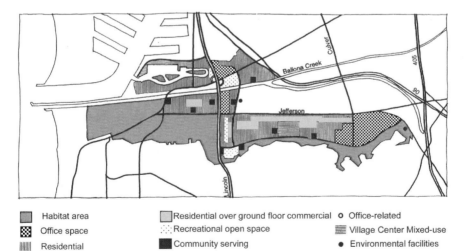

	Habitat area		Residential over ground floor commercial	○	Office-related
	Office space		Recreational open space		Village Center Mixed-use
	Residential		Community serving	●	Environmental facilities

173   Playa Vista: top site plan shows open spaces that would have been developed in the Pei/Cobb scheme; middle plan shows open spaces of the New Urbanist scheme by Duany, Plater-Zyberk, et al.; lower plan shows the land use patterns of the New Urbanist scheme. Ken Gutierrez.

are multiplied to Playa Vista's 1,087? And whether or not the latter still resembles an "authentic neighborhood" (Katz, 1994, p. 179), whatever that might mean, is entirely dubious. One of the problems of New Urbanism, not unknown to modernism, is the sloppy bantering of easy terms like community, neighborhood, tradition, and authenticity. Embedded in an ideological program, New Urbanism as a movement has the very marketable advantage over its modern predecessors, or deconstructivist peers, of being acceptable to the public. This acceptance is given for both the ideology of the traditional neighborhood and the regionalist aesthetics. Corporate developers in particular see New Urbanism as a tool for gaining entitlements, market appeal, and inexpensive construction.

174   New Urbanist site plan of Playa Vista from the early 1990s.

175   Block plan and planting scheme for the area where preserved wetlands and mixed-use development meet at Lincoln Boulevard.

176 One of the recommended street sections for Playa Vista, showing considerations of parking, traffic, pedestrians, plantings, and building massing.

Traditional small-town planning in the largest-ever urban undertaking certainly gives one pause. In the case of Playa Vista, the design politics of New Urbanism dovetail with the development campaign for public support. Playa Vista has sponsored national sustainable development meetings, a limited construction jobs program for at-risk youth, ecological reclamation of debris from demolition, and affordable housing units. These programs have won politician-advocates from the federal level down. Whether these constitute substantial efforts or propaganda ploys depends on your perspective.

Historical Perspective

Back in the 1940s, Howard Hughes bought over a thousand acres along Ballona Creek in western Los Angeles County in order to build a landing strip and aircraft facilities in the site's easternmost portion. Under contract with the government, the dashing and eccentric tycoon employed the site for defense industry experimentation with wooden aircraft, since the same materials shortages experienced by homebuilders were limiting essential war production. Hughes built a spectacular redwood hangar for construction of the Spruce Goose, a prototype cargo carrier and the largest wooden plane ever made. Eventually, some two million square feet of industrial and aircraft facilities would be built there, yet the bulk of Hughes's property remained grasslands and a few beanfields. Most significantly, a sizable wetlands comprised the western reaches, attracting migratory birds and providing the ecosystem for a variety of animal species. These wetlands, even in the forties, were not "natural," since flood controls, oil

177　Some of the Hughes industrial sheds remaining on the Playa Vista site in 1999. Photographer: Dana Cuff.

drilling, bathing resorts, and river diversions had substantially altered local ecological cycles. For a time, the site had contained the Los Angeles River at the
point where it met the Pacific Ocean. The area was, however, a small remnant of
the extensive wetlands that had since been covered by the houses and commercial development of south Venice.

It was, in part, the proximity of Hughes Aircraft that gave Westchester its
raison d'être. Where Ballona Creek now spills into the Pacific Ocean is the place
where the young Fritz Burns catapulted himself into the subdividers' big league
in the 1920s with Palisades del Rey, now called Playa del Rey (see fig. 14). Indeed,
on one panoramic photo shot from the wetlands toward Westchester, Burns had
drawn rather gleeful dollar signs across the bluffs marking the edge of Playa Vista
and his real estate dreams. Two decades later, Burns, first with Fred Marlow and
later with Kaiser, would be instrumental in the development of Westchester as
defense housing for Northrup, Douglas, as well as Hughes Aircraft.

Not long after Howard Hughes died in 1976, his heirs initiated comprehensive planning for Playa Vista. Over two decades later, earth moving finally began, though signs of construction were slow to follow. The saga of Playa Vista has
been complicated in both typical and special ways. A thousand-acre development
in a major urban center is unimaginably complex. To exacerbate matters, as

Playa Vista was being planned in the mid-seventies, the environmental conservation movement became a legitimate player in the overall development process through the mechanism of the environmental impact report. The California initiative process, well known for its obstreperous overriding of representative government (as we saw at Chavez Ravine), had put in place an extensive set of coastline regulations that would impact the Hughes property. In 1972 the citizens of California first spoke out, albeit indirectly, on the fate of Playa Vista when they passed Proposition 20: the Coastal Initiative. Californians had seen their elected representatives siding with big developers (who were also big political donors) and decided to take urban growth matters into their own hands. About half, or 560 acres, of the Hughes property fell into the coastal zone, requiring a local planning element and oversight by the Coastal Commission.

An increasingly effective cadre of community groups had been established, to a significant degree, by federal appropriations to community organizations for social programs (see Castells, 1983). No-growth advocacy had proven able to halt what had seemed like a steamroller over quality of life. In general, the seventies saw the clear and confident expansion of real property rights for those who held an interest but not a deed. The general set of property relations among actors, previously restricted to those more conventionally enfranchised, quickly grew more complex.

Since the forties, Playa Vista had been steadily surrounded by a sea of neighborhoods. Nearby residents viewed the grassy interruption as their own scruffy Central Park, an open space in an otherwise overpopulated cityscape. Although various community organizations expressed civic interest in the land, none was more focused, and eventually effective, than the conservation group called Friends of Ballona Wetlands. It was formed in 1978, just after Howard Hughes Properties set up Summa Corporation to handle its planning effort and the possibility of a Playa Vista development became apparent to the public. Six years later, the Friends of Ballona Wetlands had 1,500 active members.

Howard Hughes Properties planned its development within the guidelines set forth by the Coastal Initiative, including public workshops which took place in 1981. At the end of 1982, the LA County Planning Commission and the LA County Board of Supervisors approved the proposed land use plan and submitted it to the Coastal Commission. With some modifications, approval was granted two years later for intense recreational and commercial development.[6] In this scheme, a 209-acre "habitat management area" was allotted, but the disgruntled Friends of Ballona Wetlands, having lobbied for about 360 acres, decided to sue all parties to the plan, including the Coastal Commission and the county. As further activity on Playa Vista proceeded and the public grew more aware of the scale of development, traffic joined the wetlands as a flashpoint of

178   Vignettes for Playa Vista emphasize pastoral scenery and leisure time.

179   Vignette rendering of a village center in Playa Vista.

antagonism. According to some estimates, 200,000 car trips a day would be generated, a load comparable to the nearby LA International Airport. A series of events served to heighten public suspicion about the entire Playa Vista enterprise.

With the 1984 go-ahead from the Coastal Commission, Summa hired Welton Becket Associates, coincidentally the architectural firm that had designed Burns's exhibition homes (the Postwar House, which became the Home of Tomorrow). It may have been that same corporate futurism of limited, acceptable innovation that attracted Summa to Becket. Now, more than a model home, the firm would have the chance to plan an entire model city. In 1984, Becket Associates brought in Harry Cobb of I. M. Pei, along with landscape architects, traffic engineers, and lawyers, to create the overall physical form of Playa Vista.

Community leaders remember Summa representatives as arrogant and uninterested, presenting proposals as *faits accomplis*. Summa representatives, by contrast, recall hundreds of community meetings. In one meeting that has become an urban legend, Summa called together a group of community leaders to unveil their concept plan. "A gray velvet cover was thrown back and here was a complete model. I knew then that it was a done deal. I was mad as a wet hen," said the leader of a local resident organization.[7] The monochrome and relatively abstract model showed a well-developed central open-space spine (see fig. 173, top) lined with high-rise office towers in a field of lower-density housing. Westchester residents were incensed that the high-rises exceeded the height of their bluffs. Other neighbors saw that the automobile-based proposal would generate an unacceptable amount of traffic. The abstract high-rises were visually completed by viewers who knew, and hated, a nearby glazed tower recently completed by Summa called the Wang Building.

The councilwoman for the district, Pat Russell, had been extremely effective in helping Playa Vista gain the approvals needed to go ahead.[8] As president of the city council, her influence at City Hall was considerable. In the public eye, her allegiance to the developer rather than to her constituents sparked a bitter political struggle that ended with her later electoral defeat.

Due to the long, complicated negotiations, Playa Vista witnessed wild fluctuations of opposition and support. Friends of Ballona Wetlands came under attack in the late nineties for negotiating a deal with Playa Vista. The organization's attorney, having sued for wetlands conservation in the eighties, argued against further wetlands conservation, publicly defending the developers in the nineties. In such large undertakings, one sometimes sees early opponents negotiate solutions that convert them into advocates who must fight later opposition.

Politicians, opponents, advocates, professional consultants, and their plans are all caught in big projects' webs. As was the case at Aliso Village and Chavez Ravine, again at Playa Vista sacrificial failures preceded the implementation of a final proposal. In the Playa Vista case, lots of players have been sacrificed. Spurred by the passage of another initiative (Proposition U, in 1986) that limited development in various parts of the city, voters ousted Russell in 1987 and put in her place Ruth Galanter, an outspoken critic of Playa Vista and a city planner by training. In 1989, the development operation was substantially restructured with Maguire Thomas Partners in the lead.[9] Rob Maguire, a local developer, had recently completed several sensitive projects that had won the support of the general population as well as politicians.[10] Before long, Galanter had negotiated enough changes that she could support the project. Then in 1997, Maguire Thomas Partners would relinquish control to yet another developer, Playa Capital.

Although the displacement of Summa was as symbolic as it was substantive, community leaders saw the arrival of Maguire Thomas as a new beginning. They were hands-on: they walked the area with concerned neighbors, held open meetings, and accepted the constraints given by Galanter.[11] They rejected the abstract modern boxes epitomized by the Wang building and projected onto Summa's site model. Maguire himself stated that his new vision for Playa Vista resembled "the best from the enduring and graceful buildings and public spaces so beloved by Southern California, such as the Pasadena City Hall and its public gardens, the Santa Barbara City Hall and park, the Los Angeles Central Library and the Palisades Park in Santa Monica" (quoted in Moran, 1989).

To these ends, Maguire Thomas hired design consultants to run a series of public workshops and develop a new concept plan, beginning in June 1989. The team included the architectural firm of Duany & Plater-Zyberk of Miami, which had recently completed Seaside and was known for its ideas about traditional neighborhood design; Ricardo Legorreta, who merged a modernist aesthetic with Mexican vernacular architecture and color; and Laurie Olin, who was brought back to do the landscape plan. Two area firms were also part of this initial team: Moore, Ruble, Yuddell, led by Charles Moore, and Moule and Polyzoides, whose principals are central players in the nationwide New Urbanist movement.

Five hundred people attended the June workshop; by November, at the third and final workshop, Duany & Plater-Zyberk presented a very general site plan illustrated by numerous perspectival images, or vignettes (see figs. 180, 181). This became the team's visual strategy: parts of the scheme shown in romantic colored perspectives, detailed models all prolifically landscaped and happily populated with white, professional pedestrians. Moreover, the vignettes represented fragments. Never again would a complete massing model of the area be made (at least for public view), nor would whole plans be rendered beyond general land use or conceptual level of detail. Maguire had one of the smoothest public relations operations exactly because it was invisible. There was no public relations department; the hands-on approach precluded placing such a mechanism between the developer and the people.

The Summa and Maguire Thomas proposals were fairly similar in square footage proposed, while differing in its distribution.[12] Further concessions appeased the different interest groups. Friends of Ballona Wetlands eventually

180　Vignettes like this one show a traffic-free, Spanish colonial setting.

181　Another dream: walking to work.

182   Study model showing the architectural development of a block.

negotiated 260 acres to be preserved (a gain of 51 acres). The Vista del Mar
Neighbors Association would have its utilities placed underground and its park
improved. Kentwood Home Guardians would retain their bluff views via building height restrictions. The Villa Marina Council was granted a desired street
closure, and various groups saw to it that a proposed throughway was abandoned. Through such actions, the developers gained the support of the majority
of local community groups.

As new activists and their organizations entered the Playa Vista debates,
both amnesia and disinterest overwhelmed previously negotiated concessions.
These neighborhood-specific deals had no bearing on the regional and national
issue of wetlands conservation; hence the formation of Citizens United to Save
All of Ballona. In 1999, its many constituent groups (including the Wetlands
Action Network and the California Public Interest Research Group) sought a
legal decision to delay all construction so that a new, more thorough environmental impact statement could be prepared. Councilwoman Galanter, originally elected for her stand against Playa Vista, was targeted (unsuccessfully) for
defeat in 1999 by wetlands activists. Motivated by environmental issues and
traffic projections, an organized and sizable opposition rallied in April of 1999.
Its legal challenges are intended to initiate new negotiations between anti-
development groups and Playa Capital. When DreamWorks reversed its decision
to locate in Playa Vista in 1999, opposition groups registered a major victory.

The politics of Playa Vista mirror in exaggerated form those typifying large-scale developments. Not only is support necessary from the public and from municipal agencies and officials, but such a large undertaking also entails state and federal backing. According to Los Angeles sociologist J. William Gibson, DreamWorks and Playa Capital were offered $110 million in tax breaks and $500 million in low-interest loans and municipal bonds, including $87 million in tax-free federal housing bonds for the 417 affordable housing units.[13] It has not escaped critics that the development's major proponents were big contributors to state and local political campaigns.[14]

Earlier we saw how real estate interests opposed to public housing had worked to shift authority to local bodies and to insert multiple decision points in the approval process. Now these same practices were being used against their authors to block private development. The longer the time span between negotiations and implementation, the more opportunities for a development deal to unravel. The broader the opposition's base, the more likely that it will be able to gather steam. In the decades-long Playa Vista debates, the taxpayer revolt, public activism over traffic problems, and environmentalism became amalgamated. The strategy taken by the Playa Vista opposition follows a pattern: it is occasionally possible to stop a development and force a turn to a wholly new solution. In this way Playa Vista is comparable to Elysian Park Heights. At Chavez Ravine, the opposition managed to preclude affordable housing and build a baseball stadium. At Playa Vista, anti-development groups fought to turn a huge new-town development into an environmental preserve. If we suspend judgment on the outcomes, the processes bear some similarity.

Implications for Architects and for the Architecture of the City

52 When New Urbanists argue for traditional neighborhood development or transit-oriented districts, they have done so articulately and with almost religious conviction, developing a position that is far more cohesive than statements of principle from other contemporary design movements. The work of New Urbanists fulfills their stated goals in most cases where new development occurs in the suburban outskirts or on cleared sites within city boundaries, like Playa Vista. In other words, New Urbanism palliates large-scale operations. However, if we are going to deal with the existing city, we will have to deal with infill projects—precisely those sites where new urbanism has failed to provide good solutions.

Large-scale projects, as we have seen, come with certain disadvantages: they seek clean slates, and thus are marked by demolition and anti-preservation strategies; they exist as islands, both formally and managerially; the area will deteriorate uniformly, and thus will suggest its own replacement, again at a large scale. The built environment will present a homogeneous face, whether modern, New Urbanist, or deconstructivist. Bigness also has significant advantages and an inevitability that cannot be ignored: utopian and urban experiments are advanced with scale; economies of scale permit otherwise infeasible alternatives; nonprofit components, affordable housing, and public open space are more possible economically in large-scale than in small-scale undertakings. When such developments become mired in public contention, however, these advantages begin to evaporate.

183 The idyllic and idealized wetlands.

The five housing projects I have examined are but one kind of large-scale operation in urban development. Myriad large ventures that have taken place since the war, like Sun City, Disneyland, the Kennedy Center, Seattle's World's Fair, Houston's Post Oak, or New York's Riverside South, are comparable in various ways. In a provocative text, John Findlay describes what he calls "magic lands": planned districts that remain lands unto themselves, planned and operated by central authorities almost in opposition to the surrounding city, populated by rather distinct and homogeneous crowds, designed thematically and given spatial coherence (Findlay, 1992).[15] Findlay even includes Chavez Ravine's Dodger Stadium among his case studies. But Findlay fails to see the dark side of magic lands—that such large projects will always require some "disparaged land" (and its people) to be destroyed for the magic kingdom to come to life. Urban redevelopment practices including public housing are another type within this same tradition, of which "themed" environments are a subset. The magic lands of which he speaks are a form of extra-large move in the city. They too require eminent domain, reassembly of land, and the demolition of poor urban neighborhoods (as when the Seattle World's Fair was used as a slum clearance/urban redevelopment project).

The projects that occupy this text have less magic than Findlay's, even though the architects invested design talent where none was demanded by market considerations. Nor are they all money-making ventures, and even those that are (Westchester and Playa Vista) exert less central control than his totalizing places, creating a set of big, publicly accessible works.

184   New Yorkers demonstrate against Donald Trump's Riverside South development. Photographer: Monica Almeida.

The most relevant extrapolation from Findlay's to my work is a recent community development called Celebration, near Orlando, Florida. On nearly 5,000 acres the Disney Corporation built a suburban new town, complete with school, post office, downtown, pool, and parks. City Hall, designed by Philip Johnson, had no rationale, since the town is to be run by Disney for its first twenty years (see Kroloff, 1997; Ross, 1999). Planning and governance have been retained by Disney, and most of the residents seem perfectly content with this arrangement—odd, given the high degree of participation Celebration residents demonstrate in all other aspects of community life, and given the general national trend toward citizen participation in planning.

The residents of Celebration are quick to proclaim how important community is to them. Yet they want this "community" without the contention or disharmony that has characterized, to some extent, all the cases I have explored in Los Angeles. The most common reason given for moving to Celebration is the school, which probably serves as a code word for class if not racial isolation. And it was the school that provoked enough tension to divide the residents. When disagreement arose over its innovative pedagogy, Disney town employees led school supporters in attempts to suppress disharmony and led dissenters to leave town. If we can turn anything from the natural world (see Davis, 1997) to the neighborhood into entertainment themes, then it may be disagreement and contention that spare us from both corporate takeover and vapid harmony.

Constructive Contention for an Urban Architecture

53 If, in Celebration, disagreement leads to exile, then Playa Vista's planning may represent the other extreme, where contention reproduces itself seemingly for its own sake. While the latter model has rankled developers for some time, citizen groups have been less aware of the ways their own interests are thwarted by it.

In my own participation in community interest groups, I too have supported tactics to slow or stop unwanted development. Although I am an advocate of thoughtful urban growth, at times extreme actions have seemed warranted to halt an injustice or an irreparable act. To save one thousand units of public housing in Houston, for example, a group I was part of made demands on environmental, archaeological, and planning grounds to buy strategic time for public housing residents and their advocates. In Houston, it became clear over time that our efforts were like so many pebbles before the steamroller. The mistakes we made there contributed to the loss of public housing and to my understanding of urban upheaval. In nearly every big operation which has behind it large-scale agencies and massive funding, whether public or private, citizen groups are worn down. Perhaps more to the point, a large piece of property with real estate potential will eventually be transformed (except those few properties that become part of the public trust).

There is an optimum point in the life of a large-scale project for community interests to have an effect on the final solution. This is neither at the outset nor at some long-drawn-out conclusion, but somewhere in between. Knowing

185 Donald Trump with the model of Trump City and 150-story tower that sparked public outcry, 1988. Photographer: Chester Higgins.

when to settle a negotiation, difficult enough in itself, is further complicated by the multiple, unrelated parties privy to urban development negotiations. The all-or-nothing strategy in the fight over Playa Vista, in my evaluation, is a risky one. On the slim chance of gaining substantially larger wetlands and lesser traffic impacts, advocates risk the greater chance of eroding former agreements with other community groups. That is, further opposition may yield even fewer affordable units, higher-density development, or nonadherence to design standards. Let me restate why I have come to this conclusion, using Playa Vista as the prime example.

First, the sporadic reshuffling of the development team has not been nearly as meaningful as is sometimes portrayed. Indeed, some of the same interests, motives, plans, and actors remain firmly in power. It makes better news and it is good for group morale to find victory when there is little more than delay. At both Riverside South in New York and Playa Vista, what were billed initially as major concessions by the developers seem less significant when examined years later. Indeed, some of the concessions that were most difficult to win, such as the undergrounding of an expressway in New York, were challenged in subsequent years. The overall square footage of the Playa Vista project changed little from the antagonistic Summa Corporation to the beneficent Maguire Thomas, though there was a shift from office space to residential land use.

Second, there is no way to identify the vested negotiators. When one group's advocates settle on a compromise with the developer, neither they nor the developer have any assurance that another group will not form and reconsider the very same issues thought to have been resolved. This happened at Playa Vista when Friends of the Ballona Wetlands negotiated an agreement about the extent and management of wetlands to be preserved. After the fact, other groups, including The Wetlands Action Network, Ballona Wetlands Land Trust, and the California Public Interest Research Group, appeared on the scene to oppose the development and demand further concessions (see Berthelsen, 1997). The fact that no settlement can be considered final considerably weakens the bargaining position of the community interest groups.

Third, the court system is extensively abused, particularly by environmental concerns, as documented in the well-researched book *The Environmental Protection Hustle* (Frieden, 1979). Any savvy interest group searches for environmental issues in order to slow or stop a development, or to gain a seat at the negotiating table. Environmental tactics inadvertently and sometimes intentionally raise the costs of development overall. They also can undo the very settlements that their advocates would have supported, by causing such long delays that new actors move into the project, abandoning prior agreements. Most relevant, because legal action increases costs, the prospects of privately sponsored affordable housing as well as newly dedicated public space are made even more distant. Finally, such tactics have degraded environmental politics overall.

Fourth, open-ended citizen participation gives advantage to those groups with the greatest stability and resources. While low-income neighborhoods have battled successfully against unwanted development, the environmental justice literature demonstrates that poor communities of color also have a disproportionate number of battles to wage, and that the wealthier, long-established interest groups have the advantage. In general, stability and resources do not characterize community groups. Probably the strongest player by this measure is the state, with its entrenched policy if vulnerable politicians, followed by the late-arriving developer.

The Los Angeles Sites Revisited, and Beyond

54 The most apparent theme throughout these stories has been the importance of property-based politics to large-scale urban form. The issue of permanence also colors this conception of urban change. For any place, we tacitly identify its position on an imaginary continuum from temporary to permanent, from expendable to invaluable. When our mental conceptions differ, as was so clearly the case at Chavez Ravine between residents and public housing advocates, contention ensues. The neighborhood called The Flats was deemed blighted and provisional, making it possible to build Aliso Village. When the wetlands at Playa Vista were threatened, public interest groups argued that at least a portion should be allowed to be permanent. Because urban development in every instance means transformation, one state of existence will be threatened and another advocated. The scale of these transformations varies, but those that have captured our attention are large and inherently discontinuous. The preceding condition has little bearing upon what follows.

The sites investigated in this book continue to evolve; each has appeared in the news of late. At Aliso Village, "transitory" Russian and Mexican residents were removed in the 1940s so that "permanent" housing for low-income families could be built. In September of 1996, the three connected public housing projects at Pico-Aliso held a "Demolition Fiesta" to celebrate the destruction of buildings through HUD's HOPE VI program, by which large housing developments are reduced in size and converted to mixed-income neighborhoods. In

186 The ramadas being demolished at Aliso Village public housing in 1999. Photographer: Beth Holden.

1999, demolition in Aliso Village began with the ramadas. Once the development's most outstanding formal element, the breezeways had become dangerous areas without surveillance. It will not be long before significantly more of Aliso Village is razed.

Real estate interests and community groups insisted that federally subsidized housing, where necessary during the war, should be temporary. Plans for each unit's dismantling had to be incorporated into its construction. Thus was born Rodger Young Village, for veterans who decided that Los Angeles would be an ideal place to settle down. When the Village was disassembled and carried off over the protests of its remaining occupants, the vacant acreage was redeployed in several ways: as freeway ramps, zoo parking, playing field, and museum. Because of its fractured reincarnation, Rodger Young's site will not undergo its next upheaval as a whole. At present, a sizable area comprising the parking lot is under discussion as a site for a zoo project to demonstrate sustainable environmental planning.

Westchester explicitly reversed the process evident in The Flats and Chavez Ravine: a large parcel of land was subdivided into many small pieces of property. Although homeownership fractured property boundaries into thousands of individual parcels, large-scale upheavals have transpired nonetheless. The community's goliath neighbor, the airport, has seized neighborhoods for its own expansion and will inevitably take another bite out of Westchester's southern boundary. Property values nearest the airport are lower than in other parts of Westchester, and family incomes are commensurately low. At this juncture, Westchester resembles the patterns of The Flats and Chavez Ravine before their demolitions.

In April 1999, newspaper articles on Chavez Ravine would not have surprised readers of this book. It was reported that the Dodgers' owners were considering a move to a new stadium at the Los Angeles Coliseum site. It was proposed, without even a nod to events in the 1950s, that the Chavez Ravine site be turned into housing. No better site for it, it was claimed. Families who still return for an annual picnic to memorialize the destruction of their Chavez Ravine community must find this turn of events bitterly ironic.

Still, if you ask me, I believe that some large projects should be built. Large-scale upheavals are fundamental to urban development. They will continue to occur because of the numerous advantages to their owners, but there are advantages that could be better reaped by designers and citizens as well. Utopian experiments often need bigness, as do avant-garde schemes that will illuminate urban plans. At times, they appropriately match the scale of urban crises. There are indeed tremendous social and urban costs to large-scale development. Big projects destroy their fine-grained predecessors and, at times, their subsequent neighbors. They interrupt not only history but urban pattern, social life, architectural development, and our sense of stability. They undermine conventional thinking about historical continuity and the material record. To reduce the damage without eliminating the advantages of large-scale operations, we need new strategies for effecting bigness. For example, there can be perforations in big projects to allow for interruptions from the existing context. The retention of some buildings, infrastructure, and social relations can establish a continuity that does not now characterize bigness. A revitalized Utah Street School at the heart of Aliso Village was just such a strategy. A mechanism for uneven construction schedules could prevent whole regions from deteriorating simultaneously. Finally, better than many other types of urban change, large upheavals can contribute to the public domain. I want to conclude by focusing on this last charge.

Convulsive space exists throughout the American city because of the nature of property, real estate finance, the force of the state in the city, the recurrent attraction of big plans, and the existence of significant urban problems. From Augustus Caesar to Daniel Burnham, from the Federal Housing Administration to professional baseball clubs, those with the means have sought comprehensive solutions that will memorialize their authority in vast built form. In bursts of conviction and finance, new form supplants old to create the provisional city.

Public and private developers will inevitably seek large spaces for their projects, but architects and planners can adjust their tactics in light of this study.

Contentious developments create a focus on design. They challenge the self-determined interests of developers and their design proposals with the moral imperative of the public interest. The expanded sense of the residents' Lockean rights and the developers' duties produces fertile soil for seeds of local, semipublic, urban and regional missions. Even in smaller-scale developments, a justice is hammered out that inserts collective interests into once-private terrain. And while assertions of rights and duties fly through all the discussion, rarely do the contenders resolve contradictions among competing claims or visualize the manifestation of those assertions. All this fuels the architect's traditional motive—to control the design—but simultaneously generates another more complex role: the architect as visionary of a politicized public realm.

Where communities or special interest groups unite to establish a developer's duties, they carve out new territory in development debates—a territory that supports the design and creation of a public realm. Architects have not always taken advantage of these opportunities, for example in CIAM's treatment of recreation and transportation as functional zones rather than public domain. Ironically, the architect's task becomes the design of a solution that the paying client does not want. The idea that an architect is duplicitous is not new, though typically deception is justified not by the public interest but by architecture for its own sake. In her analysis of the contemporary architectural profession, sociologist Magali Larson states, "As a form of cultural production, modern architecture must simultaneously convince and deceive the client" (1993, p. 147). Architect Vittorio Gregotti tells her something similar in an interview: "The typical duplicity of the architect is precisely that of having in mind two different goals simultaneously—architecture as autonomous culture and the client" (Larson, 1993, p. 147). Architects in contentious developments go beyond this two-part deception, adding the creation of a public realm for an amorphous, nonexistent client. Indeed, I would argue that architects have an ethical and professional obligation to convince and (at least initially) deceive the client in this matter.

If the architect can create the opportunity for public work, it will be through what are initially planning mechanisms, then later acts of physical design. Design, in turn, will be a strategic act. To survive the corrosive process of contentious development, design proposals exhibit certain characteristics. First, the design's skeleton, both formal and conceptual, needs to be able to withstand incremental and individual demands without deteriorating the whole. As citizen groups come forward with their concerns about noise, views, parking, preservation, or adjacencies, the underlying design structure, or *parti*, can easily erode.

Its resistance depends upon a recognition of more fundamental constraints as well as desires. Second, design proposals appropriate to contentious developments make themselves clear and easily understood, so that people know and can represent to others what they are advocating. This argues for conceptual simplicity both in rhetoric and in form. The last directive to the architect of a contentious project contradicts the stereotype that the physical outcome is compromised by politicized development: the design proposal for a contentious project needs a visionary quality. In order to gain advocates, the proposal can be neither mediocre nor ambivalent, even while the most central contested terrain remains malleable.

If good design in contentious development must have an underlying concept founded on the central political concerns, with clarity and a visionary quality, then it is no wonder that so few development undertakings exhibit high design quality. These characteristics are rarely found in any architectural project, least of all one involving the most cost-conscious of all clients (developers) and the most argumentative of processes. The realm of contention has complicated the architect's job, but it simultaneously opens new avenues for doing good work. Contentious development can elevate the architect to a crucial role, as the one who makes not only conceptual synthesis out of chaos, but its physical realization as well.

Political philosophy and history justify this role for the architect. But if architecture as a profession is to survive, its visionary proposals will give priority to the public interest above the local demands of a contentious development.[16] An editorial by *Progressive Architecture*'s Tom Fisher states the case similarly: "The profession of architecture was founded to guard the public, not just the public's health and safety through building and zoning codes, but the public realm and the public interest broadly defined" (Fisher, 1993, p. 7). The architect is never neutral in the process, nor a mere mediator. Instead, the architect is an advocate for what is very often difficult to determine: the public good.

If architects were to assume stewardship of the public realm, many changes would need to take place within the profession. Such a role implies a level of education about the environment that architecture schools have yet to achieve. It implies a degree of political participation that does not presently characterize our profession. And it implies that architects understand and advocate exactly those regional issues that typically have no constituents. Filling such a role can jeopardize the architect's business function, but not to do so risks further marginalization in a society that already looks at architecture askance.

We live in the provisional city. Its convulsions continue to punctuate urban history in a morally ambiguous way: they reverberate between good and bad.

The architecture of sporadic urbanism is politically electrified, as is the planning, but it is not out of control. The shape of discontinuity is not a postmodern cliché, but the labor of the new millennium.

187, 188

Notes

I No Little Plans

1 On the postmodern city, see Dear (1999), the edited collection by Sorkin (1992), and Kling, Olin, and Poster (1991).

2 I don't believe this conference represents a turning point, or starting point, but it reflects the predominant sentiments and scholarship that led to later policy on the topics of housing, slums, and decentralization.

3 Just who does the valuing can vary from agencies with authority, like the federal government, to more populist forces, as in instances when environmental or architectural preservation groups are involved in development disputes.

4 Kevin Starr, for example, pays no attention to public housing in his book on the Depression era in California (1996).

5 It was newsworthy when Jacob Riis came to Los Angeles at the beginning of the century and "said that he had seen larger slums but never any worse." Los Angeles, Housing Commission (1909a).

6 A string of important books have been published over the past years, including those by Hayden (1995), Davis (1990), Hise (1997), Klein (1997), Ovnick (1994), Dear et al. (1996), and Scott and Soja (1996).

7 The connection between utopian politics and land development can be traced back at least to the early days of Llano del Rio, the socialist colony in the desert outside Los Angeles which thrived in the teens and is today only an archaeological ruin (see Greenstein et al., 1992, Davis, 1990). Llano del Rio was an instigator of the cooperative movement that would continue through the legacy of Upton Sinclair's EPIC Party (End Poverty in California) and eventually lead to the Mutual Housing Corporation at Crest-wood Hills (Friedland and Zellman, in press). In these movements, ideology was explicit and determining. Utopian plans were based upon socialist and progressive beliefs. Contrariwise, the projects described in the following chapters were mainstream utopias, they had their socialist and Communist players, but they were dominated by Democrats and Republicans.

8 In particular, work like that of Ed Soja about space provides a context for and contrast to my work. See, for example, Soja's "Postmodern Geographies: Taking Los Angeles Apart" (1994); also Soja and Hooper's "The Spaces That Difference Makes" (1993), and D. Massey's article "Politics and Space/Time" in the same volume (1993).

9 Another volume that takes a similar conceptual stance is Peter Jukes's *A Shout in the Street* (1990).

10 One urban historian argues that without the middle phase of 4-to-10-story mixed-use buildings, the urban infrastructure could not contain the "visual anarchy" of more recent American development (Morris 1979, p. 289).

11 Granted, there is an inbuilt stability to cities via urban systems like block patterns. In some European countries, particularly France, contemporary city structures have changed little since the fifteenth century.

12 The historian Vance (1971) pushes the date back to at least 1500 when the European urban landscape was transformed by land becoming a direct source of income, with ownership divorced from use and property producing rent. This catalyzed the end of what he calls the ordered city, and encouraged the segregation of uses that remains prevalent.

13 See R. Montgomery, in Davis (1977).

14 Los Angeles, Housing Commission (1913), p. 22.

15 Author's interview with William Hannon, associate of Fritz B. Burns and a commercial developer of Westchester, September 16, 1997.

16 See Robbins and Tilton, *Los Angeles: Preface to a Master Plan* (1941).

17 The Utah Street Project was one of several Public Works Administration housing developments proposed for Los Angeles. None of these were accomplished during the PWA era; but under the new administration of the United States Housing Authority, the Utah Street Project became Aliso Village, Aliso Extension, and Pico Gardens, and the Ann Street Project became William Mead Homes.

18 Information on Russian Town and The Flats (the former being a part of the latter) comes from the excellent study of the Molokans in the area in the early 1930s by Pauline Young (1932), a student in USC's graduate program in sociology, a branch of the Chicago School. The view that this area was one of the city's worst slums can be found in nearly every document about the place, including Aliso Village's printed program for the project's dedication ceremony on October 25, 1942.

19 From a speech by Lloyd Wright, "Aliso Village Group Housing Project: The Result of Coordinated Planning," no date (ca. 1942). Lloyd Wright Papers, UCLA Library, Special Collections, Collection 1561, Box 43, File 4.

20 Figures cited in Ovnick, 1994.

21 By far the most substantial analysis of the story of public housing in Los Angeles is Don Parson's *Making a Better World* (forthcoming). His published articles on the subject reveal some of that larger work.

II Siting Land: The Politics of Property

1 Historic maps in the possession of the Housing Authority of the City of Los Angeles show single holdouts. Disgruntlement is visible in some of the appraisal photos in this book. Other documents show that the City Housing Authority was trying to placate residents with information about relocation.

2 While these interest groups are in some way "public," they are ambiguously so in that they work for their own objectives over those of others.

3 This was also true of early American squatters who utilized land owned by others for their own gain, without any payment of rent. The most persistent architectural preservationists are perceived to be cranks by more mainstream parties to development negotiations. I suggest that preservationists assume more extensive rights over someone else's private property than society now acknowledges. They may in fact be visionary, if present trends in property relations continue to give communities even more say over environmental design. The complementary explanation would suggest that hard-line activists foresee the expansion of the developer's duties.

4 Although Blackstone was here referring to rights "inherent in every Englishman," his *Commentaries* constituted the whole of the law in America before and after the American Revolution by some accounts (Boorstin, 1941).

5 Glendon disagrees with the proposition that a frontier ethic has shaped our present view of property rights to a significant extent. Instead, she attributes greater influence to the history of law and its popular diffusion. See Glendon (1991).

6 For example, citizens in colonial townships were required to build their houses within a half-mile of the meeting house.

More recently, the federal highway program, through eminent domain, has steamrollered hundreds of neighborhoods in the name of the greater good. See Clawson (1964).

7 The Homestead Act of 1862 gave each individual a free quarter-section, or 160 acres, regardless of its suitability for cultivation versus for grazing, for example. This homogeneous policy eventually led to Dust Bowl conditions in Oklahoma (Bryant, 1972).

8 According to conservative analyst Ellen Paul (1987), federal and state power over land takes three forms: taxation, police power, and eminent domain.

9 On land as a special type of property—a nonconsumable—see the introduction to Ryan (1984).

10 Author's interview with William Hannon, Los Angeles homebuilder with Fritz B. Burns, September 16, 1997.

11 These programs specifically served the interests of builders (see Boyer, 1973; Freedman, 1969; Abrams, 1946).

12 Only the first of the Los Angeles public housing projects, Ramona Gardens, admitted the intended occupants. By the next project, war had broken out and low-wage defense workers received priority and fully occupied the public housing.

13 This is most shockingly apparent in our no-duty-to-rescue rule that removes Americans from the obligation of helping others in danger, ably described by Glendon (1991, pp. 78–89).

14 For example, a transfer of air rights occurs when one owner is permitted to build higher than her property allows by purchasing the height allowance or building envelope of another piece of property. See Coase (1960) on the market reallocation of property rights.

15 Community activists also advocate individual interests, but this is by no means the only scenario. The system of common property is not well developed by Waldron.

16 For a concise discussion of exclusionary zoning, see Bettencourt (1991) on the NIMBY syndrome.

17 On the other extreme of a dumbbell phenomenon, large landholders control even larger parcels than in earlier days.

18 Detroit's Poletown case, where General Motors was given eminent domain authority to tear down private housing to build a factory, shows just how far private benefit can be stretched (Schultz, 1992).

19 An excellent and comprehensive analysis of public housing in Los Angeles is Don Parson, *Making a Better World* (forthcoming).

20 I wish to thank Bill Deverell for bringing information about bubonic plague to my attention.

21 An informative discussion of the Housing Act is contained in Freedman (1959, esp. p. 28).

22 Both the South and the West were underrepresented at this and other such conferences. On its various committees, with a total membership of 93, there were two representatives from Alabama and one from Washington state; the other 90 came from the Northeast or Midwest (Gries and Ford, 1932).

23 From a U.S. Housing Authority pamphlet, no date. Lloyd Wright Papers, UCLA Library, Special Collections, Collection 1561, Box 43, File 3.

24 José Gámez brought Said's analysis to my attention in relation to domestic colonization in Los Angeles. See his dissertation (1999).

25 See Abrams (1946) for a thorough critique of the Ickes administration.

26 Jackson's careful study of FHA lending practices focuses on federal bias against the city and for suburbanization. His work also discloses clear biases against racial and ethnic minorities, but he acknowledges that "the precise extent to which the agency discriminated against blacks and other minority groups is difficult to determine" (Jackson, 1985, p. 209).

III Provisional Places with Fugitive Plans: Aliso Village

1 The name refers to the Los Angeles River's floodplain, through which ran the Arroyo del Poscitos. Pauline Young, in her book of 1932, called the area in question Russian Flats because of the Molokan Russians who then made up a substantial minority of the population (the other part being ethnic Mexicans). It was considered part of Brooklyn Heights for some time, according to a U.S. Geological Survey map; in her essay, Spalding (1992) labeled it the Boyle Heights Flats or The Flats for short.

2 The HOLC was created by Roosevelt to refinance personal, nonfarm mortgages and save people's homes from foreclosure. Since this meant loaning huge sums of federal money (over $3 billion in the first year of its existence), it led to a need for reliable property appraisal (Abrams, 1946).

3 Los Angeles, Housing Commission (1910), p. 10. The house courts, also called Cholo courts, were inhabited by ethnic Mexicans, and generally built by them out of salvaged materials. After a nationwide investigation, the housing commission concluded: "The Cholo court seems to be a purely local development. There is no other city in the United States, probably, that has a like condition" (Los Angeles, Housing Commission, 1909a, p. 8). More specifi-

cally, the area south of First Street seems to have had the highest concentration of house courts, but exact location of various house courts discussed is unknown since the commission did not include maps in its annual reports.

4 Photographs in the commission's reports show primarily Latino and African-American faces, but further reading indicates that Russians, Italians, Greeks, Japanese, and Slovenians are also living in substandard conditions.

5 Author's interview with Frances Camareno, April 1997.

6 Lloyd Wright, letter to Mr. Galleon, October 2, 1935, 2 pp. Lloyd Wright Papers, UCLA Library, Special Collections, Collection 1561, Box 44, Folder 1.

7 Pauline Young describes the Molokan neighborhood in the 1932 book *Pilgrims of Russian Town,* based on her doctoral study under the direction of Robert Park at the University of Southern California. The area is also documented in the 1939 housing survey done by the WPA and the city housing authority, and in the appraisal photos and report contracted by the housing authority in 1940–1941 (property of the Housing Authority of the City of Los Angeles). That study concluded that a full 93 percent of the area's housing was substandard.

8 Herman's essay, written in 1931, can be found in the Lloyd Wright Papers, UCLA Library, Special Collections, Collection 1561, Box 44, folder 4. The excerpts quoted are from pp. 5, 16.

9 I wish to thank Michael Engh and Rev. Gregory Boyle for giving me access to Ms. McMahon's diary, in the possession of Rev. Boyle.

10 Based on a map made by the Los Angeles Housing Authority prior to demolition. No date given (ca. 1941).

11 The Utah Street School teacher wrote in her diary on March 26, 1942, "The little house with the large tree at its north wall is still there. Across Kearny Street however the houses have been raised off their foundations and will soon be moved" (McMahon, 1942).

12 Home Owners Loan Corporation, "Description of Areas. Security Map #1. Metropolitan Los Angeles, California." Washington, D.C., September 18, 1936. C. C. Boyd, Field Agent. This typewritten manuscript is located in the National Archives, Federal Home Loan Bank Board, Record Group 195. I am quoting from an updated description of the Boyle Heights area (April 19, 1939; p. 401), included in the 1936 manuscript.

13 Weston, Neutra, Bauer, and Mumford explicitly sought to apply the European garden apartment, mid-rise models to U.S. projects. In the controversy over Chavez Ravine, however, Bauer argued against Neutra and Alexander's high-rise solution there. Alexander himself later came to believe that their Elysian Park plans were better unbuilt; see Eisner (1992) and Alexander (1989).

14 Lloyd Wright, letter to Mr. Goetze, January 29, 1927, 2 pp. Lloyd Wright Papers, UCLA Library, Special Collections, Box 44, Folder 4.

15 Author's interview with Jean Whinnery, February 1, 1999.

16 Lloyd Wright, "Aliso Village Group Housing Project, the Result of Coordinated Planning," p. 1. Typewritten manuscript, n.d. [ca. 1942]. 5 pp. Lloyd Wright Papers, UCLA Library Special Collections, Box 43, Folder 4.

17 Lloyd Wright Papers, UCLA Library, Special Collections, Box 269. There are no dates on either site drawing.

18 Lloyd Wright, "Aliso Village Group Housing Project," p. 2.

19 Wilson was a partner of Robert Evans Alexander, the architect later responsible for bringing Neutra into the Chavez Ravine commission. The public housing design circles in Los Angeles at this period were tight.

20 Ross Montgomery, John Kibbey, George Adams, Walter S. Davis, Bill Mullay, and Lloyd Wright were the original Utah Street Architects. In 1935 Montgomery and Kibbey resigned and Eugene Weston and Ralph Flewelling, who practiced together, were recommended by others on the team. Early correspondence from Wright argued against Flewelling because of some adverse political ties, even though elsewhere Flewelling was recommended as "a liberal and a registered Democrat." Neutra was listed as a possible member of the team, but this never came to pass. Many of these collaborations began during the Depression years when few architects had any work to speak of. In Los Angeles, architects had taken work designing sets for the film industry to get by; when the federal housing funds became available, they were competitively sought. Mullay later disappeared from the final association of architects, and Wilson appeared to take his place. Lloyd Wright Papers, UCLA Library, Special Collections, Collection 1561, Box 42, Folder 8, "California Housing Authority." See also Box 45, Folder 1.

21 At Ramona Gardens, Adams was the chief architect (with Flewelling, Wilson, Weston, Davis, and Wright). Davis brought a suit against the Utah District Housing Architects, in 1941, in reference to the Ramona Project. Davis was not a member of the Rancho San Pedro team. Lloyd Wright Papers, UCLA Library, Special Collections, Collection 1561, Box 43, Folders 3 and 4.

22 Author's interview with Jean Whinnery, February 1, 1999.

23 Lloyd Wright Papers, UCLA Library, Special Collections, Office Files, Aliso Village, notes and Change Orders, Box 19, Folder 6. Wright was a registered architect in California, but he had no formal architectural training. He graduated from the University of Wisconsin after three years with a degree in science and horticulture, going on to work with his father, Frank Lloyd Wright, in Chicago for three years, with the Olmsted brothers for two years, and then in southern California with Irving Gill for two more years. He stated his specializations as architectural design, structural engineering, landscape, and city planning.

24 Housing Authority brochure in Lloyd Wright Papers, UCLA Library, Special Collections, Collection 1561, Box 19, Folder 6.

25 Nadel's widow, Evelyn De Wolfe Nadel, is in possession of this monograph and generously permitted me to examine it.

26 Fritz Burns Papers, Center for the Study of Los Angeles, Southern California Research Collection, Loyola Marymount University, Box 1, File "Speech Material (1943–44)."

27 See comments of Raymond M. Foley, Housing and Home Finance Administrator, speaking before the National Association of Home Builders, October 18, 1950. In Fritz Burns Papers, Center for the Study of Los Angeles, Research Collection, Loyola Marymount University, Box 2, File: "National Association of Home Builders (1950–51)."

28 The architects were Reginald Johnson and the firm Wilson, Merrill and Alexander, Architects Associated, of which both Lewis Eugene Wilson and Robert E. Alexander designed projects for the Los Angeles Housing Authority.

29 From Catherine Bauer Wurster Papers, Bancroft Library, University of California, Berkeley, Box 22, Folder: Holtzendorff. A summary comparison of costs shows that Aliso Village was the most expensive of the early public housing developments in Los Angeles. Part of this expense was due to costs of slum clearance, which were included as part of land costs.

30 Author's interview with David Ochoa, 1997. See also Gordon (1993); Chuang (1997).

31 Originally intended to house 910 units, Aliso Apartments (then called the Aliso Village Extension) were completed with 500 units. Bowron Collection, Huntington Library, File: "Housing Authority of the City of Los Angeles," document: "Facts Regarding Aliso Village Extension Site, Ca. 4–14," June 13, 1951, 4 pp.

IV Temporary Abode, Industrial Aesthetic: Rodger Young Village

1 In 1947, Dreves was also the Chairman of the Mayor's Emergency Housing Commission and Executive Secretary of Greater Los Angeles Plans. The opening quotation is taken from the *Los Angeles Examiner,* 1946a.

2 The Los Angeles builder Fritz Burns testified before Congress. Fritz Burns Papers, Center for the Study of Los Angeles, Southern California Research Collection, Loyola Marymount University, Box 1, File: "Speeches and Memos on Speeches and Outlines (primarily 1943–44)."

3 In one photo in *Architectural Forum,* the horror of slums is illustrated by the delivery of a Medal of Honor to a serviceman whose family lives in such undignified surroundings.

4 See *Journal of Housing,* June 1952 and May 1955, for a description of Willow Run's

vast defense housing and production enterprise.

5 This is the wording that went along with the award of contracts for 7,400 veterans' emergency housing units in Region VI, which included California, Nevada, Arizona, and Utah. Eighty percent of these were to be placed in California, and of those Rodger Young and Basilone Homes comprised nearly 3,000 units. See *Southwest Builder and Contractor* (1946).

6 Mayor's Emergency Housing Committee, "Los Angeles Housing Study," October 30, 1947, in the Bowron Collection, Huntington Library Public Housing files.

7 Along with Los Angeles city veterans' projects, the county built temporary units in the following developments: Will Rogers (168 units), Alondra Park (144), Belvedere (100), Spadra (74), Palm Land (300), Claremont (40), La Verne (20), and Bonnie Beach (300). Mayor's Emergency Housing Committee, "Los Angeles Housing Study," October 30, 1947, in the Bowron Collection, Huntington Library, Public Housing files.

8 While the Quonset hut had a predecessor in the British Nissen hut, researchers like Young argue that the Quonset was an original design concept and only utilized the general shape of the Nissen and not its structural or fabrication system. The designers indicated on Fuller's blueprints were Otto Brandenberger, Tomasino Secondino, Dominic Urgo, and Robert McDonnell (Young, 1996).

9 Six issues of the *Rodger Young News,* spanning a year period, were sent to the author by Leota Fantl, now Smith-Flowers, who lived in the Village and wrote for the paper.

10 Hence the error that some LA historians (e.g., Eberts, 1996) have made that there

were 1,500 huts. In fact, there were 750 huts and 1,500 dwelling units.

11 Author's interviews and correspondence with former residents Dorothy Sterling and Leota Smith-Flowers.

12 Personal correspondence with the author from Rodger Young Village resident Leota Fantl, now Smith-Flowers, dated April 7, 1997.

13 Roybal Papers, UCLA Library Special Collections, Collection 847, Box 49, Folder: "Veterans Affairs and Public Housing." Quoted in total.

14 Roybal Papers, UCLA Library, Special Collections, Collection 847, Box 49, Folder: "Veterans Affairs and Public Housing." Document title "Rodger Young Village, Community Emergency Council," 11 pp.

15 Fletcher Bowron's address to the city council, headed "Office of the Mayor, City Hall," August 8, 1949, 8 pp. Bowron Collection, Huntington Library, Box 50.

V Whose Dream, America?

1 Charles Abrams, letter to Mr. Lee Johnson, February 19, 1945. Catherine Bauer Wurster Papers, Bancroft Library, University of California, Berkeley, Box 9, Folder: "Abrams, Charles 1 of 3."

2 From Charles Abrams, "Human Rights in Slum Clearance," address before the National Association of Housing Officials, May 11, 1951. Catherine Bauer Wurster Papers, Bancroft Library, University of California, Berkeley, Carton 26, Folder: "Slums."

3 Fritz Burns Papers, Center for the Study of Los Angeles, Southern California Research Collection, Loyola Marymount University, Box 2, File: "National Association of Home Builders (1950–51)."

4 For example, the shortage of construction materials might have led to price goug-

ing by suppliers had the federal government not stepped in to regulate prices and distribution.

5 See *Los Angeles Times,* June 14, 1953; "NAREB Maps Further Cure of Blight Spots" (no author), from Fritz Burns Papers, Loyola Marymount University, Scrapbook 1953.

6 Transcript of Wilkinson's speech accepting his special citation; in author's possession.

7 All this information comes from the Fritz Burns Papers, Loyola Marymount University, File: "Speeches (notes, announcements, . . . conferences)—1957."

8 In *The Realtor* (Massachusetts, January 1954), p. 4, Burns writes in "America Can Afford to Outlaw Slums": "We can get rid of blight and slums by taking three practical steps: 1. Strict enforcement of adequate and reasonable city ordinances that prohibit the use of dwellings that fall below local health, building, and sanitary standards, including demolition or removal of structures that cannot be made to conform to those standards. 2. Attraction of new construction on cleared or vacant sites in older city areas through the incentive of accelerated depreciation for federal income tax purposes. 3. Systematic improvement of city schools, parks, streets, and sewers in the areas where deterioration and neglect exist." Fritz Burns Papers, Loyola Marymount University, Scrapbook 1954.

9 Burns was chairman of CASH from 1951 through the referendum in 1952 when public housing and its reluctant advocate, Mayor Bowron, were defeated. See open letter from George M. Eason, Finance Chairman of CASH, 1951, in Bowron Collection, Huntington Library, Box 50.

10 The architects for these eight houses were J. R. Davidson, Richard Neutra, Spaulding

and Rex, Wurster and Bernardi, Ralph Rapson, Whitney Smith, Thornton Abell, and Charles Eames and Eero Saarinen (McCoy, 1977, p. 9).

11 The Postwar House was remodeled by Welton Becket into the Home of Tomorrow. "This newest residential showcase, reborn successor to the far-famed Postwar house which served as an 'experimental laboratory' in contemporary design and functionalism, is situated on the same site at the intersection of Wilshire and Highland." Fritz Burns Papers, Loyola Marymount University, File "Home of Tomorrow," Box: "Clippings."

12 These quotes are taken from "Averill, Lee. Home of Tomorrow open to Public, 400 at Gala Preview," from Fritz Burns Papers, Loyola Marymount University, Box: "Clippings" (*Daily News,* [1951]).

13 Information about the plastic house is in a report entitled "Prefabricated Plastic Houses," Henry J. Kaiser Company, Housing Division, Oakland California, January 1945, 13 pp. Kaiser Papers, University of California, Berkeley, Bancroft Library, File 315 19.

14 Author's interview with William Hannon, September 16, 1997.

VI Convulsive Suburbia: Westchester

1 Author's interview with William Goss, July 15, 1997.

2 Author's interview with Howard Drollinger, June 1997. Urban historian Greg Hise states, by contrast, that Westchester was owned and master-planned by Security-First National Bank (Hise, 1995).

3 Author's interview with William Hannon, September 16, 1997.

4 This information comes from the Westchester Historical Society's collections

housed at Loyola Marymount University's main library.

5 Author's interview with William Hannon, September 16, 1997.

6 Information about Marlow-Burns Development Company was gathered from the Fritz Burns Papers, Center for the Study of Los Angeles, Southern California Research Collection, Loyola Marymount University, Box 1.

7 Author's interview with William Hannon, September 16, 1997.

8 For just $95 down, a two-bedroom, one-bath "Victory Model" house of 850 square feet sold for $3,890, complete.

9 These were among ten building restrictions laid out for Windsor Hills. Under architectural restrictions, flat roofs were disallowed on all buildings and garages. Building setbacks, commercial property guidelines, and an architectural committee were established, all open to review by the community after 25 years. They claimed one (eventually illegal) exception: "racial restrictions are perpetual and binding forever." Fritz Burns Papers, Loyola Marymount University, Scrapbook 1953, contents about Windsor Hills dated 1939.

10 News clipping in Fritz Burns Papers, Loyola Marymount University, Scrapbook 1956–59.

11 "Digest of Housing Notes" by H. V. Lindbergh. 7 pp. In Henry J. Kaiser Papers, Bancroft Library, University of California, Berkeley, Carton 274, File: "Housing—Notes on Housing."

12 H. V. Lindbergh, letter to George M. Wolff, Henry J. Kaiser Papers, Bancroft Library, University of California, Berkeley, Carton 273, File: "Housing—Expandable Houses."

13 The first quote is from a newspaper article in the *San Francisco News,* January 2, 1946. The second is from the *Christian Science Monitor* (dateline May 10, 1945). They can be found in the Henry J. Kaiser Papers, Bancroft Library, University of California, Berkeley, Carton 315, File: "Kaiser Community Homes News Clippings 1942–45," and Carton 274, File: "Housing—Newspaper Clippings," respectively.

14 This critique comes from an editorial in the *Pacific Coast Lumber Digest,* May 15, 1945. Lumber interests were critical of Kaiser because he threatened to take the lumber out of home construction, by replacing it with steel or aluminum, which he manufactured. See Henry J. Kaiser Papers, Bancroft Library, University of California, Berkeley, Carton 315, File: "Kaiser Community Homes News Clippings, 1942–45."

15 For a description of Kaiser Community Homes' prefabrication and production methods, see *Architectural Forum,* 1945; *Business Week,* May 19, 1945, pp. 41–44; *San Francisco News,* January 2, 1946; *Washington Times Herald,* March 23, 1947; and Hise, 1995, 1997.

16 Henry J. Kaiser Papers, Bancroft Library, University of California, Berkeley, Carton 274, File: "Housing—Press Releases" (February 18, 1947).

17 Henry J. Kaiser Papers, Bancroft Library, University of California, Berkeley, Carton 274, File: "Housing—Kaiser Community Homes."

18 In the Levittown plan, the front door enters from the carport into the kitchen, with the living room at the rear of the house. The Kaiser homes place the living room at the front.

19 Author's interview with Howard Drollinger, June 1997.

20 Author's interview (September 16, 1997) with a native of Westchester who was in elementary school when the 3,000 houses were demolished along the border with the airport.

21 Special thanks to Mary Lou Crockett of Westchester for her extensive information about both the history and current real estate market of Westchester.

VII Chavez Ravine and the End of Public Housing

1 "Gestapo Housing Authority" brochure, in Bowron Collection, Huntington Library, n.d. (ca. 1951), 2 pp. Italics and emphasis quoted directly from text. Printed by "United Patriotic People of U.S.A."

2 ". . . And 10,000 More" is the name of a 12-minute film produced by graduate students from USC's Department of Cinema in 1949 for the Housing Authority of the City of Los Angeles, narrated by a young Chet Huntley, spurred by Frank Wilkinson. It dramatizes life in the slums. The film was made at the same time and with the same intention as eye-opening slum tours led by housing activists. Source: Southern California Library for Social Studies and Research.

3 Nine graphs prepared by the Office of Information, Housing Authority of the City of Los Angeles, May 1952. Bowron Collection, Huntington Library, Public Housing Files.

4 Author's interview with Frank Wilkinson, January 22, 1997.

5 Document titled "Facts Regarding Elysian Park Heights," June 13, 1951. Bowron Collection, Huntington Library, File: "Public Housing," 2 pp.

6 Author's interview with Frank Wilkinson, January 22, 1997.

7 Acreage varies from the Housing Authority's 254.4 acres to Walter O'Malley's 315 acres. (More land was purchased when Dodger Stadium was built on the site; see below.) The number of units varies by over a thousand depending on the planning scheme.

8 Rose Hills was to be designed by the architects who laid out Rodger Young Village, William Allen and W. George Lutzi. There are few extant images of the proposals for this site.

9 See Ed Roybal Papers, UCLA Library, Special Collections, Box 16, File: "Chavez Ravine—Dodgers."

10 I wish to thank Laurie Groehler, a student in my UCLA graduate seminar, for tracking down the Sanborn map that showed the houses in the photograph. Unlike for Aliso Village, I was unable to locate comprehensive appraisal documents for Chavez Ravine.

11 Bowron Collection, Huntington Library, Public Housing Files.

12 Memo dated October 14, 1952. Neutra Papers, UCLA Library, Special Collections, Box 47, File: "Elysian Park 1952."

13 Lopez was a housing authority employee and editor of the Spanish-language newspaper *El Espectador* (White, 1989).

14 "Dear Mr. Holtzendorff," draft letter from Neutra, dated April 18, 1953. Neutra Papers, UCLA Special Collections, Box 47, File: "Elysian Park, 1953," 7 pp.

15 Fritz B. Burns Papers, Loyola Marymount University, Box 2, File: "Public Housing 49–52."

16 The public housing opposition outlined their strategy in an open letter from George M. Eason, Finance Chairman, on Committee Against Socialist Housing letterhead, 1951. The letter was intended to raise money and political support. In Bowron Collection, Huntington Library, Box 50.

17 Burns held one-third interest in 25 acres purchased in 1944 (*Herald and Express,* May 28, 1952). William Hannon (interview with author, September 16, 1997) reported that Burns owned more land than this, in conjunction with Weingard, the developer of Lakeside. In Simon Eisner's oral history (1992), he states that a further development complication came when a big-name builder gave about 14 acres at Chavez Ravine to the Catholic church, which then refused to sell to the housing authority. The donor, I believe, was Burns.

18 *Los Angeles Times* negative archive, UCLA Special Collections, Box 160, caption to photo #77852, September 30, 1952.

19 One of the most remarkable documents in the file describes a foiled FBI assassination attempt on Wilkinson, a plot known to Los Angeles Police Department special forces.

20 Lee F. Johnson, "Los Angeles Give-Away," in a "Special Newsletter" of the National Housing Conference, Washington, D.C., n.d. (ca. 1954), 2 pp. Neutra Papers, UCLA Special Collections, Box 47, File: "Elysian Park, 1953."

21 This story contrasts with Poulson's, in which he says that his first meeting with O'Malley was in 1957 at the Dodger spring training camp at Vero Beach. But Poulson admits that O'Malley was already surprisingly well informed about the Chavez Ravine site, including engineering studies (Poulson, 1962).

22 Author's interview with William Hannon, September 16, 1997. Burns's office must have had an interest in the Dodger deal, since they compiled a scrapbook with every newspaper article written on the subject.

23 Ed Roybal Papers, UCLA Library, Special Collections, Box 6, File: "Chavez Ravine (Dodgers) 2."

24 The Arechiga story is a chapter all its own. The family drew tremendous public sympathy, until it was learned that they owned eleven other houses besides the one destroyed at Chavez Ravine. See the brief discussion in chapter 14 above.

25 "Facts Regarding Elysian Park Heights," Bowron Collection, Huntington Library, File: "Public Housing."

26 Bowron Collection, Huntington Library, Box 50, "Index to Exhibits"; prepared by the Office of Information, Housing Authority of the City of Los Angeles, May 1952, 9 pp. As it turned out, the highest-density project to be built by the housing authority was the Aliso Village Extension at 26 units to the acre.

27 Rose Hills and Chavez Ravine were predominantly vacant. The West Los Angeles site, between Ballona Creek and Braddock at Slauson, was entirely vacant. See Los Angeles Citizens Housing Council, "Direct Answers to Direct Questions Regarding the Current Crisis in the Public Housing Controversy in Los Angeles," December 11, 1951; Bowron Collection, Huntington Library, Box 50. Additional information comes from a document titled "Tabulation of Documents Submitted to Mayor Bowron on December 24, 1951. RE Low-Rent Program of the Housing Authority of the City of Los Angeles," dated December 21, 1951, 19 pp.; Bowron Collection, Huntington Library, Box 50.

28 The total to be paid according to one estimate was $170,145 from the eleven sites, compared to $18,490 paid by those same sites prior to their development as housing. "History of Los Angeles City Council Actions on Slum Clearance–Public Housing Program," 2 pp. Other information drawn from "Los Angeles Citizens Housing Council," December 11, 1951, 3 pp. In Bowron Collection, Huntington Library.

29 *Southwest Builder and Contractor* ran notices about prospective building and engineering projects, and announced requests for bids, bids received, and contracts awarded throughout the Southwest region and Alaska.

30 Lee F. Johnson, "Special Newsletter" of the National Housing Conference, Washington, D.C., n.d. (ca. 1954), p. 1; in Neutra Papers, UCLA Library Special Collections, Box 47, File: "Elysian Park, 1953."

31 In a press release, O'Malley, owner of the Dodgers, argues for the stadium as its plan is modeled on the official seal of the City of Los Angeles. In Ed Roybal Papers, UCLA Library, Special Collections.

VIII At the End, Playa Vista

1 The proposition did not apply to the 10,000 units of public housing planned for Los Angeles, since existing contracts were exempt. See Bowron Collection, Huntington Library, Box 50, File: "Prop. No. 10."

2 ". . . And Now We Plan," exh. cat., Los Angeles County Museum, October 22, 1941–January 18, 1942 (not paginated). The catalog quotes heavily from *Preface to a Master Plan* (Robbins and Tilton, 1941).

3 Holston (1998) and others have noted this dilemma: that any projection of a utopian future remains tied to what exists, and thus destroys, at least in part, the distinction between the two.

4 Much of the research for this chapter was undertaken with Tridib Banerjee, under the auspices of our jointly awarded National Endowment for the Arts grant to study contentious development (Cuff and Banerjee, 1994).

5 At political gatherings, these groups advocate preserving the entire Playa Vista site as wetlands and uplands. While they want to keep DreamWorks in LA, they suggested locating corporate headquarters in West Hollywood. They have coined the best rallying cry: "Leave Ballona Alone-a."

6 This plan approved 1.3 million square feet of commercial development (primarily retail and office), 5,600 new homes, 1,800 hotel rooms, about 800 boat slips in a new marina, as well as parks, bike trails, and so on. See Cuff and Banerjee (1994) for more extensive information.

7 Author's interview with Terry Conner, then President of the Villa Marina Council, 1993.

8 In less than a year and a half, according to Summa's then-Executive Vice President David O'Malley (interview with the author, 1992), the Playa Vista team had accomplished its three principal goals: annexation into the city of Los Angeles, the establishment of zoning via specific plan, and Coastal Commission permissions, including a certified environmental impact report. This is a remarkable fact, given that the subsequent developers, Maguire Thomas Partners, were not able to achieve the same in their ten years of stewardship.

9 Although advocacy groups claimed responsibility for ousting both Russell and Summa, other factors were surely at play also (see Cuff and Banerjee, 1994). When Maguire Thomas took charge, JMB Realty acquired controlling interests in Playa Vista, with Summa retaining the position of limited partner. There were other carryovers besides Summa: the new group of architects—less modernist than Harry Cobb and very much more New Urbanist—were overseen by Douglas Gardner, who had worked under Cobb before becoming Maguire's project manager. And the landscape firm Hanna/Olin, which had completed the most successful part of the Summa plan, was retained as the landscape architect on the new team.

10 The best-known project with which he was associated was the reconstruction of the beloved art deco central library, which had been damaged in a fire. To rebuild the library, Maguire transferred the library's air rights to another nearby piece of property in order to build Library Tower, the tallest building in LA.

11 These constraints included the fragility of the Ballona wetlands, the threat of serious traffic problems, the objection to high-rise office buildings, the need for affordable housing, and the need for an open planning process.

12 It is not entirely clear that the Summa proposal was actually "stopped." Some people familiar with the Hughes heirs suggest that they sold their controlling interest to Maguire because they were in need of cash, and not because public outcry was prohibitive. David O'Malley (interview with the author, 1992) makes this case, saying that Summa had all the entitlements it needed to proceed in spite of public opinion. However, this would make Maguire Thomas's actions irrational, since its reconsideration of Playa Vista's planning has led to over a decade of further negotiations. What O'Malley fails to admit is the multiple ways the development undertaking could have been ground to a halt, even with entitlements. In the same vein, the shift from office to housing development was a fortunate coincidence of a soft office market with community sentiment.

13 Before Maguire Thomas was out of the picture, the state had authorized $40 million for roadwork, and the city gave $70 million in tax credits and infrastructure as well as $410 million in special district bonds to pay for infrastructure. Thus, new negotiations with Playa Capital were already improving the position of the developers.

14 Between 1993 and 1995, DreamWorks together with Maguire Thomas and several project consultants gave a total of $346,000 in state and local campaigns; DreamWorks heads Spielberg, Katzenberg, and Geffen together gave $562,000 to Democrats in the 1996 national campaign. For that same election, Geffen alone raised $10 million for Clinton and the Democratic Party (Gibson, 1999).

15 Findlay argues that the cases he has studied have also helped to transform their surroundings, though the nature of this transformation is debatable. Certainly some of the changes that places like Disneyland have wrought, evident in the seedy strip development that rings the park, have not been positive from an urban planning and design perspective.

16 Professional survival is a real concern, given moves in Britain and New Zealand to remove the registration requirement for architects, with the express justification that architecture does not benefit public welfare.

Bibliography

General Bibliography

Aaron, Henry. 1973. "Low Rent Public Housing." In Donald J. Reeb and James T. Kirk, Jr., eds., *Housing the Poor,* pp. 192–210. New York: Praeger.

Abrams, Charles. 1946. *The Future of Housing.* New York: Harper and Brothers.

Albrecht, Donald, ed. 1995. *World War II and the American Dream.* Washington: National Building Museum; Cambridge: MIT Press.

Alexander, Robert E. 1989. "Architecture, Planning, and Social Responsibility. Oral History Transcript 1986–1987: Alexander, Robert E." Interviewed by Marlene L. Laskey. Los Angeles: Oral History Program, University of California, Los Angeles.

". . . And 10,000 More." 1949. Film. Produced by graduate students from USC's Department of Cinema, for the Housing Authority of the City of Los Angeles. Narrated by Chet Huntley; edited by Edward Lybeck and Frank Wilkinson. 12 minutes. In Southern California Library for Social Studies and Research.

Applegate, Joe. 1989. "Westchester: Suburb Where LAX Is King." *Los Angeles Times,* July 2, At Home section, pp. 2, 4.

Architectural Forum. 1942. "War Housing" (special issue). 78 (May).

Architectural Forum. 1944. "The Fighting Seabees." 80, no. 2 (February), pp. 48–58.

Architectural Record. 1994. "The Place of Public in Housing." 182, no. 1 (January), pp. 26–29, 43, 45.

Arts and Architecture. 1942a. "Community Living Units in the West." 59, no. 1 (January), pp. 32–33.

Arts and Architecture. 1942b. "Notes in Passing." 59, no. 1 (January), p. 15.

Arts and Architecture. 1942c. "Aliso Village." 59, no. 9 (October), pp. 38–39.

Arts and Architecture. 1943a. "Bunker Hill." 60, no. 6 (July), pp. 32–35.

Arts and Architecture. 1943b. "Obsolescence and Land Use." 60, no. 8 (August), pp. 38–44.

Arts and Architecture. 1947a. "House in a Factory." 64, no. 9 (September), pp. 31–35.

Arts and Architecture. 1947b. "House in Industry." 64, no. 11 (November), pp. 28–37.

Asa, Oran W. 1959. "Chavez Ravine 'Dream Stadium' Many Years Away." *News-Herald and Journal* (Highland Park, CA), January 25, p. 1.

Ashton, Patrick J. 1978. "The Political Economy of Suburban Development." In William K. Tabb and Larry Sawers, eds., *Marxism and the Metropolis,* pp. 64–89. New York: Oxford University Press.

Atkinson, W. P., David D. Bohannon, Milton J. Brock, Alan E. Brockbank, Fritz B. Burns, Edward R. Carr, Thomas P. Coogan, Harry J. Durbin, Robert P. Gerholz, Rodney M. Lockwood, Joseph E. Merrion, Joseph Meyerhoff, George F. Nixon, and Emanuel M. Speigel. 1954. *Housing U.S.A. as Industry Leaders See It.* New York: Simmons-Boardman Publishing Co.

Babcock, Henry. 1951. *Report on the Feasibility of Redeveloping the Bunker Hill Area, Los Angeles.* Los Angeles: [Community Redevelopment Agency of the City of Los Angeles].

Babcock, Richard F., and Wendy U. Larsen. 1990. *Special Districts: The Ultimate in Neighborhood Zoning.* Cambridge, MA: Lincoln Institute of Land Policy.

Baker, Erwin. 1952. "What to Do? Where to Go? 6000 Face Eviction." *Los Angeles Examiner*, February 4, sect. 1, p. 3.

Barry, Brian. 1989. *Theories of Justice*. Berkeley: University of California Press.

Bartlett, Dana W. 1907. *The Better City: A Sociological Study of a Modern City*. Los Angeles: Neuner Co. Press.

Bauer, Catherine. 1934. *Modern Housing*. Boston: Houghton Mifflin.

Bauer, Catherine. 1953. "Redevelopment: A Misfit in the Fifties." In Coleman Woodbury, ed., *The Future of Cities and Urban Redevelopment*. Chicago: University of Chicago Press.

Bauer, Catherine. 1957. "The Dreary Deadlock of Public Housing." *Architectural Forum* 106, no. 5 (May), pp. 140–142, 219–222.

Bauer, Catherine. 1965. "The Social Front of Modern Architecture in the 1930s." *Journal of the Society of Architectural Historians* 24 (March), pp. 48–52.

Beauregard, Robert A. 1985. "Politics, Ideology and Theories of Gentrification." *Journal of Urban Affairs* 7, no. 5 (September).

Beauregard, Robert A. 1990. "Bringing the City Back." *Journal of the American Planning Association* 56, no. 2 (March), pp. 210–215.

Beauregard, Robert A. 1993. *Voices of Decline: The Postwar Fate of US Cities*. Oxford: Basil Blackwell.

Bemis, George W. 1945. *Coordinated Public Works for Metropolitan Los Angeles*. Los Angeles: Haynes Foundation. 25 pp.

Berman, Marshall. 1988. *All That Is Solid Melts into Air: The Experience of Modernity*. New York: Viking Penguin.

Berthelsen, Christian. 1997. "Playa Foes Lose Suit but Win Stay." *Santa Monica Outlook*, November 7, pp. A1, A7.

Bettencourt, Philip. 1991. *Not in My Back Yard: Removing Barriers to Affordable Housing*. Report to President Bush and Secretary Kemp. Washington: Advisory Commission on Regulatory Barriers to Affordable Housing.

Blackmar, Elizabeth. 1989. *Manhattan for Rent, 1785–1850*. Ithaca: Cornell University Press.

Blackstone, Sir William. 1765–1766. *Commentaries on the Laws of England*, Books I and II. Rpt., ed. John Frederick Archbold. London: M. and S. Brooke, Paternoster-Row, 1811.

Boesiger, W., ed. 1959. *Richard Neutra: Buildings and Projects, 1950–1960*. New York: Praeger.

Boorstin, Daniel. 1941. *The Mysterious Science of the Law*. Cambridge: Harvard University Press.

Boyer, Brian D. 1973. *Cities Destroyed for Cash: The FHA Scandal at HUD*. Chicago: Follett Publishing Company.

Boynoff, Sara. 1948a. "Westchester District, War-Baby of L.A., Suffering from Growing Pains." *Daily News* (Los Angeles), February 10, p. 3.

Boynoff, Sara. 1948b. "Westchester Worries over What Will Happen if Hit by Major Emergency." *Daily News* (Los Angeles), February 11, p. 3.

Bratt, Rachel G. 1986. "Public Housing: The Controversy and Contribution." In Rachel G. Bratt, Chester Hartman, and Ann Meyerson, eds., *Critical Perspectives on Housing*, pp. 335–361. Philadelphia: Temple University Press.

Braudel, Fernand. 1972–1973. *The Mediterranean and the Mediterranean World in the Age of Philip II.* 2 vols. New York: Harper and Row. Originally published 1949 in French [no publisher given]; rpt. Paris: Librairie Colin Armand, 1966.

Braudel, Fernand. 1977. *La Méditerranée, l'espace et l'histoire.* Paris: Arts and Métiers Graphiques.

Brook, James. 1985. "Trend-Setting Quonset Hut Is Demolished on L.I." *New York Times*, August 2.

Bryant, W. G. 1972. *Land: Private Property, Public Control.* Montreal: Harvest House.

Budd, Leslie, and Sam Whimster, eds. 1992. *Global Finance and Urban Living: A Study of Metropolitan Change.* London: Routledge.

California Eagle. 1947. "Houseless? Here's Figures Will Make You Cozily Hot." June 12.

Carr, Aute Lee. 1947. *A Practical Guide to Prefabricated Houses.* New York: Harper and Brothers.

Carr, Stephen, M. Francis, L. G. Rivlin, and A. M. Stone. 1992. *Public Space.* Cambridge: Cambridge University Press.

Castells, Manuel. 1983. *The City and the Grassroots.* London: E. Arnold.

Checkoway, Barry. 1986. "Large Builders, Federal Housing Programs, and Postwar Suburbanization." In Rachel G. Bratt, Chester Hartman, and Ann Meyerson, eds., *Critical Perspectives on Housing*, pp. 119–138. Philadelphia: Temple University Press.

Chuang, Angie. 1997. "As Building Falls, So Do Tears." *Los Angeles Times*, January 17, p. B3.

Clawson, Marion. 1964. *Man and Land in the United States.* Lincoln: University of Nebraska Press.

Coase, Ronald. 1960. "The Problems of Social Cost." *Journal of Law and Economics* 2 (October).

Cohn, Jan. 1979. *The Palace or the Poorhouse: The American House as a Cultural Symbol.* East Lansing: Michigan State University Press.

Collins, Keith. 1980. *Black Los Angeles: The Maturing of the Ghetto, 1940–1950.* Saratoga, CA: Century 21 Publishing.

Cravens, Jack. 1946. "GIs Get Quonsets, Now They Need Lots." *Daily News* (Los Angeles), July 16, p. 3.

Crawford, Margaret. 1995. "Daily Life on the Homefront: Women, Blacks, and the Struggle for Public Housing." In Donald Albrecht, ed., *World War II and the American Dream*, pp. 90–143. Washington: National Building Museum; Cambridge: MIT Press.

Cuff, Dana. 1985. "Beyond the Last Resort: The Case of Public Housing in Houston." *Places* 2, no. 4 (Winter), pp. 23–43.

Cuff, Dana, and Tridib Banerjee. 1994. "Form in Contention: Design in Development Disputes." Report to the National Endowment for the Arts. Award number 92-4251-0031.

Cuomo, Andrew. 1997. "Housing Maverick" (interview). *Architecture* 86, no. 8 (August), pp. 44–49.

Daily News (Los Angeles). 1953. "Housing Needed for These Vets' Families." July 6, p. 16.

Davis, Mike. 1990. *City of Quartz: Excavating the Future in Los Angeles.* London: Verso.

Davis, Mike. 1998. *Ecology of Fear: Los Angeles and the Imagination of Disaster* New York: Metropolitan Books.

Davis, Sam, ed. 1977. *The Form of Housing.* New York: Van Nostrand Reinhold.

Davis, Sam. 1995. *The Architecture of Affordable Housing.* Berkeley: University of California Press.

Davis, Susan G. 1997. *Spectacular Nature: Corporate Culture and the Sea World Experience.* Berkeley: University of California Press.

Dear, Michael. 1999. *The Postmodern Urban Condition.* Malden, MA: Blackwell.

Dear, Michael, H. Eric Schockman, and Greg Hise, eds. 1996. *Rethinking Los Angeles.* Thousand Oaks, CA: Sage Publications.

Defense Housing Digest: A Summary of Laws, Regulations and Results. 1940. Chicago: National Association of Housing Officials.

DeMarco, Gordon. 1988. *A Short History of Los Angeles.* San Francisco: Lexikos.

Donovan, Richard. 1952. "The Great Los Angeles Public Housing Mystery." *The Reporter* (Los Angeles) 6, no. 5 (March 4), pp. 25–29.

Douglas, Mary. 1966. *Purity and Danger: An Analysis of Concepts of Pollution and Taboo.* New York: Praeger.

Dunlap, David W. 1991. "Trump and Civic Groups Team Up to Oversee Big Riverside Project." *New York Times,* April 14, sect. 1, p. 28.

Eberts, Mike. 1996. *Griffith Park: A Centennial History.* Los Angeles: Historical Society of Southern California.

Eichler, Ned. 1982. *The Merchant Builders.* Cambridge: MIT Press.

Eisner, Simon. 1943. "Urban Redevelopment." *Arts and Architecture* 60, no. 10 (December), pp. 18, 36.

Eisner, Simon. 1992. "Seven Decades of Planning and Development in the Los Angeles Region. Oral History Transcript, 1987–1989: Simon Eisner." Interviewed by Edward A. Holden. Los Angeles: Oral History Program, University of California, Los Angeles.

Eliot, Charles W. 1945. *Citizen Support for Los Angeles Development.* Los Angeles: Haynes Foundation. 12 pp.

Exploding Metropolis, The. 1958. Garden City, NY: Doubleday.

Fainstein, Susan S. 1994. *The City Builders.* Cambridge, MA: Blackwell.

Favro, Diane. 1983. "Roman Solar Legislation." *Passive Solar Journal* 2, no. 2, pp. 90–98.

Findlay, John M. 1992. *Magic Lands: Western Cityscapes and American Culture after 1940.* Berkeley: University of California Press.

Fischel, William A. 1995. *Regulatory Takings: Law, Economics, and Politics.* Cambridge: Harvard University Press.

Fisher, Thomas. 1993. "Systems of (Professional) Survival." *Progressive Architecture* (December), p. 7.

Fishman, Robert. 1987. *Bourgeois Utopias.* New York: Basic Books.

Fogelson, Robert M. 1993. *The Fragmented Metropolis: Los Angeles, 1850–1930.* Berkeley: University of California Press.

Forty, Adrian. 1986. *Objects of Desire.* New York: Pantheon.

Frampton, Kenneth. 1980. *Modern Architecture: A Critical History.* New York: Oxford University Press.

Franck, Karen A., and Michael Mostoller. 1995. "From Courts to Open Space to Streets: Changes in the Site Design of U.S. Public Housing." *Journal of Architectural and Planning Research* 12, no. 3 (Autumn), pp. 186–220.

Frantz, Douglas, and Catherine Collins. 1999. *Celebration USA: Living in Disney's Brave New Town*. New York: Henry Holt.

Freedman, Leonard. 1959. "Group Opposition to Public Housing." Dissertation, political science. University of California, Los Angeles.

Freedman, Leonard. 1969. *Public Housing: The Politics of Poverty*. New York: Holt, Rinehart and Winston.

Frieden, Bernard. 1979. *The Environmental Protection Hustle*. Cambridge: MIT Press.

Frieden, Bernard J., and Lynne B. Sagalyn. 1989. *Downtown, Inc.: How American Rebuilds Cities*. Cambridge: MIT Press.

Friedland, Roger, and Deirdre Boden, eds. 1994. *NowHere: Space, Time, and Modernity*. Berkeley: University of California Press.

Friedland, Roger, and Harold Zellman. In press. "Broadacre in Brentwood: The Politics of Architectural Aesthetics." In Michael Roth and Charles Salas, eds., *Los Angeles: Paradigms and Perspectives*. Los Angeles: Getty Center Publications.

Fuerst, J. S., ed. 1974. *Public Housing in Europe and America*. London: Croom Helm.

Fulton, William. 1991. *Guide to California Planning*. Point Arena, CA: Solano Press Books.

Gámez, José. 1999. "Building Post-colonial Los Angeles." Dissertation, architecture. University of California, Los Angeles.

Gans, Herbert. 1962. *The Urban Villagers*. New York: Free Press of Glencoe.

Garvin, Alexander. 1996. *The American City: What Works, What Doesn't*. New York: McGraw-Hill.

Gelin, Jacques B., and David W. Miller. 1982. *The Federal Law of Eminent Domain*. Charlottesville, VA: Michie Company.

Gibson, J. William. 1999. "Hollywood Sprawl." *Nation*, March 1, pp. 16–20.

Giddens, Anthony. 1979. *Central Problems in Social Theory*. Berkeley: University of California Press.

Giddens, Anthony. 1990. *The Consequences of Modernity*. Stanford: Stanford University Press.

Glazer, Nathan, and Mark Lilla, eds. 1987. *The Public Face of Architecture*. New York: Free Press.

Glendon, Mary Ann. 1991. *Rights Talk: The Impoverishment of Political Discourse*. New York: Free Press.

Godoy, Omar. 1984. *Problems of Community Development: A Case Study of the Route 2 Corridor, Los Angeles*. Los Angeles: UCLA.

Gordon, Larry. 1993. "Projected for Demolition." *Los Angeles Times*, August 27, p. B10.

Gottdiener, Mark. 1997. *The Theming of America*. Boulder, CO: Westview Press.

Gray, George Herbert. 1946. *Housing and Citizenship: A Study of Low-Cost Housing*. New York: Reinhold.

Greenstein, Paul, Nigey Lennon, and Lionel Rolfe. 1992. *Bread and Hyacinths: The Rise and Fall of Utopian Los Angeles*. Los Angeles: California Classic Books.

Gries, John M., and James Ford. 1932. *President's Conference on Home Building and Home Ownership*. Washington: President's Conference on Home Building and Home Ownership.

Habe, Reiko. 1989. "Public Design Control in American Communities." *Town Planning Review* (2), pp. 195–219.

Hamilton, Calvin S. 1995. "Seven Decades of Planning and Development in the Los Angeles Region. Oral History Transcript 1991: Calvin S. Hamilton." Interviewed by Edward A. Holden. Los Angeles: Oral History Program, University of California, Los Angeles.

Harmer, Ruth M. 1955. "Trick Play at City Hall." *Frontier.* February.

Harries, Karsten. 1997. *The Ethical Function of Architecture.* Cambridge: MIT Press.

Hayden, Dolores. 1981. *The Grand Domestic Revolution.* Cambridge: MIT Press.

Hayden, Dolores. 1984. *Redesigning the American Dream.* New York: W. W. Norton.

Hayden, Dolores. 1995. *The Power of Place.* Cambridge: MIT Press.

Henderson, Cary S. 1980. "Los Angeles and the Dodger War, 1957–1962." *Southern California Quarterly* 62, no. 3 (Fall), pp. 261–289.

Herald Express (Los Angeles). 1952. "Warn on Juvenile Crime Growth in Housing Scheme." January 1.

Herbert, Gilbert. 1978. *Pioneers of Prefabrication: The British Contribution in the Nineteenth Century.* Baltimore: Johns Hopkins University Press.

Hilberseimer, Ludwig. 1955. *The Nature of Cities.* Chicago: P. Theobald.

Hine, Thomas. 1989. "The Search for the Postwar House." In *Blueprints for Modern Living: History and Legacy of the Case Study Houses.* Los Angeles: Museum of Contemporary Art; Cambridge: MIT Press, 1989.

Hines, Thomas S. 1982a. "Housing, Baseball, and Creeping Socialism: The Battle of Chavez Ravine, Los Angeles, 1949–1959." *Journal of Urban History* 8, no. 2 (February), pp. 123–143.

Hines, Thomas S. 1982b. *Richard Neutra and the Search for Modern Architecture.* New York: Oxford University Press.

Hines, Thomas S. 1998. "The Blessing and the Curse: The Achievement of Lloyd Wright." In Alan Weintraub, ed., *Lloyd Wright,* pp. 12–37. London: Thames and Hudson.

Hise, Greg. 1995. "The Airplane and the Garden City: Regional Transformations During WWII." In Donald Albrecht, ed., *World War II and the American Dream,* pp. 144–183. Washington: National Building Museum; Cambridge: MIT Press.

Hise, Greg. 1997. *Magnetic Los Angeles.* Baltimore: Johns Hopkins University Press.

Holston, James. 1989. *The Modernist City.* Chicago: University of Chicago Press.

Holston, James. 1998. "Spaces of Insurgent Citizenship." In Leonie Sandercock, ed., *Making the Invisible Visible: A Multicultural Planning History.* Berkeley: University of California Press.

Housing Headlines (Citizens' Housing Council of Los Angeles). 1940. 1, no. 4 (September 12).

Housing News (Los Angeles). 1946a. "City Authority Announces Emergency Housing Program." 3, no. 3 (March). 6 pp.

Housing News (Los Angeles). 1946b. "L.A. War Veterans' Emergency Housing Project Dedicated." 3, no. 5 (May). 8 pp.

Housing News (Los Angeles). 1948a. "Redevelopment Commission Appointed by

Mayor Bowron." 5, no. 11 (November), pp. 1, 4.

Housing News (Los Angeles). 1948b. "Rodger Young Okayed; Keppler Grove Vetoed." 5, no. 11 (November), pp. 1, 3.

Hudnut, Joseph. 1949. *Architecture and the Spirit of Man.* Cambridge: Harvard University Press.

Hume, David. 1888. *A Treatise of Human Nature.* Ed. L. A. Selby-Bigge. Oxford: Clarendon Press.

Jackson, J. B. 1970. *Landscapes.* Amherst: University of Massachusetts Press.

Jackson, Kenneth T. 1985. *Crabgrass Frontier: The Surburbanization of the United States.* New York: Oxford University Press.

Jacobs, Jane. 1958. "Downtown Is for People." *Fortune* (April).

Jacobs, Jane. 1961. *The Death and Life of Great American Cities.* New York: Vintage Books.

Jacobs, Jane. 1992. *Systems of Survival.* New York: Random House.

Journal of Housing. 1955a. "1940–1955: The Story of World War II Housing From Construction to Disposition." 12, no. 5 (May), pp. 152–159.

Journal of Housing. 1955b. "1955 Housing Act." 12, no. 8 (August-September), pp. 263–265, 302.

Journal of Housing. 1959. "1959 Housing Act Summarized." 16, no. 9 (October), pp. 315–317.

Journal of the American Institute of Architects. Supplement. "Architects and War Housing." 8 (January), pp. 1–8.

Jukes, Peter. 1990. *A Shout in the Street.* Berkeley: University of California Press.

Katz, Peter. 1994. *The New Urbanism.* New York: McGraw-Hill.

Kelly, Burnham. 1951. *The Prefabrication of Houses.* Cambridge: Technology Press of MIT.

Kempner, Jary Jean. 1945. "Builders at War." *House and Garden* 88, no. 3 (September), pp. 88–89, 116–118.

Klein, Norman M. 1997. *History of Forgetting: Los Angeles and the Erasure of Memory.* London: Verso.

Klein, Norman M., and Martin J. Schiesl, eds. 1990. *20th Century Los Angeles: Power, Promotion, and Social Conflict.* Claremont, CA: Regina Books.

Kling, Rob, Spencer Olin, and Mark Poster, eds. 1991. *Postsuburban California: The Transformation of Orange County since World War II.* Berkeley: University of California Press.

Knetsch, Jack L. 1983. *Property Rights and Compensation.* Toronto: Butterworth and Company.

Koolhaas, Rem. 1995. *S M L XL.* New York: Monacelli Press.

Kostof, Spiro. 1985. *A History of Architecture: Settings and Rituals.* New York: Oxford University Press.

Kostof, Spiro. 1991. *The City Shaped.* Boston: Little, Brown.

Krieger, Alex, ed. 1991. *Andrés Duany and Elizabeth Plater-Zyberk: Towns and Town-Making Principles* New York: Rizzoli.

Kroloff, Reed. 1997. "Disney Builds a Town." *Architecture* 86, no. 8 (August), pp. 117–119.

Kronzek, Lynn C., and Roberta S. Greenwood. 1996. "Historical Background." In Roberta S. Greenwood, *Down by the Station: Los Angeles Chinatown, 1880–1933,* pp. 5–40. Monumenta Archaeologica no. 18. Los Angeles: Institute of Archaeology, University of California, Los Angeles.

Kruft, Hanno-Walter. 1994. *A History of Architectural Theory from Vitruvius to the Present*. London: Zwemmer; New York: Princeton Architectural Press.

Langdon, Philip, and Robert G. Shibley. 1990. *Urban Excellence*. New York: Van Nostrand Reinhold.

Larson, Magali Sarfatti. 1993. *Behind the Postmodern Facade*. Berkeley: University of California Press.

Le Corbusier. 1973. *The Athens Charter*. New York: Grossman.

Locke, John. 1960. *Two Treatises of Government*. Ed. Peter Laslett. Cambridge: Cambridge University Press.

Logan, John R., and Harvey L. Molotch. 1987. *Urban Fortunes: The Political Economy of Place*. Berkeley: University of California Press.

Los Angeles Examiner. 1946a. "Dreves Returns as Southwest Housing Czar." March 5, part 2, p. 1.

Los Angeles Examiner. 1946b. "Huts in Park Despite Suit." March 5, part 2, p. 1.

Los Angeles Examiner. 1946c. "Codes Lifted in Vet Housing." April 16, part 1, p. 3.

Los Angeles Examiner. 1946d. "Ban Radicals from Housing." October 24, part 1, p. 6.

Los Angeles Examiner. 1952a. "Vet Village End Ordered by Park Board." February 1, sect. 1, p. 1.

Los Angeles Examiner. 1952b. "Rodger Young Closing Protest Led by Mayor." March 17, sect. 3, p. 3.

Los Angeles Examiner. 1952c. "L.A. Airport One of Three Largest in U.S." May 29, sect. 1, p. 2.

Los Angeles Examiner. 1952d. "Rodger Young Extension to 1954 Voted." October 28, sect. 2, p. 6.

Los Angeles Times. 1938. "Slum Clearance Here Probable." October 14, p. 1.

Los Angeles Times. 1947. "A Modest Hope for Housing." Editorial. June 11, p. 4.

Los Angeles Times. 1951a. "Settlement Losing Battle for Its Life." August 20, sect. 2, pp. 1, 2.

Los Angeles Times. 1951b. "Council Votes to Cancel Public Housing Project." December 27, p. 1.

Los Angeles Times. 1951c. "Furious Council Debate Airs Views on Housing." December 27, p. 2.

Los Angeles Times. 1951d. "7 Councilmen Join Housing Support Suit." December 28, p. 1.

Los Angeles Times. 1951e. "Near Riot Flares Housing." December 29, p. 1.

Los Angeles Times. 1952. "Slum Clearance Reports Jostles Housing Advocates." October 30, p. 1.

Los Angeles Times. 1959. "Arechigas Agree to Get Off Land." May 15, pp. 1, 2.

Loukaitou-Sideris, Anastasia, and Tridib Banerjee. 1998. *Urban Design Downtown: Poetics and Politics of Form*. Berkeley: University of California Press.

Maher, Jerry. 1952a. "Fritz B. Burns: Mr. Housing, U.S.A." *Mirror* (Los Angeles), November 18, p. 49.

Maher, Jerry. 1952b. "High Jinks Spark Burns' Career." *Mirror* (Los Angeles), November 19, p. 54.

Marchand, Bernard. 1986. *The Emergence of Los Angeles: Population and Housing in the City of Dreams, 1940–1970*. London: Pion.

Marcuse, Peter. 1995. "Interpreting 'Public Housing' Theory." *Journal of Architectural and Planning Research* 12, no. 3 (Autumn), pp. 240–258.

Massey, D. 1993. "Politics and Space/Time." In Michael Keith and Steve Pile, eds., *Place and the Politics of Identity*, pp. 141–161. London: Routledge.

Mayer, Albert. 1934. "New Homes for a New Deal I: Slum Clearance—But How?" *New Republic* 78 (February 14), pp. 7–9.

Mayer, Albert, Henry Wright, and Lewis Mumford. 1934. "New Homes for a New Deal IV: A Concrete Program." *New Republic* 78 (March 7), pp. 91–94.

Mayer, Martin. 1978. *The Builders: Houses, People, Neighborhoods, Governments, Money*. New York: W. W. Norton.

McClintock, Anne. 1994. "The Angel of Progress: Pitfalls of the Term 'Post-colonialism.'" In Patrick Williams and Laura Chrisman, eds., *Colonial Discourse and Post-colonial Theory*, pp. 291–304. New York: Columbia University Press.

McCoy, Esther. 1977. *Case Study Houses, 1945–1962*. Los Angeles: Hennessey and Ingalls.

McDonnell, Timothy L. 1957. *The Wagner Housing Act*. Chicago: Loyola University Press.

McMahon, K. 1942. "Aliso Village." Unpublished journal of a Utah Street School teacher. Property of Mr. Gregory Boyle, S.J., at Projecto Pastoral/Jobs for a Future, Los Angeles. 57 pp.

McWilliams, Carey. 1949. "Look What's Happened to California." *Harper's Magazine* 199, no. 1193 (October), pp. 21–29.

McWilliams, Carey. 1973. *Southern California: An Island on the Land*. Salt Lake City: Peregrine Smith.

Miranda, Gloria E. 1990. "The Mexican Immigrant Family: Economic and Cultural Survival in Los Angeles, 1900–1945." In Norman M. Klein and Martin J. Schiesl, eds., *20th Century Los Angeles: Power, Promotion, and Social Conflict*. Claremont, CA: Regina Books.

Mollenkopf, John H. 1978. "The Postwar Politics of Urban Development." In William K. Tabb and Larry Sawers, eds., *Marxism and the Metropolis*, pp. 117–152. New York: Oxford University Press.

Montgomery, Roger. 1977. "High Density, Low Rise Housing and Changes in the American Housing Economy." In Sam Davis, ed., *The Form of Housing*, pp. 83–112. New York: Van Nostrand.

Montgomery, Roger. 1989. "Modern Architecture Invents New People." In W. Russell Ellis and Dana Cuff, eds., *Architects' People*, pp. 260–281. New York: Oxford University Press.

Moran, Julio. 1989. "Firm Takes Over as General Partner at Summa Project." *Los Angeles Times*, February 23.

Morris, Anthony E. J. 1979. *History of Urban Form: Before the Industrial Revolutions*. New York: John Wiley and Sons.

Mumford, Lewis. 1934. "New Homes for a New Deal III: The Shortage of Dwellings and Direction." *New Republic* 78 (February 28), pp. 69–72.

Mumford, Lewis. 1961. *The City in History*. New York: Harcourt, Brace and World.

Murguía, Edward. 1975. *Assimilation, Colonialism and the Mexican American People.* Mexican American Monograph Series no. 1. Austin: Center for Mexican American Studies, University of Texas at Austin.

National Housing Association. 1929. *Housing Problems in America.* Proceedings of the Tenth National Conference on Housing, Philadelphia, January 28–30, 1929. New York: National Housing Association.

Neff, Philip, and Annette Weifenbach. 1949. *Business Cycles in Selected Industrial Areas.* Berkeley: University of California Press.

Nelson, Howard J., and William A. V. Clark. 1976. *The Los Angeles Metropolitan Experience: Uniqueness, Generality, and the Goal of the Good Life.* Cambridge, MA: Ballinger.

Noyes, C. Reinold. 1936. *The Institution of Property.* New York: Longmans, Green.

Nozick, Robert. 1974. *Anarchy, State, and Utopia.* New York: Basic Books.

Ovnick, Merry. 1994. *Los Angeles: The End of the Rainbow.* Los Angeles: Balcony Press.

Parson, Don. 1983. "Los Angeles' Headline-Happy Public Housing War." *Southern California Quarterly* 65, no. 3 (Fall), pp. 251–285.

Parson, Don. 1993. "'This Modern Marvel': Bunker Hill, Chavez Ravine, and the Politics of Modernism in Los Angeles." *Southern California Quarterly* 75, nos. 3–4 (Fall/Winter), pp. 333–350.

Parson, Don. 1999. "'The Darling of the Town's Neo-Fascists': The Bombastic Political Career of Councilman Ed J. Davenport." *Southern California Quarterly* (Winter).

Parson, Don. *Making a Better World: Public Housing and the Direction of Modern Los Angeles.* Forthcoming.

Partlow, Vern. 1951. "Growing Pains of a Great City: Sensational Development of Westchester Outlined." *Daily News* (Los Angeles), October 19, pp. 3, 53.

Paul, Ellen Frankel. 1987. *Property Rights and Eminent Domain.* New Brunswick, NJ: Transaction Books.

People's World. 1952a. "Vets Challenge L.A. Eviction Plan." February 19, p. 6.

People's World. 1952b. "LA Vet Housing Project Saved." March 20, p. 3.

People's World. 1953a. "Tenants Organize to Save LA Project." July 14, p. 6.

People's World. 1953b. "Housing Tenants, Facing Ouster, Tell Plight; Win Hope of Stay." August 17, p. 3.

People's World. 1953c. "Evictions Speeded in Two Vet Projects." November 18, p. 3.

Perez-Pena, Richard. 1995. "Highway Plan for West Side Appears Dead." *New York Times,* July 26, pp. B1, B3.

Politi, Leo. 1966. *Tales of the Los Angeles Parks.* Palm Desert, CA: Best West Publications. Unpaginated. In the Huntington Library collection.

Porter, Douglas R., and Lindell L. Marsh, eds. 1989. *Development Agreements: Practice, Policy, and Prospects.* Washington: Urban Land Institute.

Poulson, Norris. 1962. "The Untold Story of Chavez Ravine." *Los Angeles Magazine* 3, no. 4 (April), pp. 14–18.

Poulson, Norris. 1966. "Who Would Have Ever Dreamed?" Interviewed by Doyce B. Nunis, 1962. Los Angeles: Oral History Program, University of California, Los Angeles.

Radford, Gail. 1996. *Modern Housing for America.* Chicago: University of Chicago Press.

Ramos, George. 1996. "Complaint Forces Delay in Housing Construction." *Los Angeles Times,* September 27.

Reed, Peter S. 1995. "Enlisting Modernism." In Donald Albrecht, ed., *World War II and the American Dream,* pp. 2–41. Washington: National Building Museum; Cambridge: MIT Press.

Reps, John W. 1965. *The Making of Urban America.* Princeton: Princeton University Press.

Ricoeur, Paul. 1986. *Ideology and Utopia.* New York: Columbia University Press.

Rittel, Horst W. J., and Melvin M. Webber. 1973. "Dilemmas in a General Theory of Planning." *Policy Sciences* 4, pp. 155–169.

Robbins, George W., and Deming Tilton. 1941. *Los Angeles: Preface to a Master Plan.* Los Angeles: Pacific Southwest Academy.

Rodger Young News. 1947a. "Committees Being Formed." 1, no. 9 (January 3), p. 1.

Rodger Young News. 1947b. "After the Quonsets." Editorial. 1, no. 35 (July 24), p. 2.

Rosen, Allen D. 1993. *Kant's Theory of Justice.* Ithaca: Cornell University Press.

Rosenman, Mrs. Samuel I. 1944. "Comments." *Architectural Forum* 80, no. 2 (February), p. 46.

Ross, Andrew. 1999. *The Celebration Chronicles: Life, Liberty, and the Pursuit of Property Value in Disney's New Town.* New York: Ballantine Books.

Rousseau, Jean-Jacques. 1973. *A Discourse on the Origin of Inequality.* In Jean-Jacques Rousseau, *The Social Contract and Discourses,* trans. G. D. H. Cole. London: Dent Dutton.

Rowe, Peter G. 1995. *Modernity and Architecture.* Cambridge: MIT Press.

Ryan, Alan. 1984. *Property and Political Theory.* Oxford: Basil Blackwell.

Ryan, Alan. 1987. *Property.* Milton Keynes: Open University Press.

Sandercock, Leonie, ed. 1998. *Making the Invisible Visible: A Multicultural Planning History.* Berkeley: University of California Press.

Schultz, David A. 1992. *Property, Power and American Democracy.* New Brunswick, NJ: Transaction Publishers.

Scott, Allen J., and Edward W. Soja, eds. 1996. *The City: Los Angeles and Urban Theory at the End of the Twentieth Century.* Berkeley: University of California Press.

Scully, Vincent. 1969. *American Architecture and Urbanism.* New York: Praeger.

Seligman, Daniel. 1957. "The Enduring Slums." *Fortune* 56 (December), pp. 144–149+.

Sennett, Richard. 1977. *The Fall of Public Man.* New York: Knopf.

Shevky, Eshref, and Molly Lewin. 1949. *Your Neighborhood: A Social Profile of Los Angeles.* Los Angeles: Haynes Foundation.

Shevky, Eshref, and Marilyn Williams. 1949. *The Social Areas of Los Angeles: Analysis and Typology.* Berkeley: University of California Press.

Simons, Grace E. 1952. "Project Eviction Attacked." *California Eagle* 72, no. 45 (February 7), pp. 1, 3.

Smith, Henry Nash. 1950. *Virgin Land: The American West as Symbol and Myth.* Cambridge: Harvard University Press.

Smith, Richard Candida. 1995. *Utopia and Dissent: Art, Poetry, and Politics in California*. Berkeley: University of California Press.

Soja, Edward. 1994. "Postmodern Geographies: Taking Los Angeles Apart." In Roger Friedland and Deirdre Boden, eds., *NowHere: Space, Time, and Modernity*. Berkeley: University of California Press.

Soja, Edward W., and Barbara Hooper. 1993. "The Spaces That Difference Makes." In Michael Keith and Steve Pile, eds., *Place and the Politics of Identity*, pp. 183–205. London: Routledge, 1993.

Soja, Edward W., Rebecca Morales, and Goetz Wolff. 1989. "Urban Restructuring: An Analysis of Social and Spatial Change in Los Angeles." In Robert A. Beauregard, ed., *Atop the Urban Hierarchy*. Totowa, NJ: Rowman and Littlefield.

Sorkin, Michael, ed. 1992. *Variations on a Theme Park: The New American City and the End of Public Space*. New York: Hill and Wang.

Southwest Builder and Contractor. 1946. "Contracts Awarded: Emergency Veteran Housing." 107, no. 5 (February 1), p. 39.

Southwest Builder and Contractor. 1948. "Notes and Comment." 112, no. 5 (July 30), pp. 3–4.

Southwest Builder and Contractor. 1952a. "The Editors' View of the News." 119, no. 15 (April 11), p. 7.

Southwest Builder and Contractor. 1952b. "The Editors' Views of the News." 119, no. 17 (April 25), p. 9.

Southwest Builder and Contractor. 1952c. "The Editors' Views of the News." 119, no. 21 (May 23), p. 7.

Southwest Builder and Contractor. 1952d. "Further Decline in Residential Building Costs." 119, no. 21 (May 23), p. 30.

Southwest Builder and Contractor. 1954. "Bids Being Taken: Sale and Removal of Quonset Huts." 123, no. 16 (April 16), p. 55.

Spalding, Sophie. 1992. "The Myth of the Classic Slum: Contradictory Perceptions of Boyle Heights Flats, 1900–1991." *Journal of Architectural Education* 45, no. 2 (February), pp. 107–119.

Starr, Kevin. 1996. *Endangered Dreams: The Great Depression in California*. New York: Oxford University Press.

Steidle, Harry H. 1944. "A Statement from the Prefabricated Home Manufacturers Association." *Arts and Architecture* 61, no. 7 (July), pp. 41–49.

Stern, Robert. 1981. *The Anglo-American Suburb*. Architectural Design Profile 37. *Architectural Design* 51, nos. 10–11, pp. 1–96.

Sullivan, Timothy J. 1984. *Resolving Development Disputes through Negotiations*. New York: Plenum Press.

Tabb, William K., and Larry Sawers, eds. 1978. *Marxism and the Metropolis: New Perspectives in Urban Political Economy*. New York: Oxford University Press.

Taylor, Alan. 1995. *William Cooper's Town: Power and Persuasion on the Frontier of the Early American Republic*. New York: Knopf.

Terkel, Studs. 1997. *My American Century*. New York: New Press.

Tschumi, Bernard. 1994. *Event Cities: Praxis*. Cambridge: MIT Press.

Turpin, Dick. 1954. "Big Rodger Young Village Vanishing." *Los Angeles Times,* April 4, part 2, pp. 1–2.

[UAW-CIO], International Union, United Automobile, Aircraft and Agricultural Implement Workers of America. 1943. *Homes for Workers: In Planned Communities thru*

Collective Action. UAW-CIO Publication no. 24. 62 pp.

[UAW-CIO], International Union, United Automobile, Aircraft and Agricultural Implement Workers of America. 1944. *Politics in Housing.* UAW-CIO Publication no. 42. 18 pp.

Vance, J. E., Jr. 1971. "Land Assignment in the Precapitalist, Capitalist, and Postcapitalist City." *Economic Geography* 47, pp. 101–120.

Veiller, Lawrence. 1929. "Slum Clearance." In National Housing Association, *Housing Problems in America,* pp. 71–84. Proceedings of the Tenth National Conference on Housing, Philadelphia, January 28–30, 1929. New York: National Housing Association.

Von Hoffman, Alexander. 1997. "The Curse of Durability: Federal Housing for the Poor." *Harvard Design Magazine* (Fall), pp. 47–49.

Waldinger, Roger, and Mehdi Bozorgmehr, eds. 1996. *Ethnic Los Angeles.* New York: Russell Sage Foundation.

Waldron, Jeremy, ed. 1984. *Theories of Rights.* New York: Oxford University Press.

Waldron, Jeremy. 1988. *The Right to Private Property.* New York: Oxford University Press.

Wallis, Allan D. 1991. *Wheel Estate: The Rise and Decline of Mobile Homes.* New York: Oxford University Press.

Weiss, Marc A. 1980. "The Origins and Legacy of Urban Renewal." In Pierre Clavel, John Forester, and William W. Goldsmith, eds., *Urban and Regional Planning in an Age of Austerity,* pp. 53–80. New York: Pergamon Press.

Weiss, Marc A. 1987. *The Rise of the Community Builders.* New York: Columbia University Press.

Weiss, Marc A. 1992. "Density and Intervention: New York's Planning Traditions." In David Ward and Olivier Zunz, eds., *The Landscape of Modernity: Essays on New York City, 1900–1940,* pp. 46–75. New York: Russell Sage Foundation.

Weston, Eugene. 1936. "A Review of Modern Housing in Europe." In two parts. *Southwest Builder and Contractor* 87, no. 15 (April 10), pp. 10–12, 15; 87, no. 16 (April 17), pp. 10–12.

White, Charlotte Negrete. 1989. "Chavez Ravine and the Coming of the Brooklyn Dodgers: A Peoples' Displacement." Unpublished manuscript. December. 45 pp.

White, Richard, and Patricia Nelson Limerick. 1994. *The Frontier in American Culture.* Ed. James R. Grossman. Berkeley: University of California Press.

Wilkinson, Frank. 1965. "And Now the Bill Comes Due." *Frontier* (October). 2 pp.

Wood, Edith Elmer. 1929. "Is Governmental Aid Necessary in House Financing?" In National Housing Association, *Housing Problems in America.* New York: National Housing Association.

Wood, Edith E. 1941a. "Building for Defense: Emergency Housing Proposals." *Architectural Forum* (April).

Wood, Edith E. 1941b. "Danger Points in Defense Housing." *Survey Graphic* (August).

Wright, Gwendolyn. 1981. *Building the Dream.* New York: Pantheon Books.

Wright, Henry. 1933. "The Sad Story of American Housing." *Architecture* 68, no. 3 (March).

Wright, Henry. 1934. "New Homes for a New Deal II: Abolishing Slums Forever." *New Republic* 78 (February 21), pp. 41–44.

Young, Pauline V. 1932. *The Pilgrims of Russian Town.* Chicago: University of Chicago Press.

Young, T. Luke. 1996. "The Unassuming Quonset: Survival of Semi-Circular Significance." *Cultural Resources Management* 19, no. 4, pp. 7–10.

Zukin, Sharon. 1991. *Landscapes of Power: From Detroit to Disneyland.* Berkeley: University of California Press.

Governmental Publications

Los Angeles. Housing Authority. 1938. "Questions and Answers Regarding the Program of Slum Clearance and Low Rent Housing."

Los Angeles. Housing Authority. 1939. "Preliminary Report on Certain Facts Revealed through the Operation of a Housing Survey." 3 pp.

Los Angeles. Housing Authority. 1940a. 2nd Annual Report, 1939/40.

Los Angeles. Housing Authority. 1940b. Housing Survey, City of Los Angeles, CA, Digest of Final Report. April. 20 pp.

Los Angeles. Housing Authority. 1940c. "A Report on the Dwelling and Low Income Housing Survey, City of Los Angeles." May 15.

Los Angeles. Housing Authority. 1941. 3rd Annual Report, 1940/41.

Los Angeles. Housing Authority. 1942a. "Homes for Heroes." 4th Annual Report, 1941/1942.

Los Angeles. Housing Authority. 1942b. *The Truth about Low-Rent Public Housing in Los Angeles.*

Los Angeles. Housing Authority. ca. 1942. "Low Rent American Homes for War Workers." Brochure. 4 pp. UCLA Special Collections, Collection 1561, Lloyd Wright Papers; Box 44, folder 2.

Los Angeles. Housing Authority. 1945. "A Decent Home, an American Right." 5th, 6th, 7th Consolidated Report. 1942/1943–1944/1945.

Los Angeles. Housing Authority. 1947. "Public Housing Developments in the City of Los Angeles."

Los Angeles. Housing Authority. 1948. "There is Nothing Sentimental . . ." 8th, 9th, 10th Reports. 1945/1946–1947/1948.

Los Angeles. Housing Authority. 1951. "Facts Regarding Elysian Park Heights." June 13, 1951. In Huntington Library, Bowron Collection, File: "Public Housing." 2 pp.

Los Angeles. Housing Authority. 1953. *Handbook of General Information of the Housing Authority of the City of Los Angeles.* December. 44 pp.

Los Angeles. Housing Authority. 1955. *Handbook of General Information.* October. 42 pp.

Los Angeles. Housing Commission. 1909a. *Report of the Housing Commission of the City of Los Angeles 1906–1908.* 31 pp.

Los Angeles. Housing Commission. 1909b. *Report of the Housing Commission of the City of Los Angeles 1908–1909.* 29 pp.

Los Angeles. Housing Commission. 1910. *Report of the Housing Commission of the City of Los Angeles, June 30, 1909–June 30, 1910.* 29 pp.

Los Angeles. Housing Commission. 1913. *Report of the Housing Commission of the City of Los Angeles, 1910–1913.* 66 pp.

Los Angeles County. Department of City Planning. 1947. *Conditions of Blight: Central Area, City of Los Angeles*. Los Angeles: Department of City Planning.

Los Angeles County. Housing Authority. 1944. "A Review of the Activities of the Housing Authority of the County of Los Angeles. 1938–1943."

Los Angeles County. Housing Authority. 1951. *Report, the Housing Authority of the County of Los Angeles, July 1, 1943–December 31, 1950.*

United States. Federal Housing Administration, Division of Economics and Statistics. 1938. *Housing Market Analysis, Los Angeles, California as of December 1, 1937.*

United States. Federal Housing Administration. 1939. *The Structure and Growth of Residential Neighborhoods in American Cities*. Washington: Federal Housing Administration.

United States. Federal Public Housing Authority. 1946. *Public Housing Design, a Review of Experience in Low-Rent Housing*. Washington: National Housing Agency, Federal Public Housing Authority.

United States. Public Housing Administration, Housing and Home Finance Agency, 1950. *Low Rent Public Housing: Planning, Design and Construction for Economy*. December. 94 pp.

Archives

Air Photo Archives. Department of Geography, University of California, Los Angeles.

Bauer Wurster, Catherine, Papers. Bancroft Library, University of California, Berkeley.

Bowron Collection. Henry E. Huntington Library. San Marino, California.

Burns, Fritz B., Papers. Center for the Study of Los Angeles, Southern California Research Collection, Von der Ahe Library, Loyola Marymount University. Los Angeles, California.

Drollinger, Howard, Papers. Personal property of Howard Drollinger, Westchester, California.

Hannon, William, Papers. Personal property of the Hannon estate, Westchester, California.

Housing Authority of the City of Los Angeles. Files and photographs.

Kaiser, Henry J., Papers. Bancroft Library, University of California, Berkeley.

Los Angeles City Council Files. 555 Ramirez Street, Room 320, Los Angeles, California.

Los Angeles Times Photographic Archives. Department of Special Collections, UCLA Library, University of California, Los Angeles.

Maps of Los Angeles; Photographic Collection. Los Angeles Public Library. Los Angeles, California.

Nadel, Leonard, Photographic Archives. Property of Evelyn De Wolfe Nadel. Los Angeles, California.

Neutra, Richard, Papers. Department of Special Collections, UCLA Library, University of California, Los Angeles.

Roybal, Ed, Papers. Department of Special Collections, UCLA Library, University of California, Los Angeles.

Security Pacific National Bank, Photographic Collection. Los Angeles Public Library. Los Angeles, California.

Southern California Library for Social Studies and Research. Los Angeles, California.

Still Picture Collection. National Archives, Virginia.

Westchester Historical Society Collections. Von der Ahe Library, Loyola Marymount University. Los Angeles, California.

Wright, Lloyd, Papers. Department of Special Collections, UCLA Library, University of California, Los Angeles.

Interviews (Partial List)

Frances Camareno. April 1997.

Terry Conner. 1992.

Mary Lou Crockett. April 24, 1997.

Howard Drollinger. June 26, 1997.

Leota Fantl Smith-Flowers. April 3, 1997; extended correspondence thereafter.

Douglas Gardner. 1992, 1993.

William Goss. July 15, 1997.

William Hannon. September 16, 1997.

Julie Inouye. 1993, 1994, 1997.

Ruth Lansford. 1993.

George McQuade. 1997.

Elizabeth Moule. 1993.

David Ochoa. March 1997.

David O'Malley. 1992.

Elizabeth Plater-Zyberk. 1993.

Stefanos Polyzoides. 1993.

Nelson Rising. 1992.

Pat Russell. 1993.

Dorothy Sterling. March 20, 1997.

Adele Wexler. 1992.

Jean Whinnery. February 1, 1999.

Frank Wilkinson. January 22 and 23, 1997.

Illustration Credits

Figs. 1, 26: Courtesy of Wendelyn Bone.

Figs. 2, 3, 7, 11, 15, 20, 25, 28, 31, 32, 43, 44, 47, 50, 67, 71, 72, 74, 75, 82, 85, 89, 90, 95, 96, 97, 98, 102, 103, 106, 108, 151, 154, 159, 187, 188: Courtesy of the Housing Authority of the City of Los Angeles.

Figs. 6, 22, 27, 30, 40, 76, 115, 149, 152, 153, 161, 164: Courtesy of the Housing Authority of the City of Los Angeles and Evelyn De Wolfe Nadel.

Figs. 8, 41, 104, 156: Courtesy of Security Pacific National Bank Photograph Collection, Los Angeles Public Library, and Evelyn De Wolfe Nadel.

Figs. 10, 17, 18, 29, 33, 42, 83, 91, 92, 99, 105, 165, 166: Courtesy of UCLA Special Collections.

Figs. 21, 45, 64, 66, 84, 87, 88: Courtesy of Security Pacific National Bank Photograph Collection, Los Angeles Public Library.

Figs. 23, 78, 110, 111, 112, 113, 114, 116, 118, 119, 120, 121, 123, 124, 128, 129, 132, 134, 135, 136, 137, 138, 139, 140, 141, 169: Courtesy of University of Southern California, Regional History Collection, Doheny Library.

Fig. 65: Courtesy of the Southern California Library of Social Studies and Research.

Fig. 77: Courtesy of Evelyn De Wolfe Nadel.

Figs. 80, 81, 101: Courtesy of Leota Fantl Smith-Flowers.

Fig. 93: Courtesy of Dorothy Sterling.

Fig. 122: Courtesy of University of California Berkeley, Bancroft Library. Berkeley, California.

Fig. 130: Courtesy of Westchester Historical Society Collections, Loyola Marymount University, Von der Ahe Library, Los Angeles, California.

Fig. 145: Courtesy of H. Drollinger.

Figs. 158, 162, 163, 168: Property and courtesy of Thomas S. Hines.

Figs. 171, 174, 175, 176, 178, 179, 180, 181, 182, 183: Courtesy of Maguire Thomas Partners.

Figs. 184, 185: New York Times Pictures.

Index

Sophmore year

Princeton '06-'07